UNIVERSITY OF NORTH CAROLINA
STUDIES IN THE ROMANCE LANGUAGES
AND LITERATURES

Number 28

THE CATHOLIC NATURALISM OF PARDO BAZÁN

by

DONALD FOWLER BROWN

CHAPEL HILL
THE UNIVERSITY OF NORTH CAROLINA PRESS

CONTENTS

Preface

Disciple of a misunderstood movement, Pardo Bazán has herself been widely misunderstood. Many of those who criticize naturalism most severely really do not know what it is. They only know that it has certain objectionable features and that they do not like it. Proceeding from this point, the critics either condemn Pardo Bazán thoroughly for her defense of naturalism or else, being friendly to her, they try to show that she really was not a naturalist at all. One attempts to prove that she was primarily a regionalist, another that her realism is actually Spanish in origin, still others that her admiration for Zola was only a passing fancy, and finally, there is one who describes her as an eclectic who never adhered to any system. Surely in the face of such confusion it is worthwhile to determine just what the truth may be. Nothing, however, can be proved as to the supposed naturalism of Pardo Bazán until the term itself is defined. After viewing naturalism historically and objectively, the reader should be well equipped to examine Pardo Bazán's critical reactions to the literary school. It will be found that, while making many reservations, she accepts a good share of Zola's teachings. This is further demonstrated by a study of her novels, which reveal influence not only as to concept but occasionally also as to content. When all the evidence is in, it should be apparent just how wrong many of the critics of Emilia Pardo Bazán have been. Zola himself was at a loss to explain how his chief follower in Spain could at once be a naturalist and a staunch Catholic. That problem, too, must be resolved.

D. F. B.

Hope College
Holland, Michigan

PREFACE TO THE SECOND EDITION

During the years since the first edition in 1957, this book has proved its worth not only as a study of Pardo Bazán's complicated relation to Emile Zola but also for its careful definition of just what Zola's naturalism was. Too many scholars tend to take for granted that their readers know what naturalism is when as a matter of fact it can be a most vague and distorted concept.

A Bibliography has been added this time which should prove valuable to scholars who may wish to do further research on Doña Emilia's literary achievements and ideas.

D. F. B.

Villanova University
Villanova, Pennsylvania
1971

ZOLA, MASTER OF NATURALISM

Zola was the first to apply the term naturalism to a literary system. Previously it had been purely a philosophical term, so it is important to know the history and implications of the word at the time that Zola chose it as a name for his literary system. Martino, in his interesting little book, *Le Naturalisme français*, cites a revealing list of references to and definitions of naturalism. By their chronological order one can trace successive acceptances in which the term was used. First it was used in a philosophical sense, beginning with the sixteenth century surgeon, Ambroise Paré: "... doctrines des naturalistes, épicuristes et athéistes qui sont sans Dieu."[1] Then to Diderot and the eighteenth century: "Ceux qui n'admettent point de Dieu, mais qui croient qu'il n'y a qu'une substance matérielle revêtue de diverses qualités."[1] That Littré in 1866 still understood the term in the same sense may be seen from his definition: "Système de ceux qui attribuent tout a la nature comme premier principe."[1] Naturalism as used here would imply either atheism or pantheism, with perhaps a tendency to materialism, as indicated in this quotation from Sainte-Beuve (1839): "... la doctrine du XVIIIᵉ siecle, ... le matérialisme ou le panthéisme, ou encore le naturalisme, comme on voudra l'appeler."[2] Martino also cites the fact that the *Revue de Deux Mondes* (1852) reproached the poetry of Gautier and his school as being "toute naturaliste: elle ne professe que le culte des choses de la création, et elle ne remonte point du monde visible à Dieu."[2]

All these references show that the term naturalism was first used to indicate a philosophy which was opposed to the theological idea of God and which sought the ultimate principle, if at all, in nature. It might be pantheistic or materialistic. But who would profess such a philosophy? Clearly, those especially absorbed in the study of the phenomena of nature, the scientists, the naturalists. The connection between the words naturalist, meaning scientist, and naturalism, meaning a philosophy, is now clear. A naturalist is apt to be a man who professes naturalism as his philosophy. It becomes the philosophy of science:

Les "naturalistes philosophes," résume très exactement Sainte-Beuve, en 1863, "tendant à introduire en tout et à faire prévaloir en tout les procédés et les résultats de la science; affranchis eux-

mêmes, [ils] s'efforcent d'affranchir l'humanité des illusions, des
vagues disputes, des solutions vaines, des idoles et des puissances
trompeuses."[3]

Flaubert liked to compare his work of collecting documents for
his realistic novels to that of the naturalist observing phenomena
in the world of animal and plant life. It remained, however,
for Emile Zola to popularize thoroughly the two terms hitherto
confined to the exclusive world of philosophers and savants.

C'est quand les mots *naturalisme* et *naturaliste* sont arrivés à
ce stade, riches de leur ancien sens philosophique, de toutes les
conquêtes récentes de la biologie, de tous les efforts de la peinture
vers la représentation de la réalité, et de toutes les aspirations
artistiques, politiques ou sociales de l'esprit positiviste moderne,
c'est alors que Zola les saisit, et qu'il en fait sa chose. . . .[3]

And the last definition is from the pen of Zola himself in *Le
Roman expérimental*:

Tel est le naturalisme, ou, si ce mot effraye, si l'on trouve une
périphrase plus claire, la formule de la science moderne appliquée
à la littérature.[4]

But the whole story is not found in the development of the
meaning of a word. It lies rather in the stream of ideas which
carried that word along. Let us trace that stream to its sources:

Il ne faut pas non plus perdre de vue cette grande voie droite
qui rejoint le naturalisme au positivisme, le positivisme au saint-
simonisme, celui-ci à l'idéologie, et celle-ci à la philosophie ency-
clopédiste. Le réalisme et le naturalisme n'ont été que deux
manifestations . . . d'un immense mouvement intellectuelle; leur
prestige, leur puissance de rayonnement, en France et à l'étranger,
qui fut grande, ne sont pas dus surtout à l'éclat de quelques mani-
festes littéraires, ni même à l'excellence des grandes oeuvres qu-ils
ont inspirées; leur vraie force vient du dehors; et c'est pourquoi,
si leurs formules, celle du naturalisme, surtout, sont aujourd'hui
en partie périmées et vieillottes, leur esprit est toujours vivant.
Cet esprit, c'est l'esprit même du XIXe siècle, une fois qu'il se
fut débarrassé du romantisme.[5]

Idéologie is generally dated around 1820, but for its sources the
Grande Encyclopédie goes back not only to the eighteenth-cen-
tury encyclopedists but to the philosophers of the seventeenth
century:

L'idéologie a des precurseurs nombreux: au XVIIe siècle,
Descartes et Bayle, les savants, de Galilée à Newton, les philosophes
partisans de l'expérience, Bacon, Gassendi ou Hobbes, et Locke,
qui en résume les directions diverses; au XVIIIe siècle, Fon-
tanelle, Montesquieu et Voltaire, puis leurs continuateurs, en-
cyclopédistes, philosophes, économistes. . . . En somme, l'idéologie
est un moment dans le developpement de cette philosophie scien-

tifique qui, parfois unie au christianisme et à la métaphysique ancienne, parfois les combattant ou marchant seule, s'efforce de tirer, de la connaissance positive et systématisée de l'homme et de l'univers, les règles practiques propres à diriger l'individu, à éléver l'enfant, à organiser la société.[6]

Starting with such men as Descartes and Spinoza, who believe in the all-powerfulness of human reason, we pass on in the history of philosophy to Locke, Hume, and the English empiricists. Locke is inclined to recognize some limits to what man can reason out for himself and be sure of; after all, we are very dependent on the reliability of our five senses. Indeed, Berkeley goes still farther and declares nothing is real but ideas suggested by what we call sensations. Hume doubts even our ability to be sure the sun will rise tomorrow; nothing is actually proved by analogy to what happened in the past. All this while practical men of science were making important discoveries and material progress. Galileo, Bacon, Newton contribute their discoveries in astronomy and physics. Buffon makes his name remembered in the realm of natural history. While such men as Voltaire and Diderot are attacking established religion, and metaphysics, with Hume, is abutting on universal doubt, practical science is really achieving results. What is the outcome? It may be found in Auguste Comte and the nineteenth century philosophy of positivism. No matter if we cannot be rationally sure of the existence of God, no matter if we cannot be metaphysically sure of anything, the fact remains that we live and move in a world of apparent reality. Science can help us dominate that world and make it materially better. Here is something concrete, let us stick to it. We shall not know the ultimate why of things but at least we shall know the how of things.

Le positivisme s'en tiendra aux réalités "appréciables à notre organisme," c'est-à-dire aux phénomènes perçus par les sens et à leurs lois. Une telle philosophie sera sans doute toute *relative*, puisqu'au lieu de déterminer des causes elle no saisira que des relations constantes entre des faits, mais elle sera *utile*, puisqu'elle permettra de prévoir et d'agir sur la nature; elle sera *organique*, car l'invariabilité et la concordance que nous observons entre les lois de la nature imprimeront au savoir un caractère croissant d'unité et de simplicité.[7]

Auguste Comte is generally considered a disciple of the philosopher Saint-Simon (1760-1825). The latter's most interesting belief was that society could be made the subject of a science as exact as biology or physics. In developing his new science of sociology Saint-Simon came to condemn many of the social ills of his time. He was one of the first to preach the gospel of work; everyone should work, there should be no idle parasite classes, above all no military class; inheritance was a great evil; goods should go to the state. Many of the seeds of socialism as we know it today are in the doctrine of this thinker of over a hundred years ago. One of the important ideas which Comte derived from Saint-Simon was that the phychology of the human animal was merely a part of his physiology or biology. Saint-Simon had preached that a social science could be created as definite as biology. Comte merely connected the two more closely, for sociology is individual psychology in the aggregate and

> Quant à la psychologie, Comte la reduit à n'être qu'un chapitre de la biologie dont elle empruntera la méthode d'observation expérimentale. . . . La psychologie positiviste trouvera sa place à la fois dans l'anatomie et la physiologie qui détermineront exactement les conditions organiques dont dépendent les fonctions mentales.[8]

Here we have the beginnings of that deterministic philosophy which is to become the very cornerstone of Zola's naturalism. Psychology is no more than a chapter in biology. A man's thoughts are determined by physiological causes—in short, we are being introduced to *l'homme physiologique*. But Auguste Comte was not a skillful introducer. He was a much better thinker than he was a stylist. It remained for Hippolyte Taine's lucid diction to present the physiological man to the world of French letters, and it was not until thirty years later, in 1864, that Taine published his *History of English Literature*—a work which would now be forgotten were it not for its famous Introduction. Ostensibly a prologue to a study of English authors, what the Introduction really introduced was *la bête humaine*—the human animal with his every response, both moral and physical, determined by physiological laws as arbitrary as that of gravitation.

> Que les faits soient physiques ou moreaux, il n'importe, ils ont toujours des causes; il y en a pour l'ambition, pour le courage, pour la véracité, comme pour la digestion, pour le mouvement musculaire, pour la chaleur animale. Le vice et la vertu sont des produits comme le vitriol et le sucre.[9]

What possibilities for a novelist! There is no longer for him any moral *gêne*; he may treat of any depravity so long as he accounts for it scientifically as the *savant* would describe the preparation of a poison.[10] But let us allow Taine to develop his

system further and discover for us what may be these causes
of vice and virtue:

> Trois sources différentes contribuent à produire cet état
> moral élémentaire, *la race, le milieu* et *le moment.* Ce qu'on
> appelle *la race,* ce sont ces dispositions innées et héréditaires que
> l'homme apporte avec lui à la lumière, et qui ordinairement sont
> jointes à des différences marquées dans le tempérament et dans
> la structure du corps. . . .

> Lorsqu'on a aussi constaté la structure intérieure d'une race,
> il faut considérer le *milieu* dans lequel elle vit. Car l'homme n'est
> pas seul dans le monde; la nature l'enveloppe et les autres hommes
> l'entourent; sur le pli primitif et permanent viennent s'étaler les
> plis accidentels et secondaires, et les circonstances physiques ou
> sociales dérangent ou complètent le naturel qui leur est livré. . . .

> Il y a pourtant un troisième ordre de causes; car avec les forces
> du dedans et du dehors, il y a l'oeuvre qu'ils ont déjà faite en-
> semble, et cette ouvre elle-même contribue à produire celle qui
> suit; outre l'impulsion permanente et le milieu donné, il y a la
> vitesse acquise. . . .[11]

Taine is interested in studying English literature in order to
penetrate the personality of its authors. It is people he is interested in, people who were the products of their heredity, of
their environment, and of the time in which they lived—just
as any man today presumably is the result of those three determining forces. It was not a new theory; the positivists following after Auguste Comte had said as much. The originality of
this historian of English literature lay in the fact that he applied positivism to literature. His book was accepted with
great enthusiasm by the realist writers of his day. Indeed, the
famous Introduction became a sort of Bible both to the contemporary realists and to the naturalists who followed. Even
Paul Bourget and the psychological novelists found a master in
Taine.[12] His philosophy of the determinism exercised on human
life by the three forces of *race, milieu, moment,* was to become
the backbone of the French novel for almost half a century.

One must not forget, at this point, that just five years before
Taine wrote his *History of English Literature,* Darwin had published his epoch-making work, *The Origin of the Species* (1859).
With its doctrine of the gradual development of animal life
through the geological ages, Darwin's theory was well in line
with the positivistic trend of the century, regarding man, as it
did, as merely a higher animal, determined, like his brothers of
the forest, by the mechanical forces of heredity and environment.
The theory was given solidity by another giant in the world of

science, Claude Bernard. Discarding the traditional empirical approach to medicine, he sought to apply to it the observational and experimental methods of modern biology. Proceeding under the conviction of there being an infallible determinism regulating physical phenomena in any animal organism, human included, he applied his experimental method to prove all hypotheses. He was not content to take the average result of experiments with varying outcome. The same conditions must always produce the same result—if results were different, then original conditions must have varied. No hypothesis can be considered proven until an exact series of experiments has sustained it.[13] This conception of hypotheses sounds perfectly natural to us today; we do not realize what a different rôle such conjectures played in the medical practice of former times. It was thought that disease could be reasoned out abstractly and that no practical experimentation could be made upon the complicated dual make-up of a human soul and body. But Claude Bernard marched ahead with his method in his physiological laboratory in Paris, and the practical results were nothing short of amazing to the people of his time. When he published his *Introduction to the Study of Experimental Medicine* in 1865, the book was a sensation and its author rewarded with membership in the French Academy.[14] It is hard for us today to realize the prestige enjoyed by this one savant. Like Louis XIV, who said "L'état c'est moi," Claude Bernard might have said, "La physiologie c'est moi." The *Grande Encyclopédie* sums it up very well:

> Il est presque san exemple que dans aucune science la part d'un seul homme ait été aussi considérable que celle de Claude Bernard en physiologie. Il faut être pénétré de cette vérité pour comprendre que ses admirateurs aient pu dire de lui: "Claude Bernard n'est pas un simple physiologiste: il est la physiologie même." Si l'on réfléchit en outre que ce savant s'est élevé, en quelque sorte, du rang d'expérimentateur à celui de legislateur de la méthode expérimentale—et qu'enfin, la bienveillante sérénité, l'élévation et la sincère passion de la vérité ont été les traits distinctifs de son caractère—on se fera alors une idée précise de la place qu'il a occupé dans l'affection et dans l'admiration des biologistes contemporains.[15]

We must add another element in the aggregate which made up Bernard's prestige—the tremendous popular enthusiasm for science. As Martino remarks:

> Mais la science avait alors, plus qu'aujourd'hui, des admirateurs dévots et mal informés, d'autant plus passionnés qu'ils

savaient moins. Les formules péremptoires de Zola choquèrent en réalité moins que nous ne serions tentés de le croire, tant l'ambiance était favorable à de pareilles exaggérations.[16]

When Zola came to Paris in 1858, he was a poet and a romanticist. It took him eight or ten years to find himself and to discover fully where his true talent lay. His first two naturalistic novels were *Thérèse Raquin* (1866) and *Madelaine Férat* (1868). It was not until Zola wrote the preface to the second edition of *Thérèse Raquin*, however, in 1868, that he definitely realized just what sort of literary work he was to do.[17] In this same year he conceived his great series of novels, *les Rougon-Macquart*. The manuscript plans for *La Fortune des Rougon*, in which Zola reasons with himself at this critical point in his career, are all preserved for us in the National Library at Paris. They present a most interesting study of the *enfantement* of naturalism as a literary school. Matthew Josephson, in his interesting biography of Zola, has had the kindness to quote these documents at length.

> "First," he says to himself, "I am a novelist, and I wish to dominate; now, to dominate one must convey a certainty, a truth. Taine, my master, claims that there is no great novelist whose work does not contain a philosophy. Yes, even an absurd philosophy like Balzac's. That is the capital question for me, and I have been searching for one for eight years. . . . I shall not lack for a philosophy: I shall acquire one in advance. I want a system that is entirely new; one of necessity that is taken from the movement of ideas of my own time. . . . What is it?. . . . We believe in Science. The future is there, that is the general view. In whatever direction I turn, I see nothing but scientists. Even Sainte-Beuve has declared: 'Anatomists and physiologists, I find you everywhere.' "[18]
>
> "I am," he says triumphantly, "a positivist, an evolutionist, a materialist; my system is heredity. I have found the instrument of my epoch, and there is no doubt about the power that it gives a man to feel himself holding it in his hands and aiding the natural evolution of things. I wish to be a painter of life. I must therefore ask of science to explain life to me."[19]

Zola had already dipped into scientific books and medical treatises for ideas in the construction of his two early works, *Thérèse Raquin* and *Madelaine Férat*.[20] But now he sets himself seriously to study the newest in science. He buries himself in Dr. Prosper Lucas' book on heredity and takes voluminous notes. Filled with enthusiasm, on the basis of this work he constructs (1868-69) the famous family tree of the Rougon-Macquart family.[21] This hypothetical genealogy has all the principal types of heredity as treated in Dr. Lucas' book. Starting with an abnormal ancestress subject to nervous attacks, Zola traces the effects of the *nerviosité* through four succeeding generations. There is also the heredity of alcoholism in one of the male ancestors, and that is revealed in its various manifestations of homicide and depravity. Zola composed the whole tree before writing the first novel, *La Fortune des Rougon*. The series, originally planned as ten novels, and developing later to twenty, was to trace the history of a family under the Second Empire. Heredity was to be the connecting link that would bind them all together. Thus Zola could well say, "My system is heredity." But heredity could not be all of it. We must not forget the heritage of Taine: *race, milieu, moment*. Heredity is only one third of the system. In the genealogy of the Rougon-Macquart family Zola has been careful not only to make each member a particular hereditary case but also to place each in a different environment. There will be a novel on the *nouveaux-riches* and one on the slums of Paris, one about a priest and one about a peasant, etc. The *moment* will be taken care of by the chronology of the family and also by the events of the Second Empire. The matter of historical setting is of course not so important to a novelist writing of contemporary or almost contemporary situations. It was not until Zola approached the end of his series that the lapse of time between author and scene became a major consideration for documentation. We have mentioned Taine and Dr. Lucas as sources; there remains another, the book by Dr. Charles Letourneau on the *Physiology of the Passions*.[22] It has been shown how Zola chose positivism as a unifying philosophy to underlie all his books and how he decided to turn to Science as a mentor to tell him about life. Proceeding then to Taine's three forces, he used Dr. Lucas for heredity and Dr. Letourneau to show how the physiological man reacts to his environment; and for chronology he could rely largely on his own acquaintance with the events of the Second Empire. On the basis of these three sources, then, he constructed the plan of the Rougon-Macquart family and the work was well begun.

Zola did not care particularly whether the scientific theories he appropriated were reasonably well established or not. He saw the fever of adoration with which the populace welcomed anything even savoring of the scientific. He would humor the popular fancy, and the philosophy of positivism was as good as another to give unity to his work, as he says in his *notes intimes* as of 1868:

> Il est indifférent que le fait générateur soit reconnu comme absolument vrai; ce sera surtout une hypothèse scientifique empruntée aux traités medicaux. Mais lorsque ce fait sera posé, lorsque je l'aurai accepté comme axiome, en déduire mathématiquement tout le volume. Prendre avant tout une tendance philosophique non pour l'étaler, mais pour donner une suite à mes livres. La meilleure serait le matérialisme, je veux dire la croyance à des forces sur lesquelles je n'aurai jamais besoin de m'expliquer. Le mot force ne compromet pas.[23]

One sees with what cynical purpose Zola could view his project at the start, but later on he himself must have become convinced by the torrent of his own ink. If not that, at least he was carried away by the popular enthusiasm for Science which at first he sought to flatter.[24] Furthermore, the very audacity and uncertainty of the hypothesis upon which he chose to build his enterprise undoubtedly appealed to the poetic imagination which was in Zola. Consider this quotation from *Docteur Pascal,* the last and concluding novel of the series:

> Ah! ces sciences commençantes, ces sciences où l'hypothèse balbutie et où l'imagination reste maitresse, elles sont le domaine des poètes autant que des savants! Les poètes vont en pionniers, à l'avant-garde et souvent ils découvrent les pays vierges, indiquent les solutions prochaines. Il y a là une marge qui leur appartient, entre la vérité conquise, définitive, et l'inconnu, d'où l'on arrachera la vérité de demain . . .[25]

Yes, Zola even went so far as to believe that he could discover scientific truth by means of a novel. Starting out with the acceptance of certain hypotheses merely to give his novel logical sequence, so as to "en déduire mathématiquement tout le volume," he gradually swings around to the idea that the novel is an experiment, an attempt to prove the theories assumed at the start. Just as a scientist such as Claude Bernard assumes an hypothesis and then proceeds with a series of trials to prove or disprove it, so the novelist experiments with his characters, subjecting them to the pushes and pulls at once of their hereditary equipment and of their surroundings in time and place. So vivid did this analogy become to Zola that he decided to make it the subject of a polemic in defense of naturalism, *Le Roman expérimental.* This short article of some fifty pages was first published in the Russian review, *The European Messenger.* Later it lent its name to a collection of articles first published in France in 1880. The resultant book constitutes perhaps the clearest and most famous of Zola's manifestoes in favor of naturalism. The short article on the experimental novel is placed first in the book, and this is appropriate as it may be considered the spear-point of Zola's argument.

The fortuitous analogy which the author strikes between his own procedure as a novelist and that of Claude Bernard as a physiologist is to become the crux of his naturalistic doctrine. It is important that it be understood. Let us let Zola give us an example to illustrate the procedure:

> Le romancier part à la recherche d'une vérité. Je prendrai comme exemple le baron Hulot dans *La Cousine Bette* de Balzac. Le fait général observé par Balzac est le ravage que le tempérament amoureux d'un homme amène chez lui, dans sa famille et dans la société. Dès qu'il a eu choisi son sujet, il est parti des faits observés, puis il a institué son expérience en soumettant Hulot à une série d'épreuves, en le faisant passer par certains milieux pour montrer le fonctionnement du méchanisme de sa passion. Il est donc évident qu'il n'y a pas seulement l'observation, mais qu'il y a aussi expérimentation, puisque Balzac ne s'en tient pas strictement aux faits receuillis par lui, puisqu'il intervient d'une façon directe pour placer son personnage dans des conditions dont il reste le maître. Le problème est de savoir ce que telle passion, agissant dans tel milieu et dans tels circonstances, produira au pointe de vue de l'individu et de la société . . . En somme toute l'opération consiste à prendre les faits dans la nature, puis a étudier le méchanisme des faits, en agissant sur eux par des modifications des circonstances et des milieux, sans jamais s'écarter des lois de la nature. Au bout il y a la connaissance de l'homme.[26]

Of course, there is an inherent fallacy here which must be apparent to anyone, namely, that no actual experiment ever takes place. It is all in the novelist's own mind. He starts with a *fait observé* and proceeds to compose a novel to prove the truth of it, being mindful to make his characters always react according to his "laws" governing human conduct—laws which also are hypotheses. Nothing apparently could be more unlike the chemist, who combines two liquids in his test tube and then measures the resulting precipitate. Zola tries bravely to maintain the analogy, however, and there is a certain truth in his comparison.

> Un fait observé devra faire jaillir l'idée de l'expérience à instituer, du roman à écrire, pour arriver à la connaissance com-

plète d'une vérité. Puis, lorsqu'il aura discuté et arrêté le plan de cette expérience, il en jugera à chaque minute les résultats avec la liberté d'esprit d'un homme qui accepte les seuls faits conformes au déterminisme des phénomènes. Il est parti du doute pour arriver à la connaissance absolue; et il ne cesse de douter que lorsque le mécanisme de la passion, démonté et remonté par lui, fonctionne selon les lois fixées par la nature.[27]

We are inclined to wonder what those "laws fixed by Nature" may be and whether Zola's novelist can really know them so perfectly, but if we will accept for a moment nineteenth-century man's blind faith in science, the analogy stands. Like the scientist, the author starts with certain hypotheses—the pernicious influence of slums and alcohol on an honest, hard-working couple, for instance—and with certain given materials to be opposed to certain forces. His "givens" are the hereditary temperaments of his characters. The forces are to be found in the milieu—temporal and social—in which they are to be placed and which they themselves modify. Given physiological men who are ruled by certain appetites and determined by certain rules of passion (to be found in Dr. Letourneau's book), we place them in a certain environment—perhaps a coal mining town which we have studied with care over a period of months—and we work out the results according to the constant rules of determinism. With men in such circumstances, reduced to the brute by hunger and misery, the result is likely to be very real.

Zola's whole system now derives itself from the principle of the experimental novel. The heredity and temperament of the personages are given. The milieu is then studied minutely and described completely. No determining detail may be omitted for reasons of delicacy or morals. Morals are merely products like sugar and sulphuric acid, as Taine remarked. One must tell all and withhold none of the influences which push and pull this our physiologically determined human animal across the stage. As Martino sums it up:

Roman "expérimental," roman physiologique, tares héréditaires, influence des milieux, c'est tout l'armature des Rougon-Macquart. . . .[28]

Or as Zola put it:

Tel est le naturalisme . . . la formule de la science moderne appliquée à la littérature.[29]

But Zola's naturalism was not just a reflection of the scientific spirit of his time; it may also be viewed as the climax of a long literary current going back to the beginning of the century.

Despite the magnificent display that was romanticism, there continued all the while a strong literary undercurrent of realism. Romanticism was a revolt against the fetters of the past and the materialism of the present. It was dazzling while it lasted but essentially temporary in nature.[30] We have seen how Zola originated naturalism as a new literary system, and we know that he was inordinately proud of his creation:

> "My work," he resolved, "will be in conformity with this science. I am going to picture the physiological man. This is my formula; and best of all it will be a new art, a new literature, which will be my own literature, my own art. *I, I alone will be Naturalism.*"[31]

And he was quite right; naturalism really did begin with Zola and did contribute something new to literature. Nevertheless, Zola did not wish to disown his literary ancestors; rather he would make capital of the established reputations of such realists as Balzac and Flaubert, saying that they, too, were naturalists. Regardless of terminology, it is true that Zola's naturalism includes many literary techniques which were first invented by his realist predecessors and any study of naturalism must include a study of these techniques.

In 1881 Zola published a book entitled *Les Romanciers naturalistes* in which he traces his ancestry back to Balzac, "notre véritable père."[32] Stendhal, Flaubert, and the de Goncourt brothers all are considered as forming a chain of naturalistic authors. Zola is able so to classify them by reducing his formula to its minimum essentials of analysis and experiment. It is a matter of scientific procedure, of certain general truths deriving from the development of the novel, of due regard for the determinism of phenomena, and of disregard for idealistic or spiritual phenomena—of *l'inconnu.*[33] Zola's admiration for Balzac is very great; he found in him the true beginnings of the naturalistic dynasty.

> Mais il suffit qu'il soit notre véritable père, qu'il ait le premier affirmé l'action décisive du milieu sur le personnage, qu'il ait porté dans le roman les méthodes d'observation et d'expérimentation. C'est là ce qui fait de lui le génie du siècle.[32]

Stendhal, in comparison to Balzac, seems to Zola much less complete, though he is still a naturalist for he proceeds by analysis and his novels are experiments to prove certain theories or general truths. Here we have the comparison as Zola pens it:

> Ce qui est vrai, c'est que Balzac partait en savant de l'étude du sujet; tout son travail était basé sur l'observation de la créa-

ture humaine, et il se trouvait ainsi amené, comme le zoologiste, à tenir un compte immense de tous les organes et du milieu. Il faut le voir dans une salle de dissection, le scalpel à la main, constatant qu'il n'y a pas seulement un cerveau dans l'homme, devinant que l'homme est une plante tenant au sol, et décidé dès lors, par amour du vrai, à ne rien retrancher de l'homme, à le montrer dans son entier, avec sa vraie fonction, sous l'influence du vaste monde. Pendant ce temps Stendhal reste dans son cabinet de philosophe, remuant des idées, ne prenant de l'homme que la tête et comptant chaque pulsation du cerveau. Il n'écrit pas un roman pour analyser un coin de la réalité, êtres et choses; il écrit un roman pour appliquer ses théories sur l'amour, pour appliquer le système de Condillac sur la formation des idées.[34]

The conclusion which Zola draws is that Stendhal and Balzac represent two different philosophies. The former was sixteen years older than the latter and his philosophy is that of the eighteenth century. Balzac studies the physiological man, influenced by the vast world around him. Stendhal studies only the mind and soul of man; he is the link which joins nineteenth-century naturalism directly to the preceding epoch, establishing thus an unbroken chain with the past. One can now pass over romanticism as a temporary excrescence and arrive at naturalism as a natural development of the "vieux génie français."[35]

As a concrete instance of Stendhal's incompleteness Zola cites the scene from *Le rouge et le noir* where Julien Sorel forces himself to take Mme. Renal's hand in the dark of the garden. Julien might well have been an intellectual type more or less impervious to his surroundings, but surely Mme. Renal was not such a person. She undoubtedly sensed all the voluptuous sway of the soft summer night, with all its sweetness and hushed sounds. Without this *milieu* the picture remains undeniably incomplete.[36] Compare now Balzac:

. . . Prenez un personnage de Stendhal: c'est une machine intellectuelle et passionelle parfaitement montée. Prenez un personnage de Balzac: C'est un homme en chair et en os, avec son vêtement et l'air qui l'enveloppe. Où est la création la plus complète, où est la vie? Chez Balzac, évidemment.[37]

Zola owes much to Balzac. From him he got the idea of writing a series of novels, like the *Comédie Humaine*, each one in a different milieu. The Rougon-Macquart series is a modification of Balzac's system. It has more unity, through the hereditary connection of the characters, and as a general thing Zola kept the number of characters in any one book smaller than did Balzac. But the technique of showing the varying influence of different milieus by placing each novel in its own particular section of human life undoubtedly came to Zola from Balzac, a fact that the master of naturalism does not hesitate to admit. We have also seen him take an example from Balzac (le baron Hulot) to illustrate the technique of the experimental novel.

Passing now to Gustave Flaubert, Zola underlines a number of important contributions toward the development of naturalism. Speaking first of *Madame Bovary,* Zola says that this great novel was in many respects a model for future generations to follow. Here was an everyday plot played by everyday people and told in a matter-of-fact, impersonal fashion. Henceforth the romantic plot is banned:

> On n'y rencontre plus des enfants marqués à leur naissance, puis perdus, pour être retrouvés au dénoûment. Il n'y est plus question de meubles à secret, de papiers qui servent, au bon moment, à sauver l'innocence persécutée. Même toute intrigue manque, si simple qu'elle soit. Le roman va devant lui, contant les choses au jour le jour, ne ménageant aucune surprise, offrant tout au plus la matière d'un fait divers; et, quand il est fini, c'est comme si l'on quittait la rue pour rentrer chez soi.[38]

One might remonstrate that we did not receive any such tranquil impression from the death of Madame Bovary or even from the final scenes of *Germinal* but, however that may be, one must give the naturalists credit for not having any long-lost children turn up at the last moment and for not including any fantastic prison breaks, like the Count of Monte-Cristo's. The plot of a truly naturalistic novel seems to rise naturally from the interplay of characters and milieu. Even Balzac would occasionally let his fancy run away with him, developing plots that were more romantic than realistic. He never quite lost his love for extraordinary adventures.[39] Not only so, but the author of the *Comédie Humaine* had a strong tendency to exaggerate his characters. This is rigorously forbidden from Flaubert on. It is inconsistent with the tone of everyday life which the author is trying to portray. As Zola sums it up:

> La beauté de l'oeuvre n'est plus dans la grandissement d'un personnage, qui cesse d'être un avare, un gourmand, un paillard, pour devenir l'avarice, la gourmandise, la paillardise elles-mêmes; elle est dans la vérité indiscutable du document humain, dans la réalité absolue des peintures où tous les details occupent leur place, et rien que cette place. Ce qui tiraille presque toujours les romans de Balzac, c'est le grossissement de ses héros; il ne croit jamais les faire assez gigantesques; ses poings puissants de créateur ne savent forger que des géants. Dans la formule

naturaliste, cette exuberance de l'artiste, ce caprice de composition promenant un personnage d'une grandeur hors nature au
milieu de personnages nains, se trouve forcément condamné.   Un
égal niveau abaisse toutes les têtes, car les occasions sont rares,
où l'on ait vraiment à mettre en scène un homme supérieur.[40]

In addition to weeding the extraordinary out of the novel, like
strange plots and exaggerated heroes, the author of *Madame
Bovary* also left out himself.   This is another great contribution
of Flaubert's to naturalism—the principle of *impersonnalité*.
An author must neither condone nor praise; he merely tells the
facts as such.   He does not formulate a moral at the end; he
leaves that to the reader to deduce.   Any intervention on his
part would spoil the perfection of the recital, of the artistic
whole constituted by the portion of life recorded.   All the facts
presented are perfectly interrelated in a symmetry which Zola
is wont to compare to that of *un beau marbre*.   Zola's admiration
for the genius of Balzac was ever tempered by an awareness
of the unevenness of the work of the early master.[41]   It remained for Gustave Flaubert to achieve many sane improve-
ments and make of the novel a truer and more scientific study
of life—even perhaps a more beautiful, surely a more perfect
thing.

. . . ce que Gustave Flaubert a fait du roman après lui: il l'a
assujetti à des règles fixes d'observation, l'a débarrassé de l'enflure
fausse des personnages, l'a changé en une oeuvre d'art harmonique,
impersonnelle, vivant de sa beauté propre, ainsi qu'un beau marbre.
Telle est l'évolution accomplie par l'auteur de *Madame Bovary* . . .
Son rôle a été surtout de parler au nom de la perfection, du
style parfait, de la composition parfaite, de l'oeuvre parfaite,
défiant les âges. . . .[42]

No study of naturalism would be complete without making
mention of the practice of documentation, and this, too, was a
technique first developed extensively by Gustave Flaubert.   He
would write of nothing about which he was not sufficiently—even
more than sufficiently—informed.   He sought the most minute
information.   Walking the banks of the Seine for miles in order
to describe a boat trip which the hero of *L'Education senti-
mentale* was to take on that river, reading twenty volumes on
agriculture in order to prepare for another book—these are
classic examples.   Even Zola did not often go so far in thorough-
ness of documentation.   The de Goncourt brothers, however,
were close competitors to Flaubert in this respect, if, indeed,
they did not surpass him; for after all, a number of their novels

are almost taken whole from life while Flaubert's novels rest imaginary in their ensemble. There is here a fundamental difference of technique for whereas Flaubert sought to make his characters a composite of many observed types, the de Goncourts are prone to portray actual individuals whom they have known or observed; hence they tend toward a more individualized sort of personage and must have pursued a form of documentation slightly different from that of Flaubert. For example, in *Germinie Lacerteux,* as everyone knows, they have merely given us the life of their maid—a secret life whose details were not revealed to the brothers except after much diligent inquiry and documentation after the woman's death. Starting out as historians of the manners of the eighteenth century, they carried on the same careful and minute form of research in the preparation of their novels. It was they who said, "A novel is history which might have happened." The de Goncourts have come to be looked upon as the masters of the documentary novel par excellence. Their work contains all the heritage of the realistic tradition. As Martino summarizes:

> Les frères Goncourt . . . ont réalisé plus complètement que les autres les diverses aspirations de la doctrine réaliste: le roman sociologue à la Balzac, le goût pour l'information minutieuse et méthodique, à la manière de Flaubert, la préférence pour les tableaux et les personnages empruntés aux moeurs populaires, comme le voulait Champfleury . . . La seule expression qui caractérise très complètement le roman, tel qu'ils l'ont compris, c'est celle de *roman documentaire*.[43]

Zola sustains Martino's judgment of the de Goncourts, adding further that they used documentation to add originality to their work.

> Ils veulent sortir du conte, de l'éternelle histoire, de l'éternelle intrigue, qui promène les personnages au travers des mêmes péripéties, pour les tuer ou les marier au denoûment. Par besoin d'originalité, ils refusent cette banalité du récit pour le récit, qui a traîné partout. Ce qu'ils cherchent, ce sont des pages d'études, simplement un procès-verbal humain, quelque chose de plus haut et de plus grand, dont l'interêt soit dans l'exactitude des peintures et la nouveauté des documents.[44]

Although the de Goncourts may ultimately be remembered for their mastery of the documentary novel, their most important contribution to the development of naturalism lay in their having "fait entrer le peuple dans le roman."[45] *Germinie Lacerteux* made a great scandal; it also made a very strong—and favorable

—impression on Emile Zola. He was among the few critics to praise the work upon its first appearance, thereby gaining early in his career the friendship of the two brothers. Above all, the youthful Zola seems to have found the book timed to suit the spirit of the day, a substantial merit in the eyes of this man who so cunningly set himself later to catch the breath and philosophy of his age in order to incorporate them into his own works. We have Zola's *premier mouvement* in response to *Germinie* preserved for us in the collection of articles entitled *Mes Haines* (1866):

> Nous sommes malades de progrès, d'industrie, de science; nous vivons dans la fièvre, et nous nous plaisons à fouiller dans les plaies, à descendre toujours plus bas, avides de connaître le cadavre du coeur humain. Tout souffre, tout se plaint dans les ouvrages du temps; la nature est associée à nos douleurs, l'être se déchire lui-même et se montre dans sa nudité. MM. Goncourt ont écrit pour les hommes de nos jours; leur Germinie n'aurait pu vivre à aucune autre époque que la nôtre; elle est fille du siècle.[46]

Now compare what he said fifteen years later in *Les Romanciers naturalistes*:

> Le roman, à son apparition, produisit un scandale énorme. On la déclara ordurier, la critique prit des pincettes pour en tourner les pages. Personne, d'ailleurs, ne dit le mot juste. *Germinie Lacerteux*, dans notre littérature contemporaine, est une date. Le livre fait entrer le peuple dans le roman; pour la première fois, le héros en casquette et l'héroine en bonnet de linge y sont étudiés par des écrivains d'observation et de style. En outre, je le répète, il ne s'agit pas d'une histoire plus ou moins intéressante, mais d'une véritable leçon d'anatomie morale et physique. Le romancier jette une femme sur la pierre de l'amphithéâtre, la première femme venue, la bonne qui traverse la rue en tablier; il la dissèque patiemment, montre chaque muscle, fait jouer les nerfs, cherche les causes et raconte les effets; et cela suffit pour étaler tout un coin saignant de l'humanité.[45]

It seems obvious that it was the de Goncourt brothers who marked the way for Zola toward those unsparing analyses which he himself was to make of the human animal, especially as that *genus* exists on the lower levels of society.

What then remains as Zola's own original contribution? We have seen how Balzac already had the idea of diverse milieus, and how he, too, wrote experimental novels, e.g., *La Cousine Bette*. Flaubert brought in the ordinary people with their ordinary action perfectly analysed; he also introduced systematic documentation and the impersonal style. The de Goncourts contributed the frank analysis of characters drawn from *les basses classes*; they also carried documentation a step further. There remained for Zola the matter of heredity, that hazy science "où l'hypothèse balbutie et où l'imagination reste maîtresse." Our novelist studied a reputable book on the subject, and the theories and examples therein sounded very convincing. Be that as it may, it was a grand idea for a novelist—to write a series of novels treating all the known cases of hereditary influences and to tie them all together within the history of one family! It had not been done, and it was in line with the popular enthusiasm for science and the positivist point of view. Novelists had presented the physiological man subjected to his environment; they had considered the *milieu* and the *moment* but they had neglected the first of Taine's determining forces—*race*. In constructing his Rougon-Macquart family tree, Zola capped the pyramid which his century had been building for him. Hitherto, France had seen *realists*; now she would know *naturalists,* of which Zola would be the first. We can appreciate the exultation with which he must have said to himself, ". . . my system is heredity. I have found the instrument of my epoch."

We have seen the two converging streams of scientific philosophy and literary realism of which Zola's naturalism was the culmination. Let us now look more closely at the system itself and at some of the complications to which it led. The thing to bear in mind now is that, although naturalism was the direct result of a continuous stream of thought in philosophy and aesthetics, yet at the same time there were other streams of thought, other *esthétiques*. Romanticists, Catholics, moralists, the authors of nice books for nice people—in short, all those whom Zola lumps together under the universal accusation of *idealists*—all these constituted opponents. Naturalism was a fighting word and most of what was said for and against it savors of gunpowder. The remaining romanticists found the naturalistic novel full of ugliness, bare reality, sordidness; the Catholics found it materialistic and pagan; the moralists found it perverting to virtue; the authors of nice books thought it indiscreet; and altogether the chorus of opposition shouted "Immoral!" Zola's opponents saw only the weakness of reasoning —not the analogy—in his doctrine of the experimental novel. Nor was there any lack of people to question the accuracy of his treatment of heredity. But most of the trouble arose over naturalism's attempt to show the determining force of the milieu on human life. The physiological man, pushed hither and yon by the sights, sounds, and smells around him, was called soulless and bestial. The description of the complete environment involved sordidness and above all a frankness as to sexual matters which aroused a turmoil of opposition.

It will help our understanding of naturalism to see how Zola defended his system against the opposition. First, consider his defense of *l'homme physiologique*:

> L'homme métaphysique est mort, tout notre terrain se transforme avec l'homme physiologique. Sans doute la colère d'Achille, l'amour de Didon, resteront des peintures éternellement belles; mais voilà que le besoin nous prend d'analyser la colère et l'amour, et de voir au juste comment fonctionnent ces passions dans l'être humain. Le point de vue est nouveau, il devient expérimental au lieu d'être philosophique.[47]

In his novel *L'Oeuvre* (1886), Zola could give freer rein to his enthusiasm when putting his ideas into the mouth of his *raisonneur* Sandoz:

> —Hein? étudier l'homme tel qu'il est, non pas leur pantin métaphysique, mais l'homme physiologique, déterminé par le milieu, agissant sous le jeu de tous les organes . . . La pensée, la pensée, eh! tonnerre de Dieu! la pensee est le produit du corps entier. Faites donc penser un cerveau tout seul, voyez donc ce que devient la noblesse du cerveau, quand le ventre est malade! . . . D'ailleurs, physiologie, psychologie, cela ne signifie rien; l'une a pénétré l'autre, toutes deux ne sont qu'une aujourd'hui, le mécanisme de l'homme aboutissant à la somme totale de ses fonctions. . . .[48]

And hence, some very significant conclusions as to the place of description in the novel:

> Voilà donc la réponse qu'on doit faire aux adversaires de la formule naturaliste, lorsqu'ils reprochent aux romanciers actuels de s'arrêter à l'animal dans l'homme et de multiplier les descriptions. Notre héros n'est plus le pur esprit, l'homme abstrait du XVIIIᵉ siecle, il est le sujet physiologique de notre science actuelle, un être qui est composé d'organes et qui trempe dans un milieu dont il est pénétré à chaque heure. Dès lors, il nous faut bien tenir compte de toute la machine et du monde extérieur. La description n'est qu'une complément nécessaire de l'analyse. Tous les sens vont agir sur l'âme. Dans chacun de ses mouvements, l'âme sera précipitée ou ralentie par la vue, l'odorat, l'ouie, le goût, le toucher. La conception d'une âme isolée, fonctionnant toute seule dans la vide, devient fausse. C'est de la mécanique psychologique, ce n'est plus de le vie . . .[49]

In the above passage there is an important naturalistic technique tacitly understood, which Zola does not bother to state in so many words. It is another principle developed first by Flaubert and followed wholeheartedly by Zola. Both authors reject the romantic ideal of description for description's sake. Only those things must be described which have some direct determining effect upon the characters—and the best way not to transgress this limitation is for the author to describe only what his protagonists see in the course of the story. No better example of this technique can be found than in *Le Ventre de Paris* where Claude Lentier, the artist, takes poor starved Florent on a tour of the Central Markets in the early morning. And all the orange-hued carrots, the deep green cabbages, the red meats and pungent fish are seen and smelled by us through the eyes and nostrils of the famished wanderer. Our interest in the description of the market never lags an instant as we wonder when the starving man is going to get some of this magnificent display of food.

After reading *Le Ventre de Paris* and following its people about through all of the vivid colors, acrid smells, and varied sounds of the Halles Centrales, one knows how well Zola mastered the art of personal description—and with what skill we are made aware of how the physiological man is influenced by all his five senses! But more than that, we feel as though we ourselves had lived in the Central Markets of Paris. Is this merely because Zola had so scrupulously documented himself on the markets, being able, for instance, to describe all the different sorts of cheeses each with its distinctive smell? No, he himself admits that there is something more demanded of a novelist than mechanical documentation: he must have that elusive talent called by Zola *sens du réel.* Without it even his note-taking will be incomplete, futile; one must have the eyes to see.

> Le sens du réel c'est de sentir la nature et de la rendre telle qu'elle est. Il semble d'abord que tout le monde a deux yeux pour voir et que rien ne doit être plus comun que le sens du réel. Pourtant, rien n'est plus rare.
>
> Vous peignez la vie, voyez-la avant tout telle qu'elle est et donnez-en l'exacte impression. Si l'impression est baroque, si les tableaux sont mal d'aplomb, si l'oeuvre tourne à la caricature, qu'elle soit épique ou simplement vulgaire, c'est une oeuvre mort-née, qui est condamnée à un oubli rapide. Elle n'est pas largement assise sur la vérité, elle n'a aucune raison d'être.[50]

Just as imagination was the essential quality of a novelist of the old school, so to a naturalist the sense of the real becomes the primary talent. For the plot of a novel now has become the least of an author's worries. It should arise naturally in his mind once he is through with his documentation, as Zola says:

> Ce serait une curieuse étude que de dire comment travaillent nos grands romanciers contemporains. Ils établissent presque toutes leurs oeuvres sur des notes, prises longuement. Quand ils ont étudié avec un soin scrupuleux le terrain où ils doivent marcher, quand ils se sont renseignés à toutes les sources et qu'ils tiennent en main les documents multiples dont ils ont besoin, alors seulement ils se décident à écrire. Le plan de l'oeuvre leur est apporté par ces documents eux-mêmes, car il arrive que les faits se classent logiquement, celui-ci avant celui-là; une symétrie s'établit, l'histoire se compose de toutes les observations receuillies de toutes les notes prises, l'une amenant l'autre, par l'enchaine-ment même de la vie des personnages, et le denoûment n'est plus qu'une conséquence naturelle et forcée. On voit dans ce travail combien l'imagination a peu de part.[51]

As a matter of fact, that seems to be just the way Zola composed some of his best works, notably those in which the milieu is all important—even the chief character, one might say; examples are *Le Ventre de Paris, L'Assommoir, Germinal, La Terre*. Take the last named as a case in point. One of the longest novels Zola ever wrote, its plot could be put on half a page. The novelist in the course of his documentation has observed the fierce love of the peasant for his land; from this love comes a fierce avarice stronger than family feeling, because the love of the land also is stronger. The lot of an old man in this society is not a happy one. The book should trace the gradual loss of prestige of such an old peasant, describe the constant hunt for his buried *magot*. Another fact observed is the clannishness of the peasants. They are slow to accept outsiders. Show this in their attitude toward a member of the Macquart family who comes from elsewhere to share their life. They will never accept him though he live among them for fifty years and have children by their daughters. A true peasant girl will love a true peasant, no matter how brutal, because of their common passion for the land. Of the old man's two sons one has his heredity, one is a ne'er-do-well —resultant complications. The whole novel is an experiment working out and proving these general observations, and there you have it!

Now in presenting a complete case for the influence of milieu on man, the novelist must be careful to omit no significant detail from that milieu. And most of the furor over naturalism arose from this very principle of complete frankness—especially frankness as to sex. And yet there are few motivations in man's environment more powerful and more important for a true understanding of him than this very matter. Naturalism started in a century when it was the fashion to cover, disguise, and idealize everything connected with the relation of the sexes. It is no wonder that naturalistic frankness caused such an outcry. But Zola was equal to the combat. According to his argument it was the idealizers who were corrupting the youth of his day.

> L'idéal engendre toutes les rêveries dangereuses; c'est l'idéal qui jette la jeune fille aux bras du passant, c'est l'idéal qui fait la femme adultère ... Prenez les romans et les drames romantiques, étudiez-les à ce point de vue; vous y trouverez les raffinements les plus honteux de la débauche . . . Sans doute, ces ordures sont magnifiquement drapées; ce sont des alcoves abominables dont on a tiré les rideaux de soie; mais je soutiens que ces voiles, ces réticences, ces infamies cachées offrent un peril d'autant plus grand que le lecteur peut rêver à son aise, les élargir, s'y abandonner comme a une récréation délicieuse et permise. Avec les oeuvres naturalistes, cette hypocrisie du vice secrètement chatouillé est impossible. Elles épouvantent peut-être; elles ne corrompent pas. La vérité n'égare personne.[52]

Truth was the great passion of the realists and naturalists. It was the universal excuse. Was it not the same passion for truth which had produced men like Claude Bernard and advanced the bounds of human knoweldge? How could it be immoral to tell the truth?

> Ainsi ces jeunes filles si pures, ces jeunes hommes si loyaux de certains romans ne tiennent pas à la terre; pour les y attacher il faudrait tout dire. Nous disons tout, nous n'idéalisons pas; et c'est pourquoi on nous accuse de nous plaire dans l'ordure. En somme, la question de la moralité dans le roman se reduit donc à ces deux opinions; les idéalistes prétendent qu'il est nécessaire de mentir pour être moral, les naturalistes affirment qu'on ne saurait être moral en dehors du vrai.[53]

The question of morals was always involved in any discussion of naturalism. The crux of the matter to the naturalist was that to idealize meant to falsify and this, to him, was the only possible immorality. One should neither idealize nor hesitate to set down the whole truth:

> . . . et les audaces de langage, la conviction que tout doit se dire, qu'il y a des mots abominables nécessaires comme des fers rouges,

qu'une langue sort enrichie de ces bains de force; et surtout l'acte sexuel, l'origine et l'achèvement continu du monde, tiré de la honte où on le cache, remis dans sa gloire, sous le soleil.[54]

The accusations against the naturalists were intensified because of their impersonal style, their refusal to moralize or comment upon the scenes presented. If the personages behaved immorally and the author did not protest, the public assumed that he gave his tacit approval to their actions. This was perhaps a natural misunderstanding and Zola had to combat it in his polemics, telling the public that what the naturalist seeks to present is a truly objective recital, like a scientific document. He says, "Here are the facts, laugh or tremble before them, draw whatever lesson you choose from them, my only concern has been to place before you the true evidence."[55] Any interpolated exclamations of sorrow or joy on the author's part would not only spoil the objective and artistic unity of the work, they would actually lessen any moral value which might really lie in the material presented. That Zola actually did expect the reader to derive conclusions, that he considered his work to have scientific and social significance, can be amply sustained; consider this grandiose statement of his:

Nous cherchons les causes du mal social; nous faisons l'anatomie des classes et des individus pour expliquer les détraquements qui se produisent dans la société et dans l'homme. Cela nous oblige souvent à travailler sur des sujets gâtés, à descendre au milieu des misères et des folies humaines. Mais nous apportons les documents nécessaires pour qu'on puisse, en les connaissant, dominer le bien et le mal.[56]

Dominate good and evil! But how can one do that if all is rigorously determined and subject to the unchangeable forces of *race, milieu, moment*? Zola has his answer ready:

Il faut préciser: nous ne sommes pas fatalistes, nous sommes déterministes, ce qui n'est point la même chose . . . Du moment où nous pouvons agir, et où nous agissons sur le déterminisme des phénomènes, en modifiant les milieux par exemple, nous ne sommes pas des fatalistes . . . Je résume notre rôle de moralistes expérimentateurs. Nous montrons le mécanisme de l'utile et du nuisible, nous dégageons le déterminisme des phénomènes humains et sociaux, pour qu'on puisse un jour dominer et diriger ces phénomènes. En un mot, nous travaillons avec tout le siècle à la grande oeuvre qui est la conquête de la nature, la puissance de l'homme décuplée.[57]

It all comes back to the question of the experimental novel, which, as I said before, is the heart of Zola's system. Such a novel naturally and inevitably concludes something, just as would an experiment in science. Granted that the novelist had the conclusion when he started to write, granted that all his novel does is prove it, not discover it; yet the analogy holds, for there is observation, evidence, and a conclusion. Granted the result is not formulated in so many words; nevertheless, it is plainly implied. An experimental novel cannot be just *un lambeau d'existence*, as some of the realistic novels are described by Zola.[58] Surely, it is safe to say that there is scarcely one of the twenty novels in the Rougon-Macquart series which does not suggest some definite general truth or underline some social evil. Even though we object that the novelist cannot discover anything from the mechanics of putting his novel together, still could he not have discovered something in the course of his documentation? Does not *Germinal* preach socialism as its implicit conclusion? And would Zola have known what was the plight and what the possible salvation of the coal miner, had he not set himself to write a well-documented novel on their milieu? One must give credit where credit is due.

Finally, what is naturalism according to Zola, summed up in a few sentences? It is both a philosophy and a literary formula built around that philosophy. Its view is that man is not a duality but one organism, of which mind is but one of the functions. This physiological man is rigorously determined by his heredity, his environment, and the time in which he lives. Nevertheless, with the acquisition of sufficient knowledge and enlightenment he can and does modify his environment. The problem of the novelist is to present a true picture of a certain section of life, as interpreted from the standpoint of this philosophy. He will first choose a certain milieu and period in which to place his novel. He will then study that environment seriously, finding out how time may have changed it, consulting books and friends about it, observing personally all he can in the time at his disposal. This may give rise to general conclusions in his mind, which the evidence of the novel will later suggest to the reader. Now in the particular case of Zola, at least, the author will have certain characters with definite hereditary temperament and tendencies to place in the setting of the story, i.e., some member of the Rougon-Macquart family tree. He must then consider the possible results of the interplay of the given heredity and the environment studied. Other characters will suggest themselves, no doubt, from the author's observations of life in the milieu. Gradually, then, in the course of meditating upon all these forces, a simple plot suggests itself naturally. Henceforth it is a problem of distribution—what actions to use as vehicles in order to carry certain necessary descriptions, etc. In telling the story, the author will never step in on his own account; it must remain strictly objective and impersonal as far as he is concerned, while at the same time all descriptions must be so incorporated into the action that the reader feels he is seeing everything through the eye of some personage in the book. Furthermore, no details shall be omitted for reasons of delicacy or false moral scruples; all facts definitely influencing the characters will be included. If the documentary study has been thorough and the author is endowed with a sense for the real and with at least a modicum of literary style, the resultant novel should be both successful and instructive.

Few writers have set forth more detailed instructions to imitators than did Emile Zola. All the directions for constructing a naturalistic novel are carefully set forth. Yet very few of his most faithful followers attained any degree of success. In fact, it seems the more literally they followed his instructions, the more mediocre was the result. The novel is, as Zola says, to become a simple *procès-verbal*, nothing more—the plain, straightforward recital of the facts, such as may be found in court record or newspaper. The novelist has merely to go to a certain milieu, document himself minutely, record what he has seen faithfully, being careful in his character analysis and being sure to omit no details, however ugly or indelicate, and out will come a naturalistic novel of the best. Many poor disciples of both Flaubert and Zola did just that, but their work was inane and little read. They recorded all they saw but they did not see what Zola would have seen. Therein perhaps lay his genius. As Pardo Bazán very succinctly remarks in her book *El Naturalismo*:

Situad a cualquiera que no sea Zola ante un mercado, una taberna, una mina, un almacén de novedades, un huerto abandonado, una casa de vecindad, y no verá allí más que lo inanimado, lo insignificante, la prosa llana, la ganancia, la pérdida, la conveniencia de arrancar las ortigas o lo abundante del marisco. A lo sumo, un artista verá colores, formas, líneas, efectos de luz, fondo para escenas. Zola verá vivir con extraña vida, con vida imaginaria, con vuelo y resuello de dragón o grifo, con serpenteos

> de melusina, al mercado, al almacén, al huerto, y les prestará
> una personalidad simbólica que ya, para nosotros, han de conservar
> siempre. He aquí la obra de la creadora fantasía, la obra propia
> de Zola. Como Homero daba voz y pasiones a los ríos, Zola presta
> amor al huerto abandonado, misterio maléfico a la mina, fatalidad
> atrayente a la taberna. . . .[59]

To anyone who thinks of Zola only as a dealer in crudity who
owed most of his success to the spicy details and consequent
perverse sex interest in his novels, the above comment of Pardo's
should come as somewhat of a jolt. Here is another:

> Los que, como Max Nordau, insinúan que el alboroto originado
> por algunos libros de Zola se debió principalmente a curiosidades
> de baja ley, podrían hacerse cargo de que muchos escritores han
> ido en ese terreno más allá que Zola, sin conseguir . . . ni escanda-
> lizar siquiera.[60]

One may be reasonably certain that Pardo Bazán's interest
in Zola, at least, did not derive from "curiosidades de baja ley."
But no intelligent student can close his eyes to the fact that most
of the scandal about Zola did arise from his frank treatment of
sex. Not only that, but I will say that the sex interest of his
novels was responsible for a large share of their power. Remember this, however,—and here is the crux of the matter—
Zola was not a humorist. To him sex is serious, legitimate, and
beautiful. As the sap carries life to the trees, so the sexual act
is the basis of the *fécundité* of human life. It is only custom
and false shame that make perverse interests possible. Nevertheless, Zola did admit in 1866 that:

> Mon goût, si l'on veut, est dépravé; j'aime les ragoûts lit-
> téraires fortement épicés, les oeuvres de décadence où une sorte
> de sensibilité maladive remplace la santé plantureuse des époques
> classiques. Je suis de mon âge.[61]

No doubt there was a progression here and Zola did start
out with a somewhat depraved taste, manifest perhaps in such
an early work as *Thérèse Raquin*—one which Pardo Bazán apparently never read. Later, he found an excuse for his delight
in the over-seasoned in the tenets of naturalism, making it an
ideal to tell the whole truth under all circumstances. Gradually
the excuse became reality for him and he came to think of himself as a sort of apostle or prophet destined to drag the sexual
act "out from the shame where it is hidden, out under the sun
in all its glory."[62] In such a book as *La Faute de l'Abbé Mouret*
Zola surely did succeed in this aim, but in *Pot-Bouille* the social
corruption revealed by removing the lid of shame can hardly be

called a glory; it is more like a witch's brew! At any rate, Zola felt himself to be a man with a purpose and his rallying cry was: Away with the taboos and restrictions of the past! Let us be of our age, let us seek truth where it may be found, let us dig into human relationships with fingers of iron and be what we find repulsive or be it beautiful, we shall not hesitate to set it forth!

And, strange to say, a surprising number of times, under Zola's reputedly brutal pen, the result is beautiful, not repulsive. Even when ugliness and filth is the composite impression, there is yet a sort of poetic grandeur to the concept that makes up in power what it lacks in beauty. Many have remarked the poetic qualities manifest in Zola. Much of his early work is strewn with lyrical and fanciful passages which the author was wont to blame on his early romantic training—passages which he sought to weed out of his later work, and from whose lack those later novels suffer. But even in his most brutally realistic books there is a certain epic grandeur verging on the Homeric.[63] Pardo Bazán shows her admiration for this quality in Zola by her comment on *Germinal*:

> El romanticismo, el temperamento poético (poeta de la miseria humana, pero poeta al fin) de Zola, brotan en *Germinal* como el fuego *grisú* de las fisuras de la cueva, y hacen que, si la mitad de *Germinal* es de verdadera y tremenda observación, la otra mitad sea de una fantasía épica, desatada. Con todo eso, parcialmente, es la obra de Zola donde sus facultades peculiares se desarollan más impetuosas, se afirman con mayor potencia creatriz, en descripciones magníficas, en trozos de factura magistrales, como el del paso de la horda que pide pan.[64]

The best appreciation of Zola's epic genius that I have found comes from the pen of the Argentine writer, Alberto Gerchunoff, who compares the great Frenchman to Homer and then cites passages to back up the statement.

> Recuerdo que una vez, paseando con Leopoldo Lugones, conversábamos de Zola, coincidiendo en nuestra admiración por su genio. Lugones, para sintetizar su entusiasmo, dijo: —Es homérico. Ya sé que leyendo a Homero oiré caer el guerrero, y las armas y el escudo harán ruido enorme en la caída, pero me emociono y me estremezco. Lo mismo me pasa con Zola. Es como Jehová: sopla el barro y sale el mundo.[65]

To be sure Gerchunoff here quotes Lugones, but let us see what the former has to say of his impressions resulting from certain

passages of Zola. First the scene of Goujet at the forge from
L'Assommoir:

> Tenéis la sensación de una apuesta entre héroes, que acompasa
> el ritmo formidable del martillo, en el calor de la fábrica, en el
> cual el hierro se transforma, como en los hornos de Vulcano, en
> maravillas enormes.

And then from *Germinal*:

> Cuando el jefe de la huelga se dirige a sus compañeros de la
> mina, renace en su palabra bronca y breve, la ira de los pueblos.
> Por su boca salen las convulsiones subterráneas como expresadas
> en un coro helénico por los elementos sublevados contra el dominio
> milenario de los dioses. El hundimiento del caderamen en las
> galerías negras, tiene la grandeza terrible de un cataclismo.

Last a scene from *La débâcle*:

> En nuestra alma seguirá atronando el ruido bárbaro de la
> tropa de caballos en el ímpetu de una carrera feroz, sin ginetes y
> sin rumbo, por los campus desolados, entre montes de cadáveres
> y extensiones en que palpita, bajo el vuelo de los cuervos, la
> agonía sin fin.[66]

Pardo Bazán made many reservations in her Spanish adaptation of naturalism but her enthusiasm for the genius of Zola
as novelist and poet, apart from his literary theories and their
philosophical basis, was almost unbounded. Let the student consider carefully the portions of Zola's work which especially appealed to her, as she sets them forth in her *Cuestión palpitante*:

> Pasajes y trozos hay en sus libros que, según su género pueden
> llamarse definitivos, y no creo temeraria aseveración la que nadie
> irá más allá. Los estragos del alcohol en el *Assommoir*, con aquel
> terrible epílogo del *delirium tremens*; la pintura de los mercados
> en *El Vientre de Paris*; la delicada primera parte de *Una página
> de amor*; el graciosísimo idileo de los amores de *Silverio* y *Miette*
> en *La fortuna de los Rougon*; el carácter del clérigo ambicioso en
> *La conquista de Plassans*; la riqueza descriptiva de *La falta del
> cura Mouret*, y otras mil bellezas que andan pródigamente sem-
> bradas por sus libros, son quizá insuperables. Con la manifesta-
> ción de un poderoso entendimiento, de una mirada penetrante,
> firme, escrutadora, y a la vez con la copia de arabescos y fili-
> granas primorosísimas, Zola suspende el ánimo. Tengamos el
> arrojo de decirlo una vez que todos lo piensan: en el autor del
> *Assomoir* hay hermosura.[67]

If one were to take merely this passage of Pardo Bazan's and the
one quoted on pages 25-26, no doubt many conclusions could be
drawn with regard to those qualities which especially appealed
to Pardo Bazán in Zola. But it is much too early to summarize
and the object at this point is merely to show that there are
qualities in Zola—power, poetry, epic imagination—which are

not inherent in his theoretical principles, qualities which appealed to Emilia Pardo Bazán and which may have influenced her work. As later chapters will reveal, she never fully accepted his ideology, yet, together with Tolstoy, he remained her literary hero.

> La filosofía de Zola se cae hacia el materialismo escueto: la de Tolstoy se precipita al misticismo delirante. Ninguno de los dos es mi filósofo, ni siquiera mi pensador: entrambos son mis dos grandes, excelsos y incomparables novelistas entre los qui viven.[68]

And in *La Cuestión palpitante*, after finding a good deal of fault with Zola's system, she still can make this admiring conclusion:

> ¿Qué le queda, pues, a Zola, si en tan deleznables cimientos basó el edificio orgulloso y babilónico de su *Comedia humana*? Quédale lo que no pueden dar todas las ciencias reunidas; quédale el verdadero patrimonio del artista; su grande e indiscutible ingenio, sus no comunes dotes de creador y escritor. Eso es lo que permanece cuando todo pasa y se derrumba; eso es lo que los siglos venideros reconocerán en Zola (aparte de su inmensa influencia en las letras contemporáneas).[69]

II

EMILIA PARDO BAZÁN

Countess Emilia Pardo Bazán was born in 1851 in the Galician city of La Coruña. She was fortunate in having parents who were not only wealthy and aristocratic but also wise beyond measure in that they did not discourage the questioning curiosity and voracious reading of their only daughter.

> Los padres, en vez de impedir las lecturas de su hija y burlarse de sus aficiones, las miran con buenos ojos, y la niña, además del cariño acendrado que le calienta el alma, encuentra la aprobación que tan grata y estimulante es, cuando sentimos que nuestras aspiraciones la merecen.[1]

Describing her own childhood, Pardo says:

> Era yo . . . de esos niños que leen cuanto cae por banda, hasta los cucuruchos de especias y los papeles de rosquillas; de esos niños que pasan el día quietecitos en un rincón cuando se les da un libro, y a veces tienen ojeras y bizcan levemente a causa del esfuerzo impuesto a un nervio óptico, endeble todavía.[2]

Besides reading everything that came to hand, she was "una niña preguntona ansiosa de saberlo todo."[1]

We have here an indication of the beginnings of that universal curiosity which led her to investigate so many subjects and to become in later life the versatile and erudite person known to us all. But not only were her parents wise enough to satisfy the child's thirst for knowledge and books; they were careful to start her out on such classics as the Bible, *Don Quijote,* the *Iliad,* Plutarch's *Lives,* and the *Conquest of Mexico* by Solís. García Ramón attributes many of Pardo's virtues to this early reading, notably among them her tolerance.[3] Be that as it may, surely no child was ever hurt by such a start in the world of letters. We must remember, too, that hers was a very different world from ours. It was decidedly not the fashion for girls to attend the universities and often they received little or no formal schooling. As a matter of fact, even after the institutions of higher learning grudgingly agreed to admit feminine students, it was years before public opinion calmed down sufficiently so that any but the boldest of women would dare face the ridicule. Although, as Espasa[4] tells us, Doña Emilia completed the course of "un elegante colegio de la corte," she was forced to be the author of her own higher education. That she did not advocate this for others will be apparent to anyone who will study her efforts in the cause of feminism in Spain.

We have the picture, then, of a little girl in a big *casa solariega* avidly reading everything she can find, including many of the masterpieces of universal literature. It is not long before she makes an attempt to do some writing on her own account— a few verses inspired by a Spanish victory in Morocco, poetry whose merits, she tells us, we may estimate by the fact that "yo frisaba en los años en que la Iglesia católica concede uso de la razón a los parvulitos."[5] Later, more verses and a short tale or two were published here and there,[6] but three great events which all happened in the same year were scheduled to interrupt the literary output of young lady Emily: "Tres acontecimientos importantes en mi vida . . . se siguieron muy de cerca: me vestí de largo, me casé y estalló la revolución de Septiembre de 1868."[7] The reader will please remember that our heroine was not born until 1851, but a wedding, to a Spanish girl of good family, meant more liberty rather than less. Her innocence no longer needed to be guarded so closely in what she read or through surveillance of her actions. Indeed, for Doña Emilia it seems to have brought a great deal of freedom, for she speaks of summer days spent in the open in the backwoods of Galicia, on horseback and afoot. If in those first eight years[8] after her marriage she did not actually do any writing, one cannot help considering them—as González-Blanco remarks[9]—among the most productive of her life, for they were the inspiration and the documentation for much of her best literary work. As she says herself in her prologue to the collection of short novels and tales issued under the title of *La Dama joven*:

> *Bucólica* y también *Nieto del Cid* son apuntes de paisajes, tipos y costumbres de una comarca donde pasé floridos días de juventud y asistí a regocijadas partidas de caza, a vendimias, romerías y ferias; tierra original de Galicia, que he recorrido a caballo y a pie, recibiendo el ardor del sol y la humedad de su lluvia, y ha dejado en mi mente tantos recuerdos pintorescos, que no cabían en el breve recinto de *Bucólica* y fué preciso dedicarles otro lienzo más ancho. . . .[10]

In addition to the summer life outdoors in Galicia, her marriage also took her out of her secluded environment in the winter months, which were now spent in gay Madrid.[11] Of Pardo Bazán's husband, Don José Quiroga, very little is known. He was the father of her children[12] and he served to give her social standing in a society that had no use for old maids. He also took her to Paris frequently and even to London. Let her tell of her first two trips to the French metropolis:

—Je viens à Paris pour la première fois,—me dit-elle—en 1871, mariée depuis peu et jeune encore: je n'avais pas accompli ma seizième année le jour de mon marriage. Je vins à Paris avec toute ma famille: mon père . . . ma mère, mon oncle et mon mari. . . .[13]

Elle reprend:

—Je revins à Paris en 1874, de passage pour Londres, où je séjournai un mois avec mon mari. Au retour je ne pus pas ne pas m'arrêter à Paris. C'est alors que je connus Victor Hugo et de la discussion que j'eus avec lui au sujet de l'inquisiiton, je ne puis vous dire que je n'aie déjà dit dans l'autobiographie qui précède Los Pazos de Ulloa et que vous n'avez sûrement pas lue, car les jeunes gens d'aujourd'hui ne lisent pas les vieux livres.[14]

The reference here is to the Apuntes autobiográficos, which unfortunately were not published with later editions of Los Pazos de Ulloa, but the account of her visit to Victor Hugo is quoted at length by Pagano in his Al través de la España literaria.[15] It is very entertaining and demonstrative of Pardo's ever-ready wit and gallardía in conversation. It seems the French patriarch of letters had been lamenting the disastrous effects of the Inquisition on Spanish life and literature. Young Emilia replied that she had read in French historians about some things called Saint Bartholomew's Day and the Reign of Terror, compared to which the Spanish Inquisition was "tortas y pan pintado." The old Frenchman smiled at that and remarked, "Voilà bien l'Espagnole!"

The chronology of the years from her marriage in 1868 to the publication of her first novel in 1879 (Pascual López) cannot be itemized in detail, but we know that she spent numerous summers enjoying country life in Galicia, that she travelled to Paris at least twice, and that she pursued a self-assigned and systematic course of studies at home in La Coruña. She studied philosophy, both the modern German schools and the ancient Greek.[16] She also tried to study some sciences although, as she tells us in the prologue to La Dama joven, she soon gave up the idea of acquiring anything but a superficial knowledge of them, for she realized the "imposibilidad práctica de conseguir nada de provecho en ciencias que reclaman la vida entera del que aspira a profundizarlas."[17] However, her interest in science is manifest in her work—in the study she made of Feijóo (with which she won a prize in 1879), in her first novel, *Pascual López*, where chemistry verging on alchemy plays a part, and in her later admiration for modern medicine, manifest in many novels and tales. The worship of science was in the air, and Pardo Bazán was the product of her times.

But turning away from science and philosopsy as a child turns away from toys which are too heavy, she directed her study to the great poets and novelists. The first result was the publication in *Ciencia Cristiana* of a work called *Los poetas épicos cristianos: Dante, Tasso, Milton*. And as the outcome of her study of the novel—English, Italian, and French—we have her own first effort in the genre. *Pascual López* was written in a sort of archaic Spanish style and its content is quite inferior to that of her later novels. That Pardo was aware of its short-comings is evident from the fact she did not republish it with her *Obras completas*.

Taking up the story at this point, González-Blanco says:

> Distraída algún tiempo de la novela por una racha de sedante misticismo, cuyas causas con tan encantadora ingenuidad describe en sus *Apuntes*, da a luz su formidable *San Francisco de Asís*, que fué seguido casi inmediàtamente por *Un viaje de novios*, novela que marca la introducción del naturalismo en España, y que quedará como piedra miliaria. Desde entonces se puede decir que la Sra. Pardo Bazán no tiene biografía . . . De la mujer no sabemos nada, sino que trabaja . . .[18]

The date of *Un viaje de novios* is 1881 and González-Blanco wrote his book in 1908. In the intervening years Emilia Pardo Bazán was very much in the public eye; yet he can say, "de la mujer no sabemos nada." Surely, it was before the day of popular biographies and human interest stories about prominent people, at least in Spain. From then on her biography is a literary history of her novels, polemics, critical writings, short stories, and lectures, although we do have this hint from Galdós, written in 1887: "Reside habitualmente en la Coruña, su patria; tiene una rica biblioteca, estudia y trabaja sin cesar, pasa en Paris todos los años una larga temporada y en Madrid otra más corta."[19]

This three-fold environment of the Countess of Pardo Bazán is reflected in her novel *La Quimera* (1905), which, like Zola's *L'Oeuvre*, contains much autobiographical material. Its action takes place partly in Galicia, partly in the world of fashionable society in Madrid, and partly in Paris, the three milieus which

Pardo knew so well. France was almost a second fatherland to Doña Emilia. De Tannenberg regrets that she did not write a history of Spanish literature,[20] but we do have a history of *French* romanticism, naturalism, and lyricism from her pen—a work that runs into four full-sized volumes. Indeed, she often felt more at home in Paris among her French friends and admirers than in Madrid, where she did not lack for enemies and where the atmosphere of prejudice and intolerance was oppressive to her spirit.[21] Hers was a mind which was often too big for her country. Her culture was European rather than national. None was better equipped to introduce naturalism to Spain and in 1883, when the movement was well on its way in France but still little known south of the Pyrenees, that was just what she did.

In her prologue to *Un viaje de novios* (1881), Pardo makes some comments on Zola and his naturalism, but they are largely uncomplimentary, and the novel itself, aside from the descriptions, is not outstandingly naturalistic. However, one can see from this prologue that naturalism had made its initial strong impression upon the mind of the young novelist. Two years later there appeared, first in the columns of a newspaper (*La Epoca*) and later in book form, her series of articles under the general title of *La Cuestión palpitante*. The book was a firebrand. And yet it stands today as one of the fairest evaluations of Zola and of the naturalistic movement that was ever written. Emilia Pardo never lost her calm common sense and her unbiased sense of values. She was swayed neither by her own enthusiasm nor by the violent prejudice around her. She condemned Zola's overly deterministic philosophy and defended him as an artist. In the midst of Zola's triumph in France and the unreasoning prejudice against him in Spain, Pardo could see what was lasting in Zola and what was dross.

> No hay cosa esencial en un autor o doctrina que se le pasa por alto, y así logra darnos una opinión objetiva, imparcial, completa. Sus estudios sobre Zola, Goncourt, Barbey d'Aurévilly y algunos otros, me han producido la impresión de lo definitivo, como si en cuanto al juicio crítico no hubiera nada que modificar jamás en ellos. Dijérase la opinión permanente y eterna, la opinión del sentido común y del juicio sano.[22]

Manuel Gálvez wrote that in 1921, almost forty years after the book in question, so he should have had ample perspective to add weight to his opinion. One would think, however, that if

Doña Emilia's judgments were so very fair and sound, then her
Cuestión palpitante could not have aroused much opposition.
Not so. Zola had penetrated into Spain just enough to shock
and revolt. The aristocracy, which was by policy conservative,
put him down as indelicate and opposed to the status quo; to the
clergy he was anathema—both immoral and blasphemous; to
great writers he was a renovator, a destroyer of the methods
to which they owed their success, and not only that, he said
things which they had never dared say. Away with him! But
Pardo wrote on in the midst of the general furor, keeping her
head and her calm judgment intact.[23] Here is her own comment
on the battle, a comment written nineteen years later upon the
occasion of Zola's death and showing that there were still people
in Spain who looked askance at her; she seasons her remarks
with her usual *gallardía*:

> A mi iniciativa se debió que el naturalismo fuese discutido, no
> tan lánguidamente ni tan desde afuera como aquí suelen discutirse
> las novedades literarias. Cierto que lo conseguí a costa de mi
> pellejo (perdónese el vulgarismo). Escribía entonces Leopoldo
> Alas (Clarín): "Sabe la autora simpática, valiente y discretísima
> de este libro (*La Cuestión palpitante*) a lo que se expone publi-
> cándolo. Yo sé más: sé que hay quien la aborrece, a pesar de que
> es una señora, con toda la brutalidad de las malas pasiones irri-
> tadas . . ." Aun hoy, a la vuelta de cuatro lustros, respiran por
> la herida los furiosos de entonces, y en un periódico de los que leen
> "las familias" acabo de encontrar un párrafo donde me anuncian
> que pronto moriré y me presentaré ante Dios sin más bagaje que
> los *Rougon Macquart*. Para ganar algún mérito, ya que mi fin
> se acerca, les perdono, porque saben lo que hacen, conocen bien sus
> lectores . . . pero no saben lo que escriben, y menos lo que escribo
> yo.[24]

Nevertheless, the name of Emilia Pardo Bazán carried considerable prestige. As Gómez de Baquero remarks, the fate of
a new literary movement depends largely on the proportions
of its champion.[25] Pardo Bazán's shoulders were broad, both
literally and figuratively speaking. We must not forget the
"linajuda familia" from which she came. Also, it was a tra-
ditionalist society in which she moved, and had she not written
a book about the Christian epic poets and the memorable life
of Saint Francis Assisi. Surely so Catholic a lady would
not advocate anything in which there was not some good. And
Pardo did not stop with *La Cuestión palpitante*, but proceeded
to write *La Tribuna* (called a *pastiche* of *Zola* by de Tannen-

berg),[26] *El Cisne de Vilamorta,* and *Los Pazos de Ulloa,* all in
the space of three years. In each were manifest obvious traces
of naturalism, and their undoubted merits as novels spoke volumes in favor of the system. Not content with taking all Spain
by the ears and turning its face toward Paris in her *Cuestión
palpitante,* Doña Emilia continued to astonish her contemporaries with the quantity, quality, and variety of the literature
which constantly issued from her busy pen. Even so great a
scholar and so decided an opponent of naturalism as Menéndez
y Pelayo could not but pause to voice his *asombro:*

> Al lado de un ensayo crítico sobre el darwinismo y de artículos
> sobre las más recientes teorías de la Física, vemos figurar un
> estudio sobre los poetas épicos cristianos, un ensayo sobre el P.
> Feijoo, apreciado en los múltiples aspectos de polígrafo, y princi-
> palmente en el campo de la filosofía experimental; y mezcladas
> con todo esto aparece una serie de cartas de ardentísima polémica
> sobre la cuestión del naturalismo artístico, y nada menos que cinco
> novelas, en la mayor parte de las cuales la tendencia naturalista
> se ostenta sin rebozo, contrastando de una manera palmaria con
> este otro libro tan idealista y tan místico que ahora tengo entre
> manos, y que es a un tiempo la vida de un santo, la síntesis his-
> tórica de su época, . . . la crónica abreviada de su Orden, y la
> reseña rápida, brillante y animadísima del arte, de la filosofía y
> de la literatura del período más interesante de la Edad Media.
> Todo esto producido sin intermisión, y de un solo aliento, en el
> breve espacio de siete u ocho años; que no hará más que yo leí por
> primera vez páginas suyas en la *Revista de España,* siguiéndola
> desde entonces con interés creciente, mezclado con verdadero
> asombro.[27]

Menéndez y Pelayo voiced his astonishment thus in 1885; no
doubt the fifth novel he was thinking of was *Bucólica,* a short
novelette of some seventy-five pages which was first published
in the *Revista de España* in 1884. Later it was republished in
a collection of short stories going under the general title of *La
Dama joven* (1885). This was the first of Pardo's volumes of
cuentos of which the final figure is nine. After her masterpiece,
Los Pazos de Ulloa (1886), she wrote and published no less than
fifteen other novels. In addition to this there were travelogues,
uncounted magazine articles, books of criticism, books of polemics. and studies of various kinds. But the Countess is chiefly
known for her work in the three fields of novel, *cuento,* and literary criticism. Opinions differ as to her merits in the three
genres. Some prefer her as a novelist[28] and others as a critic.
As a *cuentista* she enjoyed great facility and was inclined to

dash off stories without too much attention to perfection of style or composition. I do not think she will be primarily remembered as a short story writer. However, Manuel Gálvez, whose judgment of her in other respects is of the soundest, says he prefers her in this shorter genre. Be that as it may, he is probably right in preferring her as a critic rather than a novelist.[29]

An outstanding monument to Pardo Bazán's ability as a literary critic is her *Nuevo Teatro Crítico,* a monthly periodical of which she was editor and sole correspondent for three years (January 1891 to December 1893). The title of the work is explained when one considers her acquaintance with Feijóo and the fact that the latter also published a *Teatro crítico* which was quite famous in its day.[30] Some of her best critical work appeared in her periodical. She often included there her articles and *cuentos* which had been published in other magazines.[31] Also, some of the articles in the *Nuevo Teatro* were later included in collections published in book form.[32] Furthermore, when she wrote a prologue for a book, she would sometimes publish it also in the periodical, thus helping to announce the book.[31] But that the work grew burdensome at times is indicated by several facts: in 1892 she published the September number two months early so as to have a vacation during the summer;[33] in 1893 she actually discontinued publication for a period of months; and finally, at the end of that year she gave up the task completely, as being too confining and a strain on her health.[34] Certainly the five thick little volumes filled by the periodical in its bound form represent enough labor to constitute a burden even to so vigorous an individual as Emilia Pardo.

For ten years after the publication of *Los Pazos de Ulloa* Pardo Bazán continued to produce novels of good quality—some eight titles in all—but after 1896 there was a turning point. It was partly because she was too busy to do good work, and partly, too, because she turned away from realism to the imaginative and fantastic, a sort of facile production whose literary merit was as limited as the time it took her inventive mind to produce it. Commenting on this in 1903, de Tannenberg said:

> Ses plus sincères admirateurs s'alarment un peu de la voir aujourd'hui dépenser son activité littéraire en des besognes inférieurs et faciles, traductions, nouvelles rapides, articles de revues ou de journaux: la vie de Madrid est si absorbante qu'elle laisse peu de loisir; le journalisme n'est pas toujours une bonne école.

Ils regrettent parfois pour elle le temps où, dans sa retraite de la
Corogne, elle pouvait s'isoler au milieu de ses livres et osait
entreprendre les longues tâches.[34]

Answering his accusation in the September issue of *La Lectura*
for the same year, Doña Emliia was indignant: " 'Rápidas novelas cortas' . . . no lo entiendo. ¿Serían peores por rápidas?
Lo que pasa es que mi última novela corta tendrá de fecha siete
u ocho años. Cuentos sí he escrito. . . ."[35]

It is too bad, but for the most part the facts seem to be on
the side of the French critic. When Pardo says her last short
novel was written some seven or eight years back, she is probably thinking of one called *Un drama* which appeared in three
successive issues of *España Moderna* for 1895. But from *Memorias de un solterón* in 1896 to 1903 and the beginning of publication of *La Quimera* (577 pages), one finds just four minor
and rather fanciful novels, two of which at least (*El tesoro de
Gastón* and *El niño de Guzmán*) have only about 150 pages
apiece. *El saludo de las brujas* is the story of an aspirant to the
throne of an imaginary kingdom; it is classified as "exotic" by
González-Blanco.[36] The fourth, *Misterio*, is a rather romantic
story woven around the life of the ill-fated prince, Louis XVII
of France. It does not appear in her *Obras completas*. During
these seven or eight years Emilia Pardo Bazán published five
volumes of *cuentos* and two travelogues; she gave a lecture in
Paris on *L'Espagne d'hier et celle d'aujourd'hui*; she gave a political discourse at La Coruña on the occasion of *los juegos
florales*; and she was publishing the first instálments of her
History of French Literature. How could she do all that and
find time to write a worthwhile novel? And yet in 1903 she
began publishing *La Quimera*, the longest and one of the best
of her novels.

With regard to translations, however, Doña Emilia succeeded
in refuting de Tannenberg. It seems at this time Pardo was engaged in publishing what she called *La biblioteca de la mujer*, a
collection of volumes by and about women and devoted largely
to the cause of feminism, in which Pardo was interested. Naturally, this library contained numerous translations, which de
Tannenberg assumed to be from Doña Emilia's pen. This was
not true and the lady in question claims to have saved the re-
ceipts signed by the translators she employed. She is only guilty
of two translations, which she did "por compromisos de amistad."

It has been possible to trace these to the two which she finished
in the year 1891.   One is of Edmond de Goncourt's *The Brothers
Zemganno.*[37]

Nevertheless, despite all this activity we find that in this
decade—the late nineties and early 1900's—there was a sort of
conspiracy of silence against the Countess.   Most big people
seem to have a faculty for creating enemies among the little
people.   Evidence of this wilful ignoring of Doña Emilia may be
obtained merely by going through a file of a magazine such as
La Revista contemporánea.   After almost constant references
to the author and her work, there suddenly and quite unaccount-
ably ceases to be any mention of her.   In 1893 alone she has no
less than six articles or short biographical paragraphs devoted
to her.   From that year until 1900, when the periodical ends,
she has only one article devoted to her and that is a rather uncomplimentary one about *El tesoro de Gastón*, in 1897.   More
direct evidence is to be found in Luis Morote's book *Teatro y novela* (chapter dated 1905) :

> De algún tiempo a esta parte la insigne escritora Doña Emilia
> Pardo Bazán está como olvidada, no del público, pero sí de los
> periódicos y de los críticos.   Publica una novela y como si la
> publicara en otro planeta.   Nadie le dedica dos renglones, para
> censurarla o aplaudirla.   Yo no sé ni me importa averiguar si
> existe conspiración del silencio, algo como un *boycottage* contra
> la autora de cuarenta y siete volúmenes, según mi cuenta, algunos
> de ellos muy notables, que consagrarían la gloria de cualquier
> escritor en cualquier país del mundo. . . .
>
> Comparad, por ejemplo, el ruido hecho alrededor de *La cuestión
> palpitante* o de *La piedra angular* o de *Insolación*, y el silencio de
> ahora, y os quedaréis asombrados.   Esa desigualdad en el elogio
> de ayer, algunas veces incluso exagerado, y este abandono de hoy,
> incluso para la censura, para lo que se llama "un palo" es de una
> tan grande injusticia que subleva.[38]

One of the causes contributing to this hostility was the lecture
she gave in Paris in 1899 on the Spain of yesterday and the
Spain of today. She wrote it and gave it in French and later
published it in a polyglot edition in Madrid.   Doña Emilia was
proud of her French, and it seems, as one scans the two versions,
that the Spanish is rather a translation of the French than vice
versa.   Be that as it may, it was the content of the article which
riled the Spaniards.   The truth hurts sometimes and after the
disastrous Spanish-American war, Spain was feeling very ten-
der.[39]   Just as Zola revealed in his *La Débâcle* the rottenness of

French officialdom before the downfall, so the Spanish Countess put her probing fingers into the society and officialdom of her nation to reveal the empty boastfulness, the hollow decadence, which were really responsible for the loss of Spain's last shreds of empire. Like Zola, Pardo Bazán thought there could never be anything wrong with saying the truth about things, however painful it was to hear; it was false patriotism to misrepresent; only through facing the truth could Spain pull herself out of the morass of ignorance, political corruption, and slothfulness into which she had fallen. Those were not pleasant things to hear. They were wounding to the masculine vanity of many people who already resented the measure of success which the portly Countess[40] had achieved in a man's world. Was she going to tell the men now how they should run the country? González-Blanco paints an indignant picture of the Spanish equivalent of the pool-hall hound who never does anything all his life to contribute to the world's work, and yet is quite able to sit in judgment on all questions and to speak disparagingly of the tireless lady from Galicia: "Ahí está la inevitable doña Emilia con su late consabida."[41] That Pardo was ever *in medias res* is shown in that nickname: *la inevitable*. And the resentment felt toward her was doubtless an unreasoning dislike for any female's being so much in the public eye.

After 1905 she continued active, publishing *Sirena Negra* in 1908, a few more *cuentos* and finally, her last novel, *Dulce Dueño*, in 1911. These years were characterized by a growing mysticism already noticeable in *La Quimera* and becoming more prominent later. All three novels terminate in the religious conversion or saving penitence of the chief protagonist. Despite this religious undercurrent, *La Quimera* and *Sirena Negra* rank among the best of her work and as late as 1911 Tenreiro has this to say of the veteran authoress:

> La condesa de Pardo Bazán . . . sabe encontrar en su viña, nueva cosecha de sazonados racimos al llegar cada otoño . . . , cuando la mayor parte de sus coetáneos han entrado ya en el definitivo silencio. . . . Difícil ley, la de callarse a tiempo—encuentra ella manera de conservar un altísimo asiento en nuestro Parnaso, a través de dos generaciones literarias que apenas nada tienen de común entre ellas. Y no ¡viven los cielos! porque se haya mantenido, anfibiamente, en un segundo término, desteñido y correcto, sino que en la hora de las luchas literarias, entrábase brava, repartiendo mandobles por donde era mas recia la pelea, llevando

en alto, con mano segura, el fiamante estandarte de su artístico credo, y aun ahora, llegada a los más preclaros puestos en la milicia de las musas . . . vibran en sus escritos a las veces, no sé qué vagas inquietudes bélicas, clamor de clarines, redobles de tambores, que chocan con la insulsez de nuestro pobre ambiente.[42]

Tenreiro has undoubtedly caught that spirit of *gallardía* which hangs about the figure of the indomitable old Countess. Another man who remembers this quality in her is Gutiérrez-Gamero, who recalls in one of his volumes of memoirs:

Cuando volvió de Orense fuí a su casa, y excuso de decir que charlamos a cántaros. . . .

Habló de política . . . Ah, si ella pudiera hablar. . . .

—Por desgracia las mujeres están imbécilmente esclavizadas por el "homo sapiens" (¡sí, sí, vaya un "sapiens"!)—se interrumpió doña Emilia;—pero ya llegará nuestra vez, y entonces . . .[43]

To conclude, after 1911 Doña Emilia did not write very much.[44] Aside from a lecture (1917), in which she speculates on the future of literature after the war, and a few more *cuentos*, she seems to have known how to "callarse a tiempo." She died in 1921, not having quite finished her sixty-ninth year. Galdós preceded her to the grave by about a year, and

Muerto Galdós, era la condesa de Pardo Bazán la primera figura literaria de la actual España. Lo era por la vastedad, la solidez y la trascendencia de su obra; por su contribución incesante a la modernización de la prosa castellana; por su gran talento y su inmenso saber; por la influencia que ejerciera sobre los escritores de las generaciones que vinieron después de ella; y aun por su obra de cultura, mediante la cual España trabó conocimiento con los mejores espíritus de las grandes naciones europeas.[45]

It was the Argentine novelist, Manuel Gálvez, who wrote that sincere eulogy of *la gran Pardo*. Few of her fellow-countrymen would have been as generous, at least in 1921.

III

PARDO BAZÁN'S OPINION OF ZOLA

Emile Zola had no use for Catholicism. To him it was something which the modern world had outgrown, a dead thing—even the symbol of death in its hatred of life. The Church of Saint Eustace, standing there in its gloom hard by the Central Markets of Paris with their teeming life, was to him a pitiful relic of the past—the empty home of a God who had departed.

> ... Saint-Eustache au beau milieu des Halles Centrales ... C'est l'art moderne, le réalisme, le naturalisme comme vous voudrez l'appeler, qui a grandi en face de l'art ancien. ...
>
> Avez-vous remarqué quelles églises on nous bâtit aujourd'hui? Ça ressemble à tout ce qu'on veut, à des Bibliothèques, à des Conservatoires, à des Pigeonniers, à des Casernes; mais, sûrement, personne n'est convaincu que le bon Dieu demeure là-dedans. Les maçons du bon Dieu sont morts, la grande sagesse serait de ne plus construire ces laides carcasses de pierre où nous n'avons personne à loger. ... Depuis le commencement du siècle on n'a bâti qu'un seul monument original, un monument qui ne soit pas copié nul part, qui ait poussé naturellement dans le sol de l'époque; et ce sont les Halles Centrales.[1]

To be sure, that was the opinion of the artist, Claude Lentier, about contemporary architecture; but Claude was obviously the author's *raisonneur* and there is no doubt that Zola also thought it vain to construct churches "où nous n'avons personne à loger."

Zola's attitude toward the Church is clearly revealed in his *La Faute de l'abbé Mouret*, where he subtly portrays the symbolism of the sun representing life, while the crucifix stands for death. Consider this poetic description of the little rural church on a May morning as the young priest says his daily mass to the empty chairs:

> Le soleil à l'appel du prêtre venait à la messe. Il éclaira de larges nappes dorées la muraille gauche, le confessionnal; la Mère de Dieu, dans une gloire, dans l'éblouissement de sa couronne et de son manteau d'or, sourit tendrement à l'enfant Jesus, de ses lèvres peintes; l'horloge rechauffée bâtit l'heure, à coups plus vifs ... Au dehors, on entendait les petits bruits du reveil heureux de la campagne, les herbes qui soupiraient d'aise, les feuilles s'essuyant dans la chalure, les oiseaux ... Même la campagne entrait avec le soleil ... et par les fentes de la grande porte, on voyait les herbes du perron, qui menaçaient d'envahir la nef. Seul, au milieu de cette vie montante, le grand Christ, resté dans l'ombre, mettait la mort, l'agonie de sa chair barbouillée d'ocre, éclaboussée

de laque. Un moineau vint se poser au bord d'un trou . . . Un
second moineau . . . des moineaux descendirent, se promenant
tranquillement à petits sauts, sur les dalles. . . .

Le prêtre . . . n'entendait point cet envahissement de la nef
par la tiède matinée de mai, de flot montant de soleil, de verdures,
d'oiseaux, qui débordait jusqu-au pied du Calvaire où la nature
damnée agonisait.[2]

And the theme continues. Outside is life and beauty and love;
inside the church, death, asceticism. In the church dwells the
same God who drove Adam and Eve out of the garden for having
learned the secret of love and of life. And just as he drove out
that first human pair, so he will drive Serge and Albine forth
from their Paradou under sentence of death. If there is any
positive doctrine in Zola it is his belief in the acceptance of life,
that one should enjoy its delights and rejoice in the beauty of
its fecundity. This belief is increasingly evident toward the end
of the Rougon-Macquart series and finally, in the last of the
twenty books, Dr. Pascal sums it up: "Dans l'inquiétude de
l'au delà, tout au fond, il y a la peur et la haine de la vie."[3] In
his critical writings the master of naturalism is even more
frank to declare his irreligion:

Encore un coup ce n'est pas moi, le naturalisme; c'est tout
écrivain qui, le voulant ou non, emploie la formule scientifique,
reprend l'étude du monde par l'observation et l'analyse, en niant
l'absolu, l'idéal révélé et irrationnel. Le naturalisme, c'est Diderot,
Rousseau, Balzac, Stendhal, vingt autres encore. On fait de moi
une caricature grotesque, en me présentant comme un pontife,
comme un chef d'école. Nous n'avons pas de religion, donc personne ne pontifie chez nous.[4]

It would seem that rejection of religion was almost a *sine qua
non* in the classification of an author as a naturalist. To be
sure, the prime requisite was use of the scientific method of
analysis and observation, but to Zola's reasoning this necessarily
implied rejection of anything so unscientific as revealed truth
or religious dogma.

Imagine his amazement then, upon hearing that the exponent
of his beloved naturalism in the world of Spanish letters was a
devout Catholic. That his apologist should be a woman was
surprising enough, but that she also should be enrolled in the
ranks of orthodox religion was even more paradoxical. In an
interview with Soriano, editor of *La Epoca,* he is reported to
have expressed his astonishment—mixed with admriation—as
follows:

De novelas españolas conozco muy poco: ya he dicho que en
Francia somos muy ignorantes. La Sra. Pardo Bazán ha escrito
una obra que he leído: *La Cuestión Palpitante.* Es libro muy bien
hecho, de fogosa polémica; no parece libro de señora; aquellas
páginas no han podido escribirse en el tocador. Confieso que el
retrato que hace de mi la Sra. Pardo Bazán, está muy parecido, y
el de Daudet, perfectamente. Tiene el libro capítulos de gran
interés, y, en general, es excelente guía para cuantos viajen por
las regiones del naturalismo y no quieren perderse en sus encruci-
jadas y obscuras revueltas. Lo que no puedo olcultar es mi extrañeza de que la Sra. Pardo Bazán sea católica ferviente, mili-
tante, y a la vez naturalista; y me lo explico sólo por lo que oigo
decir de que el naturalismo de esa señora es puramente formal,
artístico y literario.[5]

Just how far Zola's conjectural explanation of the paradox may
have been correct and just how well Pardo Bazán may have succeeded in reconciling the unreconcilable are basic problems which
I hope to resolve in the course of this study.

In seeking a solution we must bear in mind first of all that
Pardo Bazán had the faculty of keeping a calm head in the
midst of conflicting opinions. Also, Zola was misled when he
thought of her Catholocism as "militant." Her religious viewpoint was unswerving but certainly not fanatical or militant.
González-Blanco describes it well: "Un cristianismo enérgico
sin agresividades, tolerante sin transigencias acomodaticias, sereno y firme como la verdad, sin los radicalismos de un Tolstoi,
sin los utopismos de un Fogazzaro."[6]

In an effort to see how much such a Christian spirit reacted
to Zola one must refer for principal authority to her book, *La
Cuestión palpitante,* although other writings of hers often throw
much light on the problem. Ostensibly a work about naturalism
in general, it is nevertheless chiefly concerned with setting forth
her reactions to Zola himself. This she is frank to admit:

Si al hablar de la teoría naturalista la personifico en Zola, no
es porque sea el único a practicarla, sino porque la ha formulado
clara y explícitamente en siete tomos de estudios crítico-literarios,
sobre todo en el que lleva por título *La novela experimental.*[7]

After some introductory chapters on naturalism she proceeds to
outline the rise and fall of romanticism and then to trace naturalism's literary ancestry through Stendhal, Balzac, Flaubert,
and the de Goncourt brothers. Frequent references to Zola and
parallels in procedure indicate that these chapters were based
on the latter's book, *Les Romanciers naturalistes* (1881).[8] In-

cluding a chapter on Daudet before going on to the *chef d'école,* she then devotes three chapters to the leader himself, followed by one chapter on morals in literature, in which she upholds Zola's stand. Three chapters treating the status of the English and Spanish novel conclude the work. Obviously, the very organization of the book reveals the tremendous impact of Zola's personality upon the Spanish countess. But our concern here is not to review the work in its entirety but rather to establish just what points of Zola's system Pardo rejects, what she accepts, and what she seeks to modify. In doing this, let us see first what she says of his basic philosophy and of his literary formula, and finally, what she has to say of morals in literature.

Commenting on Zola's philosophy, she certainly does not seem to share his enthusiasm for the physiological man:

> Curioso libro podría escribir la persona que dominare con igual señorío letras y ciencias, sobre *el darwinismo en el arte contemporáneo.* En él se contendría la clave del pesimismo, no poético a la manera de Leopardi, sino depresivo, que como negro y metífico vapor se exhala de las novelas de Zola; del empeño de patentizar y describir la *bestia humana,* o sea el hombre esclavo del instinto, sometido a la fatalidad de su complexión física y a la tiranía del medio ambiente; de la mal disimulada preferencia por la reproducción de tipos que demuestran la tesis; idiotas, histéricas, borrachos, fanáticos, dementes, o personas tan desprovistas de sentido moral, como los ciegos de sensibilidad en la retina.[9]

Nor does she accept the Darwinian theory, upon which the idea of the physiological man is based. See how cleverly she throws back at Zola his own condemnation of those who accept things without proof and have faith in *l'absolu:*

> Pero, en resumen, limitándome a exponer el dictamen de los más calificados e imparciales autores, indicaré que el darwinismo **no pertenece al número de aquellas verdades científicas demostradas** con evidencia por el método positivo y experimental que Zola preconiza, como, por ejemplo . . . la gravitación . . . ; sino que, hasta la fecha, no pasa de sistema atrevido, fundado en algunos principios y hechos ciertos; pero riquísimo en hipótesis gratuitas, que no descansan en ninguna prueba sólida, por más que anden a caza de ellas numerosos sabios especialistas allá por Inglaterra. . . . Ahora bien: como quiera que en achaque de ciencias exactas, físicas y naturales tenemos derecho para exigir demostración, sin lo cual nos negamos terminantemente a creer y rechazamos lo arbitrario, he aquí que todo el aparato científico de Zola viene a tierra, al considerar que no procede de las ciencias seguras, cuyos datos son fijos e invariables, sino de las que él mismo declara que empiezan aun a balbucir y son tan tenebrosas como rudimentarias. . . .[10]

Rather than proceed on the basis of such shaky science, Doña Emilia prefers to stick to the old idea of the duality of the human make-up—mind and body. Moreover, she is not pleased with the artistic results of depicting the physiological man, constant prey as he is to physical and material stimuli. The resultant literature seems to her to be untrue to life and to present an unbalanced, even an artificial picture, bordering on affectation.

> Tocamos con la mano el vicio capital de la estética naturalista. Someter el pensamiento y la pasión a las mismas leyes que determinan la caída de la piedra; considerar exclusivamente las influencias físico-químicas prescindiendo hasta de la espontaneidad individual, es lo que propone el naturalismo y lo que Zola llama en otro pasaje de sus obras "mostrar y poner de realce la bestia humana." Por lógica consecuencia, el naturalismo se obliga a no respirar sino del lado de la materia, a explicar el drama de la vida humana por medio del instinto ciego y la concupiscencia desenfrenada. Se ve forzado el escritor rigurosamente partidario del método proclamado por Zola, a verificar una especie de *selección* entre los motivos que pueden determinar la voluntad humana, eligiendo siempre los externos y tangibles y desatendiendo los morales, íntimos y delicados: lo cual, sobre mutilar la realidad, es artificioso y a veces raya en afectación, cuando, por ejemplo, la heroína de *Una página de amor* manifiesta los grados de su enamoramiento por los de temperatura que alcanza la planta de sus pies.[11]

But if Pardo Bazán finds naturalism extreme in its effort to explain all human conduct by natural or physical stimuli, she does not side with those at the other extreme, the idealists in literature.

> A fin de esclarecer esta teoría, diré algo del idealismo, para que no pesen sobre el naturalismo todas las censuras y se vea que tan malo es caerse hacia el Norte como hacia el Sur. Y ante todo conviene saber que el idealismo está muy en olor de santidad, goza de excelente reputación y se cometen infinitos crímenes literarios al amparo de su nombre.[12]

It was characteristic of Emilia Pardo Bazán to find the truth in the middle of the road and not to be easily swung to extremes. Quite consistently, then, she apparently chooses to throw in her lot with neither combatant. And to her No-Man's-Land she gives the name of *realism*.

> Si es real cuanto tiene existencia verdadera y efectiva, el *realismo* en el arte nos ofrece una teoría mas ancha, completa y perfecta que el *naturalismo*. Comprende y abarca lo espiritual, el cuerpo y el alma, y concilia y reduce a unidad la oposición del naturalismo y del idealismo racional. En el realismo cabe todo,

menos las exageraciones y desvaríos de dos escuelas extremas, y por precisa consecuencia exclusivistas.[13]

It seems obvious that Pardo is using the term *realism* in its generic sense as derived from the term *real*; she is not seeking membership in any established literary school called *realism* but merely trying to steer a middle course between extremes.

Upon the basis of these quotations from *La Cuestión palpitante* one would surely conclude that there are few, if any, naturalistic elements in her literary formula. How could there be when her Catholicism prevented her from accepting the very scientific views and philosophy upon which Zola based his whole system? When she rejects his *bête humaine* and rebels at the idea of an absolute determinism in human life? What is there left to naturalism, if one does not believe in determinism? There would then be no need for depicting the complete environment, no need for documentation, and the whole system would fall.

It is at this point that some unwary critics have been led astray. They have taken her statements in *La Cuestión* too seriously without troubling to check them against other statements from her pen. Let them consider this short paragraph from an article of hers written in 1884:

> Creemos los católicos en el albedrío humano y nos sonreímos cuando Zola atribuye la honestidad de Dionisia Baudu al buen estado de su salud, pues la observación nos demuestra que hartas vírgenes enfermas saben ser virtuosas. Sin embargo, no separándonos un ápice de las enseñanzas de la Iglesia, admitimos que el cuerpo influye en los movimientos del alma, que los estados totales y parciales del sueño, de enfermedad, de embriaguez, de pasión, de cólera o de locura, motivan resoluciones inexplicables en ánimos equilibrados, que las circunstancias empujan de un modo eficaz, aunque no irresistible, al hombre, que la naturaleza humana está viciada por el pecado, y que no somos espíritus puros, por lo cual, rechazando la tesis materialista de Zola, aceptamos sus investigaciones reales y verdaderas, y algo de su pesimismo en lo que se refiere al convencimiento de la miseria humana.[14]

Here we see that, while unwilling to go all the way with Zola, she yet could go considerable distance along the road to naturalism. Without imitating the extremes of determinism to be found in the work of her French master, she still could in conscience write an acceptable naturalistic novel in which heredity and environment would be presented as strong, but not absolute, forces in human life. Her common sense, perhaps more than her religion, kept her from falling into the exaggerations which often mar the completely realistic impression of Zola's novels.

But Emilia Pardo, with all her balance and critical penetration, seems never quite to have caught the true significance of what Zola meant by the experimental novel. Let us follow her development of the subject in *La Cuestión palpitante*:

> Prescindir del conato científico en Zola, es proponerse deliberadamente no entenderlo, es ignorar dónde reside su fuerza, en qué consiste su flaqueza y cómo formuló la estética del naturalismo.
>
> Su fuerza digo, porque nuestra época se paga de las tentativas de fusión entre las ciencias físicas y el arte, aun cuando se realicen de modo tan burdo como en los libros de Julio Verne.[15]

So far, so good; she has realized the basic importance of science both to the formation and to the subsequent popularity of Zola's formula. But—

> Digo su flaqueza, porque si es verdad que hoy exigimos al arte que estribe en el firmísimo asiento de la verdad, como no tiene por objeto indagarla, y la ciencia sí, el artista que se proponga fines distintos de la realización de la belleza, tarde o temprano, con seguridad infalible, verá desmoronarse el edificio que erija. Zola incurre a sabiendas en tan grave herejía estética, y será castigado, no lo dudemos, por donde más pecó.[16]

Obviously, she was not taken in by Zola's grandiose view of the future of the experimental novel, destined to sound out the rotten beams in the moral structure of society, to point out the weak points to the men of science who will follow after like carpenters to repair the damage, so that all may be set right and man may come to dominate good and evil.

> Nous cherchons les causes du mal social; nous faisons l'anatomie des classes et des individus pour expliquer les détraquements qui se prodiusent dans la société et dans l'homme . . . Nous sommes les actifs ouvriers qui sondons l'édifice, indiquant les poutres pourries, les crevasses intérieurs, les pierres descellées, tous ces dégâts qu'on ne voit pas du dehors et qui peuvent entrainer la ruine du monument entier. N'est-ce pas là un travail plus vraiment utile, plus sérieux et plus digne que de se planter sur un rocher, une lyre au bras, et d'encourager les hommes par une fanfare sonore?[17]

A more maliciously inclined critic might intimate that Zola is here merely invoking a noble-sounding excuse for indulging in his admitted taste for the over-seasoned. Not so, Pardo; she elects to refute his pretensions on the basis of aesthetics. He is proposing utilitarian ends as an ideal in literature, whose only ultimate goal should be beauty. Literature should be based on scientific truth, well and good, but it should not seek to discover that truth. Consider the subtle suggestion of this argument by analogy:

> . . . los brillantes destinos de la novela experimental, llamada a regular la marcha de la sociedad, a ilustrar al criminalista, al sociólogo, al moralista, al gobernante . . . Dice Aristófanes en sus *Ranas*: ". . . y al divino Homero ¿de dónde le vino tanto honor y gloria, sino de haber enseñado cosas útiles, como el arte de las batallas, el valor militar? . . ." Ha llovido desde Aristófanes acá. Hoy pensamos que la gloria y el honor del divino Homero consisten en haber sido un excelso poeto.[18]

Perhaps some day Zola, too, will be remembered as a writer of epics rather than for his discoveries in heredity and for the skill with which he sounded out the rotten beams underlying the Second Empire!

In a polemic written a year after *La Cuestión* we find Doña Emilia still sticking to her guns on this point:

> No conformándome yo con el parecer de Zola respecto al carácter de utilidad docente del arte, está demás que me pregunte "¿qué moral defienden Vds.? . . ." Por centésima vez, el objeto del arte no es defender ni ofender la moral, es realizar la belleza. Para defender la moral, salgan a la palestra los moralistas.[19]

But seven years later, in 1891, she wrote *La Piedra angular*, a novel with an obvious moral teaching against capital punishment; and that this is not the only experimental novel that Pardo Bazán wrote—whether she was conscious of it or not—will be shown in a later chapter.

Don Juan Valera, coming upon a copy of the French translation of *La Cuestión palpitante* some years after its first appearance in Spanish, was moved to write an essay on *The New Art of Writing Novels*. Written in his own inimitable way, he admits on page 19 that he is not going to examine naturalistic novels themselves (laziness preventing his reading them) but what he proposes to do is to refute their atrocious ideas.[20] Nevertheless, it soon becomes apparent that he has read two or three of Zola's most famous novels, as may be seen from Don Juan's reaction to the idea of an experimental novel:

> Otra sofistería no menos chistosa es la de llamar *novela experimental* a la del nuevo género. Pasaría yo porque se llamase *novela observadora*, si no hubiese en ella sino la narración fiel, sin añadir, trocar o brodar, de algo sucedido; pero el experimento, ¿dónde demonios está? . . . ¿Se apodera de un hombre, le derriba de un tejado para que se rompa una pierna, le hace luego beber unas copas, y así, paso a paso me le lleva, como quien no quiere la cosa, a morir bailando el más espantoso baile que se puede ima-

> ginar? Si algo de esto hiciese Zola, podría llamarse experimental
> su novela, o sea el libro en que contase su experimento; pero
> como nada de esto hace, gracias a Dios, su novela es tan fingida
> como la de otro cualquier novelista.[21]

Valera has here put into words, in as clear a fashion as may be,
the obvious fallacy in Zola's dogma, the weak point which is
apparent to anyone's common sense. It is somewhat disappointing to find that even in her final word on naturalism (*El Naturalismo*, 1914), Pardo has not got any farther than Valera
toward understanding the analogy which Zola sought to draw
between his own work as a documentary novelist and that of
Claude Bernard using the human documents that came to his
laboratory. Her final judgment coincides very closely with that
of Valera, voiced years before:

> Del modo de ejecutar ese experimento fuera del laboratorio,
> sobre la mesa de escribir; de como se producen y dirigen los
> fenómenos del alma—digamos del cerebro, si Zola la prefiere,—
> nada nos enseña Zola. En realidad, la única experimentación
> factible envuelve un regreso a la teoría romántica: sólo cabría
> experimentar en sí propio, y henos ya de cabeza en el subjeti-
> vismo.[22]

First she condemns the idea of an experimental novel as utilitarian and then she points out to us that no experiment exists
except in the author's mind—a purely subjective process. On
the other hand, in writing on *Doctor Pascal* in 1893, she admits
that although the now finished Rougon-Macquart series has
taught her nothing in the realm of philosophy, yet

> . . . en cambio sobre lo relativo y finito—la sociedad, el hombre,
> las costumbres, las pasiones, los vicios, las virtudes y los problemas
> de nuestra edad—he aprendido tanto en esas páginas luminosas,
> que sólo se puede comparar el efecto de su lectura con el de la
> lectura de Shakespeare. . . .[23]

One wonders where Zola could have got this immense store
of wisdom, as comparable only to Shakespeare's. Was it all a
subjective process? Did it all leap fully armed from the mind
of genius? Or did he not rather get it from his constant observation of life, from his voluminous notebooks full of human
documents, from his study of so many walks of human life? It
is not a very involved subjective process to conclude that the
manifold misery of the working classes in Paris or in a mining
town comes from poor working conditions, poor pay, or alcoholism. The effort was required in visiting the *milieu*, absorbing
its atmosphere, observing its phenomena. Granted that work-

ing out a novel to prove the conclusions derived from the documentation is a subjective process, nevertheless the analogy is there—the balancing of forces, the combining of materials, the problems of arrangement—and the result of the whole process of constructing a documentary novel is very apt to be the discovery of social truths. Pardo Bazán's admission of the great amount she had learned in the pages of Zola's colossal series demonstrates the point and sustains Zola in the actual, instructive value of an experimental novel. In fact, this instructive value is one of the first aspects of naturalism that seem to have attracted the young Doña Emilia; as she says in the preface to her *Viaje de novios* in 1881:

> De la pugna surgió ya algún principio fecundo, y tengo por importante entre todos el concepto de que la novela ha dejado de ser obra de mero entretenimiento, modo de engañar algunas cuantas horas, ascendiendo a estudio social, psicológico, histórico— al cabo, estudio.[24]

It is too bad the Countess missed the force of the analogy contained in the idea of an erperimental novel; that she fully appreciated the value of the product, as a social study, I think is apparent.

So much for the clash of science and religion and for the doctrine of experiment in the novel. We have seen how Pardo Bazán was able to reconcile her religion to at least a very considerable partial determinism exercised over human life by the forces of heredity and environment, while still not accepting Zola's physiological man as such. We must now ask how much of the Frenchman's formula for the construction of a deterministic novel she was inclined to accept. First of all, on the matter of hereditary influences on fictional characters we find that she takes sharp issue with Zola. To begin with, she condemns the whole basic idea of his Rougon-Macquart series, saying that it led him to present too many exceptional cases.

> Pecado original es el de tomar por asunto no de una novela, pero de un ciclo entero de novelas, la odisea de la *neurosis* al través de la sangre de una familia. Si esto lo considerase como un caso excepcional, todavía lo llevaríamos en paciencia; pero si en los Rougon se representa y simboliza la sociedad contemporánea, protestamos y no nos avenimos a creernos una reata de enfermos y alienados, que es, en resumen, lo que resultan los *Rougon*. A Dios gracias, hay de todo en el mundo, y aun en este siglo de tuberculosis y anemia, no falta quien tenga mente sana en cuerpo sano![25]

But the overabundance of neurotics is not the only fault she has to find with Zola's personages; they are too logical, too predictable in their reactions. She prefers the people depicted by the de Goncourt brothers:

> Es verdad que no procedan como Balzac, ni como Zola, quienes crearon personajes lógicos que obran conforme a los antecedentes sentados por el novelista, y van por donde los lleva la fatalidad de su complexión, y la tiranía de las circumstancias. Los personajes de los Goncourt no son tan automáticos; parecen más caprichosos, más inexplicables para el lector, procedan con independencia relativa, y sin embargo, no se nos figuran maniquíes ni seres fantásticos y soñados, sino personas de carne y hueso, semejantes a muchos individuos que a cada paso encontramos en la vida real, y cuya conducta no podemos predecir con certeza, aun conociéndoles a fondo y sabiendo de antemano los móviles que en ellos pueden influir.[26]

Quite apparently the system used by the de Goncourts in creating characters appealed to her. Certainly it was safer to base one's fictional characters on real observed persons than to imagine possible hereditary types and then seek to endow such mechanical men with the gift of life. Pardo Bazán believed in the force of heredity and took it into account in her novels, but not in the artificial, mechanical fashion of the Rougon-Macquart series. She reveals her attitude on this point very clearly whenever she comes to compare her two literary heroes, Zola and Tolstoy:

> Zola, que alardea de tan minuciosa instrucción documental, desdeña muy a menudo la realidad humilde y amasa la carne de sus personajes con una ideología matemática, por lo cual resultan tan lógicos, tan rectilíneos, que aun cuando a primera vista nos engañen, luego se ve que son teorías, ideas, conceptos, encarnados en una fantasma.
>
> La vida es más compleja y más inconsecuente: tiene sus leyes, no cabe duda, pero secretas, que encubre una apariencia de irregularidad, produciendo lo que suele llamarse misterios del corazón, arcanos del alma, contradicciones que entretejen nuestros actos, y que Tolstoy con tan ingenua profundidad anota y registra. Podrá Zola superar a Tolstoy en maestría técnica: no en franqueza, no en verdad.[27]

The upshot of the matter is that Zola's subjectively imagined personage, with his predetermined type of inherited tendencies and his thoroughly known background and present environment, seems to us altogether too logical a person. We are not used to knowing our fellow man so well. Indeed, it is very doubtful if anyone could ever know an actual individual so well. Now the de Goncourts were wont to depict people they had actually

known rather than to compound a personage based on certain
hypothetical laws of heredity; naturally, then, their people were
less mechanical, less consistent, and consequently more real.
Such a procedure appeals to Pardo's hard common sense more
than the practice of the master of naturalism himself.

However, by the same token the idealized heroes of the romantic school are even more objectionable to her than those of
Zola, for at least he did not create any people of the proportions
of Lamartine's Raphael:

> Ustedes creerán que Rafael se conforma con pintar lo mismo
> que su homónimo, esculpir como Canova y poetizar como Job, el
> Tasso, Shakespeare y Byron en una pieza. ¡Quia! El autor
> añade que, puesto en tales y cuales circunstancias, Rafael hubiese
> tendido a todas las cimas, como Cesar, hablado como Demóstenes y
> muerto como Catón. Así se compone un héroe idealista de la
> especie sentimental. ¡Cuán preferible es retratar un ser humano,
> de carne y hueso, a fantasear maniquíes![28]

The ultimate in her vocabulary of opprobrium seems to be that
a personage should appear to be a mere manikin or puppet
responding mechanically as the author pulls the strings. The
character must seem to be of flesh and blood. But this is not
enough; he must have individuality. Pardo's preference for
painting individuals seems to have grown upon her. Her later
novels, La Quimera (1905) and La Sirena negra (1908), present
a central character in each case who is a most interesting and
unique personality. That the creation of such persons finally
became an ideal with her is indicated by this selection from an
article she wrote on Brunetière in 1907:

> Para mí no cabe duda: toda obra maestra de arte, encierre o
> no confesiones y autoanálisis, es personal e individual, en el sentido
> de que destaca y afirma al individuo sobre la colectividad, y retrata
> al individuo, y por el estudio del individuo se engrandece . . . Este
> individualismo se ha calificado de "creación de caracteres": y de
> hecho, el autor que no ha suscitado individuos no ha suscitado sino
> abstracciones y generalidades pálidas. . . . Nunca conseguirá el
> mejor artista interesarnos con el hombre, sino con hombres diver-
> sos, mejor cuanto más individualizados.[29]

And if there is no direct influence of Zola on Pardo Bazán in
this respect, at least she follows others of the same literary
school, namely, the de Goncourts.

But it is not only in character study that our Countess admired the de Goncourt brothers; their colorful word paintings
were perhaps the chief aspect of their work to appeal to her.

No doubt an interesting study could be made of the influence of these other naturalists on Pardo Bazán. Here I can only touch on the subject, to establish the fact that their influence was no greater than that traceable to the historian of the Rougon-Macquart. As Doña Emilia says in *La Cuestión*:

> Llegando a hablar de los hermanos Goncourt me ocurren dos ideas: la primera, que temo elogiarlos más de lo justo, porque me inspiran gran simpatía y son mis autores predilectos, y así prefiero declarar desde ahora cuanta afición les tengo, confesando ingenuamente que hasta sus defectos me cautivan. "La muchedumbre—dice Zola—no se prosternará jamás ante los Goncourt; pero tendrán su altar propio, riquísimo, bizantino, dorado y con curiosas pinturas, donde irán a rezar los sibaritas."—Soy devota de ese altar, sin pretender erigir en ley mi gusto, que procede quizá de mi temperamento de colorista.—La segunda idea que me asalta es maravillarme de que haya quien califique a los realistas de meros fotógrafos, militando en sus filas los dos escritores modernos que con mayor justicia pueden preciarse de *pintores*.[30]

And some pages farther on:

> Los procedimientos de los Goncourt, levemente atenuados, los adoptó Zola en sus mejores descripciones; Daudet a su vez tomó de ellos las exquisitas miniaturas que adornan algunas de sus páginas más selectas, y todo escritor colorista habrá de inspirarse, de hoy más, en la lectura de los dos hermanos.
>
> ¡Cuán bella y deleitable cosa es el color![31]

No one who has read *La Madre Naturaleza* will question that Pardo Bazán was herself an *escritor colorista*. Color was undoubtedly one of the things she most admired in the de Goncourts; it is also to be found in Zola. And in her own handling of description she seldom forgot the naturalistic principle—discovered by Flaubert and followed by all the naturalists—of not describing anything which could not be seen through the eyes of one of the personages. Continuing her discussion of the de Goncourts, she shows approval of their naturalistic technique for making a novel out of what Zola called "a small rag of life" with little emphasis on plot and much on giving a real picture of everyday life.

> Nadie aplicó más radicalmente que los Goncourt el principio recientemente descubierto de que en la novela es lo de menos argumento y acción, y la suma de verdad artística lo importante. En algunas de sus novelas, como *Sor Filomena* y *René Mauperin*, todavía hay un drama, muy sencillo, pero drama al cabo: en *Manette Salomon, Carlos Demailly, Germinia Lacerteux*, apenas se encuentra más que la serie de los sucesos, incoherente al parecer, y lánguida a veces, como acontece en la vida. . . .[32]

Passing on in her next chapter to the consideration of Alphonse Daudet, observe what she has to say of his documentary method:

> . . . y bien se puede asegurar que no hay pormenor, carácter ni acontecimiento en sus novelas que no esté sacado de esos cuadernos o del rico tesoro de su memoria. Zola dice acertadamente que Daudet carece de imaginación en el sentido que solemos dar a este vocablo, pues nada inventa: solamente escoge, combina, dispone los materiales que de la realidad tomó. Su personalidad literaria, lo que Zola llama temperamento, interviene después y funde el metal de la realidad en su propia turquesa. Notable engaño el de los que creen que, por ajustarse al método realista, abdica un autor su libre facultad creadora, y lo afirman con tono doctoral, lo mismo que si formulasen irrecusable axioma estética![33]

Pardo Bazán continues her defense of the naturalistic method in description in one of her succeeding chapters on Zola, and points out the bad precedent already set in this regard by the writers of the idealistic or romantic school itself:

> Las descripciones largas fueron y son imputadas a la escuela naturalista; mas ¡cuántos *prezolistas* hubo en lo tocante a describir! Sólo que en las antiguas novelas inglesas lo pesado e interminable era la pintura de los sentimientos, afectos y aspiraciones de héroes y heroínas, y sus grandes batallas consigo mismos y sus querellas amorosas, y en Walter Scott, todo, paisajes, figuras, trajes y diálogos. ¿Quién más prolijo en extender fondos que Rousseau?[34]

But Zola goes into too much detail at times, according to Pardo:

> . . . ¿Ha visto el lector alguna vez retratos al óleo hechos con ayuda de vidrio de aumento? ¿Observó cómo en ellos se distinguen las arrugas, las verrugas, las pecas y los más imperceptibles hoyos de la piel? Algo se asemeja la impresión producida por estos retratos a la que causan ciertas descripciones de Zola. Gusta más mirar un lienzo pintado a simple vista con libertad y franqueza.[34]

One might argue this point with the Countess, did she not herself say that it applied only to "certain descriptions" by Zola. At any rate, her criticism of him cannot remain adverse for long and she hastens to add:

> No por eso es lícito decir que las descripciones de Zola se reducen a meros inventarios. Debieran los que lo aseguran probar a hacer inventarios así; ya verían como no es tan fácil hinchar un perro. Las descripciones de Zola, poéticas, sombrías o humorísticas (nótese que no digo *festivas*), constituyen no escasa parte de su original mérito y el escollo más grave para sus infelices imitadores. Esos sí que nos darán listas de objetos, si como es probable les

niega el hado el privilegio de interpreter el lenguaje del aspecto de las cosas, y el don de la oportunidad y mesura artística.[34]

The descriptive power of Zola, his ability to make an entire environment come alive, was a subject that never failed to excite the admiration of Emilia Pardo Bazán. As late as 1914 we find her still admiring his ability to produce beauty out of the multiplicity of trivial and even ugly details:

> También se inicia, en *La ralea*, la absorción y anulación de los seres humanos por los objetos y el medio. Plenamente se mostrará en *El vientre de París*. No hay allí más héroe que el mercado (Halles centrales), y así como en *La ralea* cantan en coro estrofas de perversidad los vegetales raros, en *El vientre* lo hacen los olores de las vituallas, dominando los quesos. Aparece el procedimiento favorito del novelista: sacar de lo repugnante y trivial lo hermoso, mediante el relieve y energía de la descripción . . . El caso de una novela en que los personajes interesen menos que el fondo, no era nuevo, por otra parte: recuérdese *Nuestra Señora*, de Victor Hugo, donde la heroína no es Esmeralda, sino la Catedral. La nueva estética es diferente en que reemplaza a la Catedral el Mercado, o el gran Almacén de novedades, o la mina, o la red de caminos de hierro, o la Bolsa.[35]

Despite her admiration for Zola's presentation of the complete environment, Pardo Bazán never adopted the documentary method in its entirety. She did not conscientiously sally forth, notebook in hand, to document herself on a certain milieu before writing about it. Hers was an indirect documentation—derived from experience and observation, to be sure, but not so formalized a process as was practiced in France. As she says in 1891:

> Además, la cuestión del naturalismo o de *documentarismo*, como quiere Goncourt que se diga, tiene muy diferente aspecto visto desde España que vista del bulevar. Aquí no se han escrito novelas *documentarias*, sino novelas realistas, enlazando la tradición rancia y venerable de nuestra novela de los siglos XVI y XVII, con lo poco de espíritu moderno que llegó hasta nosotros.[36]

Be that as it may, there are critics who find the novels of Pardo Bazán refreshing for their international point of view and modern technique as opposed to those of such authors as Pereda, who followed *la tradición rancia* more closely.

In any treatment of naturalism a discussion of documentation and of the description of a complete environment is followed closely by the question of frankness about sex and all the consequent discussion of morals in the novel. In the main, as I have said before, Pardo Bazón stood behind Zola on the fundamentals of the moral issue in literature. However, here as elsewhere, she considered him an extremist and refused to go quite all the way with him. To her it was all more a matter of taste than of morals; the only thing really immoral about Zola's works was their excessive belief in determinism.

> Son imputables en particular al naturalismo—no huelga repetirlo—las tendencias deterministas, con defectos de gusto y cierta falta de selección artística, grave delito el primero, leve el segundo, por haber incurrido en él los más ilustres de nuestros dramaturgos y novelistas. Lo que importa no son las verugas de la superficie, sino el fondo.[37]

But what led Zola to display such poor taste and faulty artistic selection? That the commercial motive was not absent, Pardo is ready to admit:

> En un principio convenía el ruido, las protestas, la curiosidad sana o malsana, para lograr lo que se logró; romper el ánimo y amotinar a ese París, donde un motín vale por un triunfo; después era preferible derramar aceite sobre las encrespadas olas, que ya cortaba, viento en popa, la nave del discutido naturalismo. . . .[38]

And yet it was also a question of temperament with Zola:

> De tiempo en tiempo sale un Zola, es decir, un artista brutal, un vándalo del lenguaje, que al profanarlo, lo fecunda. Así fué Rabelais, y a ése sí que le cae muy bien el epiteto de sucio. El realismo, y sobre todo el actual . . . no tiene la culpa de la aparición de esos *temperamentos*.[39]

Ostensibly an apology, there is yet an undeniable ring of admiration in that comment. And perhaps there is something of the eternal feminine in the attraction she found in the very brutality of the giant of Médan. Nevertheless, the same quality of femininity manifests itself in a certain delicacy which refuses to enjoy some of the more crude excesses indulged in by the author of *Pot-Bouille*. The master of naturalism hoped that Daudet, in his gentle, humorous way, would be an entering wedge whereby later the more violent of naturalistic novels might come to repose on the dainty shelves of the boudoirs of Paris. Doña Emilia is not so hopeful:

> Tengo para mí que esas puertas no se franquerán jamás a todas las obras de Zola, aunque envíe delante a cien Daudets allanando obstáculos. Daudet pertenece a la misma escuela que Zola, es cierto; pero se contenta con acusar la musculatura de la realidad, mientras el otro la descuella con sus dedos de hierro y la presenta al lector en láminas clínicas. Pocos estantes de palo de rosa gemirán bajo el peso de *Pot-Bouille*.[40]

Again Pardo was torn between her common sense and the

attractions of Zola's brutal strength.   Or perhaps I should say that her feminine admiration was incapable of overcoming her equally feminine delicacy.   Be that as it may, she again drew the line half way.   In her ultra-naturalistic novel, *La Tribuna,* she describes a child-birth scene—not from the doctor's viewpoint but rather from that of those who, not admitted to the chamber, must nonetheless suffer the anguish of waiting and uncertainty.   Despite the somewhat softened naturalism of such a procedure, critics protested her unwarranted frankness.   One of these she very ably answers in a polemic:

> Así estuviese yo tan segura de imitar a los grandes clásicos en el talento como lo estoy de quedarme muy atrás de ellos en la libertad del pincel, aunque apunte V. en la cuenta de mis licencias los detalles de obstetricia de *La Tribuna,* harto más sucintos y velados que los que a cada instante se oyen en conversaciones y diálogos de gente bien educada, de señoras que se refieren mutuamente sus andanzas en tan apurado trance. . . .
>
> Para narrar ese episodio tremendo de la vida femenina, que debe caber en el arte, esa suprema crisis de la maternidad, donde no hay nada de licencioso o provocativo e impera la austeridad profunda del dolor, he rehuído la descripción clínica de Zola en *Pot-Bouille,* haciendo que la tragedia se represente entre bastidores, y que el oído supla a la vista.[41]

And a few pages farther on she sums up her stand on the matter of frankness or freedom in description:

> Opiné y sigo opinando que se debe poner el límite muchísimo más allá que Octavio Feuillet y otras novelistas de agua con azucarillo, y harto más acá que Zola; pero esto en rigor es cuestión de gusto y acaso de remilgos, que algunos tendré yo como cada quisque.[42]

Her taste merely delights in a somewhat less highly seasoned product than that of Zola.   However, she does not abandon him in principle, and always defends his right to tell whatever details he saw fit.   For she maintains that the ultimate conclusion of Zola's books is not to incite the reader to vice, however much of evil may be described therein.   No more does *La Tribuna,* her own book, paint erotic freedom in very glowing colors.

> No sé lo que inspirará a las mujeres arrebatadas e indoctas el naturalismo: por la parte que toca a *La Tribuna,* no será de fijo el *amor libre,* dogma de la iglesia romántica *jorgesandiana,* nunca de la naturalista.[43]

Compare this quotation with one from Zola's *Le Roman expérimental:*

> Or, rien n'est dangereux comme le romanesque: telle oeuvre,

en peignant le monde en couleurs fausses, détraque les imagina-
tions, les jette dans les aventures . . . Avec nous ces perils dis-
paraissent. Nous enseignons l'amère science de la vie, nous don-
nons la hautaine leçon du réel. Voilà ce qui existe, tâchez de vous
en arranger.[44]

And now back to the *Cuestión palpitante*:

En cuestiones religiosas y sociales, los naturalistas proceden
como sus hermanos los positivistas respecto de los problemas meta-
físicos; los dejan a un lado, aguardando a que las resuelva la
ciencia, si es posible. Abstención mil veces menos peligrosa que
la propaganda socialista y herética de los novelistas que les pro-
cedieron. . . .

En cuanto a la pasión, sobre todo la amorosa, fuera de los
caminos del deber, lejos de glorificarla, diríase que se han em-
peñado los realistas en desengañar de ella a la humanidad, en
patentizar sus riesgos y fealdades, en disminuir sus atractivos. De
Madame Bovary a *Pot-Bouille*, la escuela no hace sino repetir con
fatídico acento que sólo en el deber se encuentra la tranquilidad y
la ventura.[45]

It is obvious that Zola and Pardo Bazán see very much eye to
eye on the matter of morality in literature. While they differ
on the degree of frankness advisable, they do not disagree on
the basic proposition that frankness is a question of taste rather
than morals.

One reason why the brutal frankness of the naturalists made
such a strong impression on those who were first exposed to it
was the impersonal, factual way in which the story was told.
The reader kept expecting the author to step into his novel and
shake his head sadly over so much wickedness. But, no, he
merely presented the scenes and actions objectively and seemed
to say, "Here is life, draw your own conclusions." It took a
famous court trial to establish the fact that Gustave Flaubert
was not trying to corrupt French morals with his *Madame Bovary*. The public thought, since the author did not interrupt his
story to condemn the sins of his heroine, that he must be ad-
vocating sin. They were misled by Flaubert's impersonal style.
Upon looking closer they could see that Emma Bovary's tragic
story did not invite emulation on the part of anyone. Indeed,
in its stark presentation it was a stronger argument against
adultery than it would have been if accompanied by any amount
of sermonizing on the author's part.

It is interesting to see how Pardo Bazán reacted to the matter
of impersonal style as employed and advocated by Flaubert and

Zola. First, we have an early comment from the Preface to her *Viaje de novios* (1881):

> Yo de mí sé decir que en arte me enamora la enseñanza indirecta que emana de la hermosura, pero aborrezco las píldoras de moral rebozadas en una capa de oro literario. Entre el impudor frío y afectado de los escritores ultranaturalistas y las homilías sentimentales de los autores que toman un púlpito en cada dedo y se van por esos trigos predicando, no escojo; me quedo sin ninguno.[46]

As I will show later in more detail, this Preface reveals merely her immature first reactions to naturalism and is to be taken with a grain of salt. So in the above quotation we find her already condemning the moralizing novelists but not yet ready to join the naturalists. The best answer to how much our author subscribed to the principle of *impersonnalité* is to be found in the study of her novels themselves. There it will be seen that she wrote books which were impersonal in the main and more or less interlarded with generalizations and bits of wisdom. This tendency of hers she summarizes very well in the prologue to *La Quimera* (1905):

> De la contemplación del destino de Silvio he sacado involuntariamente consecuencias religiosas, hasta místicas, que sin respetos humanos vierto en el papel. No me complacen las novelas con fines de apología o propaganda; pero cuando, sin premeditación se incorpora a la obra literaria lo que no quiero llamar *convicciones* ni *principios*, porque son vocablos intelectuales y militantes, sino *sentires y llamamientos*; si bajo la ficción novelesca palpita algún problema superior a los efímeros eventos que tejen el relato; si un instante el soplo divino nos cruza la sien, ¿por qué ocultarlo? ¿No es esto tan verdad como las funciones del organismo?[47]

Again, then, in the matter of impersonal style, her acceptance of this naturalistic principle is a partial acceptance. She reserves her feminine right to become personal once in a while as the spirit moves her, while striving in the main to tell a straightforward story.

Despite his insistence on *impersonnalité* and the resemblance between the ideal style and *un beau marbre*, Zola was not blind to the necessity that style express the man; if the man is a nonentity he cannot have style.

> Je connais des romanciers que écrivent proprement et auxquels on a fait à la longue un bon renom littéraire. Ils sont très laborieux, ils abordent tous les genres avec la même facilité. Les phrases coulent toutes seules de leurs plumes. . . .
> Le malheur est qu'ils n'ont pas l'expression personnelle, et c'en est assez pour les rendre à jamais médiocres . . . Jamais les phrases

ne sortent de leur personnalité, ils les écrivent comme si quelqu'un par derrière les leur dictait; et c'est peut-être pour cela qu'ils n'ont qu'à ouvrir le robinet de leur production. . . . Ils ont, au lieu d'un cerveau créateur, un immense magasin empli des phrases connues. . . .

Au contraire, voyez un romancier qui a l'expression personnelle, voyez M. Alphonse Daudet, par exemple. . . .[48]

Surely no one will deny that Alphonse Daudet has style. Doña Emilia endorses the master of naturalism in this, although she seems to wish he had been more explicit:

. . . si el arte moderno exige reflexión, madurez y cultura, el arte de todas las edades reclama principalmente la personalidad artística, lo que Zola, con frase vaga en demasía, llama el temperamento. Quien careciere de esa quisicosa, no pise los umbrales del templo de la belleza, porque será expulsado.[49]

Certainly the temperament of Zola himself was directly opposed to any simple, neat, and cold way of expression, much as he may have set them up as ideals. As Pardo remarks:

Conviene Zola en que su estilo, lejos de poseer esa hermosa simplicidad y nitidez que aproxima en cierto modo la naturaleza al espíritu y el objeto al sujeto, y esa sobriedad que expresa cada idea con las palabras estrictamente necesarias y propias, está recargado de adjetivos, adornado de infinitos penachos y cintajos y colorines que la harán tal vez de inferior calidad en lo venidero. ¿Débense realmente tales defectos a la tradición romántica? ¿No será más bien que esas puras y esculturales líneas que Zola ambiciona y todos ambicionamos, excluyen la continua ondulación del estilo, el detalle minucioso, pero rico y palpitante de vida, que exige y apetice el público moderno?[50]

It is evident that the Countess commends the richness of his style and is merely pointing out the discrepancy between his doctrine and his practice. However, at times she feels that his prose is too worked over:

El jefe del naturalismo carece de naturalidad y sencillez; no lo niega, y lo achaca a la leche romántica que mamó. Artista lleno de mátices, de primores y de refinamientos, diríase, no obstante, que su prosa carece de alas, que está ligada por ligaduras invisibles, faltándole aquel grato abandono, aquella facilidad, armonía y número que posee por ejemplo, Jorge Sand. Su estilo, igual y llano, es en realidad trabajadísimo. . . .

Hasta el valor eufónico de las palabras, y, sobre todo, su vigor como toques de luz o manchones de sombra, está combinado en Zola para producir efecto, lo mismo que el modo de usar los verbos. Si dice "iba" en vez de "fué," no es por casualidad o descuido, es porque quiere que nos representemos la acción más aprisa; que el personaje eche a andar a vista del lector.[51]

The practice of employing the imperfect tense for vividness

seems to have been one of the things our author took from French naturalism, as will be evident to anyone who reads her novels. As for the lack of "aquel grato abandono" in Zola's style, this touches upon a sore point between the two authors. Zola's ulterior motives, his constant planning for effect, success, or scandal, constituted a quality in him which to her was unbearable. "Siempre el cálculo, cálculo en un cierto modo frío, cálculo que daña. Tolstoy no calcula, y sus crudezas no hieren como las de Zola."[52]

In general, what can we conclude about her reactions to Zola's style? That she admires him when he is most spontaneous and lyrical seems evident. When his writing shows evidence of too much planning for effect, she is both aware of it and distressed by it. It is then that she perceives the feet of clay beneath her idol. His *cálculo* seems to her a crime against his own outstanding ability as a spontaneous artist, a debasement of his art for ulterior motives.

There was another tendency in Zola's artistic procedure which never failed to arouse a protest from Doña Emilia. That he should magnify some of his lyrical word pictures to Homeric proportions was all very well, but that he should constantly tend to exaggerate the evil in a world already black enough was unpardonable. From the very first we find this tendency to have been a fly in the ointment of her admiration for the great Frenchman. Thus she says in the preface to her early work, *Un Viaje de novios* (1881):

> No censuro la observación paciente, minuciosa, exacta, que distingue a la moderna escuela francesa; al contrario lo elogio; pero desapruebo . . . más que todo, un defecto en que no sé si repararon los críticos: la parenne solemnidad y tristeza, el ceño siempre torvo, la carencia de notas festivas y de gracia y soltura en el estilo y en la idea. Para mí es Zola, con su inmenso talento, el más hipocondríaco de los escritores habidos o por haber; un Heráclito que no gasta pañuelo, un Jeremías que así llora la pérdida de la nación por el golpe de estado, como la ruina de un almacén de ultramarinos. Y siendo la novela por excelencia trasunto de la vida humana, conviene que en ella turnen, como en nuestro existir lágrimas y risas, el fondo de la eterna tragicomedia del mundo. . . .[53]

And in *La Cuestión palpitante* Zola suffers by comparison to Daudet in this respect: "Aquella nota festiva que en la vida no falta y sí en las novelas de Zola, la posee el teclado de Daudet. . . ."[54] It is partly a question of Zola's deficiency in that

quality of which Pardo Bazán had so generous a share—a sense
of humor. But it is more than that:

> ¿No hay en la galería de sus personajes alguno que no padezca
> del alma o del cuerpo o de ambas cosas a la vez? Sí los hay: pero
> tan nulos, tan inútiles, que su salud y su bondad se traducen en
> inercia, y casi se hacen más aborrecibles que la enfermedad y el
> vicio . . . Lo activo en Zola es el mal: el bien bosteza y se cae de
> puro tonto. ¡Cuidado con la singularisima mujer honrada de *Pot-
> Bouille*! ¡Pues y el sandio protagonista de *El vientre de Paris*!
> Es cosa de preferir a los malvados, que al menos están descritos
> de mano maestra y no se duermen.[55]

That the Spanish author was not the only one to remark this
tendency in the early work of Zola may be seen from this parallel French comment on *Son Excellence Eugène Rougon,* the novel
which preceded *L'Assommoir*:

> Le fait est que dans ce nouveau roman, on a beau chercher,
> on ne trouve pas, dans le plus petit coin, l'ombre d'un honnête
> homme ni d'une honnête femme. Eh! quoi! tant d'appétits
> mauvais, tant de luxure, tant d'affronteries, tant de fièvre de
> débauche et d'ambition, est-ce possible?

> A Marmontel, croyons-nous, ou à Florian . . . on rapprochait de
> n'avoir mis un loup dans la bergerie. Nous ferons la reproche
> contraire à M. Zola. Il manque un mouton parmi ses loups. Une
> vertu eût relevé la sauce.[56]

But it was in *Pot-Bouille* that this procedure of Zola's reached
its most striking proportions; indeed, the book becomes to Pardo
a sort of horrible example of all that is worst in Zola. However,
the tendency to exaggerate, Doña Emilia finds, is intimately
connected with his poetic love of metaphor or, as she terms it,
symbolism. We have already had an example of this in Zola's
attitude toward religion as shown through the allegory underlying *La Faute de l'Abbé Mouret*; and just as in the earlier book
the sun symbolized life and the crucifix death, so in *Pot-Bouille*
we have the allegory of a sort of witch's cauldron in which all
the vices of the French bourgeoisie are stewed up for us under
one lid—or as Pardo puts it in *La Cuestión*:

> . . . mas por lo que toca a *Pot-Bouille* la exageración me parece
> indudable; y mejor que *exageración* le llamaría yo *simbolismo*, o si
> se quiere *verdad representativa*. Aunque suena a paradoja, el
> símbolo es una de las formas usuales de la retórica zolista: la
> estética de Zola es en ocasiones simbólica como . . . ¿lo diré? como
> la de Platón. Alegorías declaradas (*La falta del cura Mouret*), o
> veladas (*Nana, La Ralea, Pot-Bouille*), sus libros representan
> siempre más de lo que son en realidad. . . .[57]

Furthermore:

> . . . yo me figuro que el método de *acumulación* que emplea Zola sirve para hinchar la realidad, es decir, lo negro y triste de la realidad, y que el novelista procede como los predicadores, cuando en un sermón abultan los pecados con el fin de mover a penitencia al auditorio. En suma, tengo a Zola por pesimista, y creo que ve la humanidad aun más fea, cínica y vil de lo que es. Sobre todo más cínica, porque aquel *Pot-Bouille*, mejor que estudio de las costumbres mesocráticas, parece pintura de un lupanar, un presidio suelto y un manicomio, todo en una pieza.[58]

However, with the appearance of *L'Argent* (1891), Doña Emilia is glad to change her tune, although she still condemns his *La Bête humaine*, published the year before:

> Como obra de arte, paréceme *El Dinero* superior a *La Bestia humana*, que empieza de un modo admirable y acaba con una serie de crímenes dignos de la *Galería fúnebre de espectros y sombras ensangrentadas. El Dinero* es de los libros *maduros* de Zola, donde el ilustre épico sabe refrenar el vuelo de su desatada fantasía y no *acumular*.[59]

It is rather ironical that despite Pardo's praise for Zola's restraint and maturity in *L'Argent,* this work has remained one of the least popular of his Rougon-Macquart series. It was not until she wrote her book, *El Naturalismo* (1914), that Pardo Bazán seems finally to have realized that it was in *L'Assommoir* that Zola really achieved his masterpiece, the reason being that it contains the least exaggeration and is therefore the most true to life of all his novels.

> . . . en el *Assommoir* . . . dió Zola la nota sobreaguda de su originalidad, se mantuvo en los límites de la verdad y de la verosimilitud (muy repugnantes, convenido), equilibrando bien el elemento descriptivo y el narrativo, cuya medida ha solido perder en otras obras. . . . La suma de verdad posible en la novela, está en el *Assommoir* . . . Las ideas, sentimientos y mentalidad de sus personajes sangran de puro reales y causan la impresión, ya cómica, ya dramática y a veces trágica, de lo que cabe en tal vivir. Lo cómico—sin ingenio, cómico amargo y pesimista—abunda más en el *Assommoir* que en ninguna otra novela de Zola. Son modelos acabados las escenas del lavadero, las bodas de Gervasia y Coupeau, el banquete en el taller de planchado, el entierro de la vieja. . . .[60]

And in contrast to *Pot-Bouille,* the balance of *L'Assommoir* is even more apparent:

> . . . pero la obra (*Pot-Bouille*) peca, por el procedimiento tan característico en Zola, de condensar y hacer comprimidos de cuanto de vil, mezquino y miserable existe en el medio ambiente, eliminando lo que puede producir la sensación completa de la vida.

Olvidar que tambien existe lo bueno, y en especial lo indiferente, es grave error de perspectiva. En el *Assommoir* había algunos obreros honrados, y hasta excelentes, como *Gola de oro*; la heroína era, en el fondo, una bondadosa mujer, y lo propio su marido, y lo serían siempre, a no mediar el alcohol; *Pot-Bouille*, en puridad, no presenta un solo ejemplar humano que no merezca ir a presidio, excepto aquel novelista, en que Zola se representa a sí propio.[61]

Strange that it took the Countess so long to remark the balance manifest in Zola's epic of the dramshop, and that when, in her *Cuestión palpitante*, she was lamenting the predominance of *malvados* in *les Rougon-Macquart* as opposed to the few sympathetic nonentities, she did not think to consider Goujet, Gervaise, or Coupeau.

Nevertheless, I think any student of Zola will admit that the strong force in his novels is that of unmitigated selfishness. The good characters are few, and many of them remain in one's mind as pale and rather ineffectual creations. Noteworthy exceptions are to be found in the heroines of *Au Bonheur des Dames, La Joie de Vivre, L'Argent,* and *Docteur Pascal*; also the names of Jean Macquart and Dr. Pascal, himself, stand out on the optimistic side. However, Zola frequently writes as if the barest essentials of Christian charity had never been known on earth. In many of the books all of his people are at heart purely selfish, purely wolfish. They present a picture of society as it would be were all virtue and altruism dead; even common human sympathy is often lacking. There is some truth in the rabid accusations of a certain clerical critic of Pardo's time:

Ahora bien: en este caso el naturalismo ha abierto el proceso más formidable, más atroz, más implacable contra el positivismo y la sociedad contemporánea. Lo que está pintando no es una sociedad corrumpida, por el idealismo . . . sino una sociedad corrumpida, viciada, envilecida hasta la médula por el materialismo . . . Ya nos ha dicho lo que es una sociedad sin Dios, lo que será el día en que se aparte totalmente de Dios: inmenso cubil de mónstruos y fieras sedientas de cieno y de sangre.[62]

The Padre's vitriolic pen perhaps exaggerates but he makes a point with which Pardo Bazán is in essential agreement. We see this especially when she comes to compare Zola with Tolstoy and the Russian naturalists:

Escribir como si Cristo no hubiese existido, ni su doctrina hubiese sido promulgada jamás, fué el error capital de la escuela, que procedía directamente del modo de ser de Zola, cuya escasa disposición para estudiar la psiquis de la fe y del misticismo se demostró sobradamente en la figura de Sergio Mouret y en la artificiosa construcción de *El ensueño* (*Le rêve*). Y el misticismo eslavo le derrotó, prolongando al mismo tiempo la era del naturalismo en la novela, pero naturalismo con ventanas y respiración, sin pseudo-ciencia y sin positivismo barato.[63]

Her reactions to Zola in this respect are those of a Christian believing in the old conflict of the flesh *versus* the spirit, whereas Zola seeks to eliminate the latter entirely, presenting us with a society made up completely of physiological men, i.e., men who have no other drive or motive than the lusts of the flesh. Indeed, she intimates that Zola's overly black picture of society could be used by any theologian to prove how dark life could become if all the spiritual forces were removed from it. Thus she says in her 1914 essay on naturalism:

La imaginación de Zola, en cierto respecto (y por más que se refugie en el socialismo), está muy impregnada de algunos dogmas del ascetismo cristiano. En este sentido, no pudo escamotear lo religioso, como probablemente creyó hacerlo. Su hombre es el de naturaleza pervertida y viciada por el pecado original; su humanidad, una humanidad doliente, enferma, siempre aguijoneada por la concupiscencia y los apetitos corporales. . . .[64]

The idea of tracing the successive developments of Pardo's attitude toward what she terms exaggeration or accumulation in Zola, suggests the idea of tracing the evolution of her attitude toward naturalism in general. By her Preface to *Un viaje de novios* (1881) she is generally credited with having introduced naturalism to the Spanish reading public; and to be sure, the Preface does read like an introduction:

La escuela de noveladores franceses que enarbola la bandera realista o naturalista, es asunto de encarnizada discusión y suscita tan agrias censuras como acaloradas defensas. Sus productos recorren el globo, mal traducidos, peor arreglados, pero con segura venta y número de ediciones incalculable. Es de buen gusto horrorizarse de tales engendros, y ciertísimo que el que más se horroriza no será por ventura el que menos los lea. Para el experto en cuestiones de letras, todo ello indica algo original y característico, fase nueva de un género literario, signo de vitalidad, y por tal concepto, más reclama detenido examen que sempiterno desprecio o ciego encomio.[65]

As usual, she pleads for a sane and fair consideration for the new school, in place of the blind disapproval and hasty horror which was "de buen gusto."

De la pugna surgió ya algún principio fecundo, y tengo por importante entre todos el concepto de que la novela ha dejado de ser obra de mero entretenimiento, modo de engañar gratamente unas cuantas horas, ascendiendo a estudio social, psicológico, histórico—al cabo, estudio. Dedúcese de aquí una consecuencia que a muchos les sorprenderá: a saber, que no son menos necesarias al novelista que las galas de la fantasía, la observación y el análisis. Porque en efecto, si reducimos la novela a fruto de lozana inventiva, pararemos en proponer como ideal del género . . . las *Mil y una noches*. En el día—no es lícito dudarlo—la novela es traslado de la vida, y lo único que el autor pone en ella, es su modo peculiar de ver las cosas reales: así como dos personas, refiriendo un mismo suceso cierto, lo hacen con distintas palabras y estilo.[66]

So far so good. The young author already felt a strong attraction toward this new school of writers who sought to lift the novel from the pale of mere entertainment to that of a serious social *study*. Henceforth the novel is to be based solidly on reality and, being the product of careful observation and analysis of character, it will recommend itself for the very truth of its contents. It is significant to note, however, that her reaction to the violent frankness of Zola and his followers is still an immature and excessively negative reaction which she will later come to modify:

> Hay realismos de realismos, y pienso que a ésa le falta, o más bien le sobra algo, para alardear de género de buena ley y durable influjo en las letras. El gusto malsano del público ha pervertido a los escritores con oro y aplauso; y ellos toman por acierto suyo lo que no es sino bellaquería e indelicadeza de los lectores. No son las novelas naturalistas que mayor boga y venta alcanzaron, las más perfectas y reales; sino las que describen costumbres más licenciosas, cuadros más libres y cargados de color. . . .[67]

Of all Zola's novels *L'Assommoir* probably sold the most copies and made the most noise; according to Pardo's statement, then, it would not figure among the most perfect but merely among the most licentious. Is this the same author who, in *La Cuestión palpitante*, defends Zola's stand on morals in literature and passes off as but a matter of poor taste his excessive frankness? Is she the same person who could say in 1914, "No sería justo desconocer que entre las novelas de Zola, y a pesar de crudezas y brutalidades, el *Assommoir* es, en su género, una obra maestra."[68] It would certainly seem that our novelist exercised her woman's privilege and changed her mind. Again, she says in the same Preface: ". . . pero desapruebo . . . la prolijidad nimia, y a veces consada, de las descripciones. . , ,"[69] The reader will recall the citations already made from her *Cuestión palpitante* in which she refutes this, her own criticism, in a masterly fashion, declaring it was in romanticists like Walter Scott that endless description was truly boring, whereas in Zola the descriptions form no small part of his especial merit.

It should be apparent that the statements made by the Countess of Pardo Bazán in this early Preface are not to be taken as reliable guides to her artistic and literary principles. A great deal of confusion has arisen because critics have regarded the Preface as a definite manifesto on her part. To me it is just an indication of her first reactions to naturalism; it is not an example of inconsistency or insincerity, as some have insinuated, nor yet is it to be quoted as authority to show how little of French naturalism she ever would accept. The arguments pro and con about this question will be discussed in another chapter after some of the evidence from her novelistic work has been presented.

Now let us see what progress there was in Pardo's attitude toward Zola after the publication of *La Cuestión* in 1883. When the fourth edition of the book came out in 1891, it had a new Preface in which the author remarked: ". . . Si intentase *corregir* o *refundir*, tendría que *añadir mucho* sin *variar esencialmente* nada."[70] Another quotation from her *Neuvo Teatro Crítico* for 1891 further illustrates her continued satisfaction with what she had said in *La Cuestión* some eight years before:

> Hace años, cuando expuse y defendí el naturalismo, lo hice con muchas reservas, considerando ese gran movimiento de las letras contemporáneas una especie de oportunismo, la hora presente, no la del porvenir. Parecíame pueril y quimérico, negar lo que saltaba a la vista, y creía, como sigo creyendo ahora, que es preferible *comprender* a *escandalizarse*, porque en estética, el escándalo no prueba nada.[71]

Turning now to a magazine article dedicated to Zola in 1902, shortly after his death, we find the Countess still steadfast in her admiration for him as a great naturalist author, although she does not share in the popular enthusiasm over his activity in the Dreyfus case. Unlike some, who think of Zola's heroic defense of Dreyfus as a final act of atonement for all of his previous sins and errors, Pardo Bazán will continue to admire him as a great writer:

> Sólo gratos recuerdos tengo del que acaba de bajar al sepulcro; importábame consignarlo, refrescar memorias de mis polémicas para que a Zola se tributase aquí la atención que merece—antes de separarme y situarme a toda la distancia posible de la actual

pseudo-admiración, más fabricada y falsa, si cabe, que aquellos alardes de ignorancia y grosería de magnate mal educado con que antaño se acogían las obras del maestro de Medan.

Mas para no equivocarse infantilmente respecto de Zola, incluyéndole en el Santoral y en el Martirologio; para leer claramente en su alma, hay que representársele atleta que lucha su propia lucha, y que, con acierto absoluto, cree y profesa que para Zola no hay nadie, ni Dreyfus, tan importante como Zola. Otro tanto podría creer de sí Juan Peranzules, ya lo sé: la diferencia es que individuos como Zola nos comunican su persuasión, y que Zola, importante para sí, lo es para nosotros, en altísimo grado. Y ¡viven los cielos! no es por filántropo por lo que nos importa; y ¡alégrese su sombra! filántropos hay más que grandes escritores.[72]

And if she did not appreciate the master of naturalism as a philanthropist, no more did she esteem him as a social evangelist. There is a note of vague regret for the good old days in the following comment (1907) :

El análisis de Brunetière ejerció su acción enérgica y desintegradora, preparando la disolución de la escuela *como escuela*, y llevando a su pontífice por caminos insospechables cuando se publicó *L'assommoir*; compeliéndole a buscar el idealismo en *Le rêve*, y más tarde, no ignoramos con qué escaso tino y felicidad, la tesis y la novela social en los *Cuatro Evangelios*.[73]

Further evidence that she was not impressed by Zola's later manner is to be found in *El Naturalismo* (1914) : "De los últimos, las *evangelistas*, poco trató la crítica seria, e hizo perfectamente. Apenas pertenecen al arte."[74] And a few pages farther on: "Cuando, años despues, extraviado por la política, escribirá la rapsodia de *Trabajo* . . . sentenciada a los limbos de la obras falsas y mediocres. . . ."[75]

We have seen how Pardo Bazán's common sense and remarkable equilibrium ever kept her from going all the way with Zola. Even in *La Cuestión* she condemns his exaggerations, not only his exaggerated pessimism through his method of accumulation but also the excessively mechanical determinism manifest in his work. His system was too perfect, too limiting, and he followed it too closely. The result was inevitable—naturalism à la Zola, naturalism as a *literary school,* was doomed by its very artificiality. Not so the Russian naturalists, and to them the Countess of Pardo Bazán now gives homage (1910) :

Obsérvase—para distinguir el realismo y el naturalismo ruso del francés—la transformación del último en *escuela literaria*. Si hay algo incompatible con la genialidad rusa es esta transformación, la flor natural convertida en flor de trapo, la retórica sustuyendo a la vida. Y en retórica y en procedimiento degeneró el naturalismo, bajo la influencia de Zola y sus discípulos; de eso murió tan pronto, y por eso Zola dió el espectáculo que presenciamos no sin extrañeza, de acabar su vida imitando a Sué y a Víctor Hugo, y creyendo imitar a Tolstoi, o al menos atribuirse el papel del apóstol y nuncio de la revolución social . . . En Rusia, los novelistas no cerraron el movimiento dándole cánones y leyes; no lo empapelaron en preceptos. Y así el naturalismo ruso continúa su evolución, cuando ya hace tiempo que en Francia se ha desgregado atomísticamente esa escuela y aun las que la sustituyeron con alardes idealistas.

And, coming more to the point, she says in the same article:

La misma aspiración científica, en la novela de Zola, revestía carácter de limitación, presa en la cárcel de un determinismo positivista que sólo representa, a lo sumo, un momento de la evolución científica de nuestro siglo; y lo que es de un momento lleva en sí, la caducidad. Mucho se clamó contra los excesos del naturalismo, sus palabras gruesas y sus desnudeces, y es el caso—no sospechado por los timoratos—que el naturalismo murió, no por lo que cometía, sino por lo que omitía. A la hermosa Venus miliense que se llama la Verdad, le cortó el naturalismo, no sólo los brazos, sino más de la mitad del cuerpo, dejando sólo, de la soberana estatua, las regiones inferiores.[76]

After that last simile one feels moved to ask the worthy Countess, "Who is exaggerating now?" But the reader will observe that she is really maintaining here, in 1910, exactly the same attitude that she first took in 1883, i.e., endorsing Zola's stand on morals while condemning his physiological man and the narrow determinism to which he subjected him. Fundamentally there has been little change in her opinion of naturalism—a literary school or formula based upon a pseudo-scientific philosophy, containing much exaggeration and limitation and yet bringing its very considerable contribution to the progress of literary art. The skepticism of Zola himself as to the infallibility of his system is apparent from intimate conversations of his, recorded in the Goncourts' journal.[77]

Es preciso reconocerlo: para entender las causas y razones suficientes de la estrepitosa y pronta caída de lo que se llamó *naturalismo*, hay que conciliar el hecho de esta caída con la afirmación de que algo del naturalismo no puede morir. Lo que cayó de un modo definitivo allá por 1891, fué el naturalismo de escuela, la fórmula de Zola, que por tantos estilos no se tenía en pie, en la cual ni Zola mismo creía, y a la cual nunca se adhirieron formalmente ni Daudet, ni Maupassant, ni los Goncourt.[78]

Lo que descuella en la labor de Zola, es principalmente el estudio de costumbres populares, *La Taberna*; el de la vida minera,

Germinal; el de la historia contemporánea, *El desastre*. Lo demas, aunque merezca atención, es, a mi ver, inferior a estas obras, sobre todo considerándolas como documentos.[79]

The novel as a study of a certain environment, as a true picture of a section of human life—that, in a word, is the lasting contribution of the naturalistic school.

We set out to trace the evolution of Pardo Bazán's attitude toward naturalism and Zola, and strangely enough we find it evolved so very little that the conclusion to her whole stand on the subject may be found in a polemic published just a year and a half after *La Cuestión*:

> . . . donde radicalmente me aparto de Zola es en el concepto filosófico: ya sabe V. que en *La Cuestión palpitante*, hace año y medio, me adelanté a rastrear sus doctrinas deterministas, fatalistas y pesimistas, declarando que por esos cerros ningún católico podía seguirle. . . .
>
> Aun por eso insisto en que aceptemos del naturalismo de Zola lo bueno, lo serio, el método, y desechemos lo erróneo, la arbitraria conclusión especulativa, *anti-metafísica* que encierra. . . .[80]

Once more the discussion comes back to the fundamental difference of outlook between Catholic and positivist. And to Doña Emilia the conclusion implicit in *Docteur Pascal*, the last of the great series that contains Zola's finest work, is one of frustration, of the futility of human science, of the constant yearning of our hearts toward the ideal, the mysterious unknown:

> Desde la cruz a la fecha, si algo demuestra la última novela de Zola, es que, en efecto, la ciencia, a fines del siglo XIX, ha dado en quiebra estrepitosamente y las ilusiones de nuestros tatarabuelos . . . serían candideces en nosotros. . . .
>
> En suma, la impresión definitiva que produce el *Docteur Pascal*, es que Clotilde tenía razon cuando, boca arriba sobre los candentes guijarros de la era, en estrellada y magnífica noche, pedía el cielo y no quería que se lo arrebatasen en nombre de filosofía ninguna. Y así acaba la serie de los *Rougon-Macquart*, y así, del conjunto de crueles y repugnantes estudios anatómicas que adornan como sangrientos trofeos la magna obra zolaesca, álzase, a modo de columna de incienso quemada al pie del altar, la perpetua aspiración de nuestras almas, siempre doloridas y tristes, siempre orientadas hacia el ideal, aunque parezcan muy entretenidas en considerar tanta cosa fea y estrambótica como sucede de tejas abajo. . . .[81]

I think we may conclude that, far from being a handicap, the Countess Emilia's Catholicism kept her from accepting what was most exaggerated and impermanent in Zola's system, while at the same time her well-balanced critical judgment made her accept of naturalism all of its good and lasting contributions to literature: notably, the sharp and detailed observation of life and of special *milieux*, the need for the events to be logically connected, with that strong partial determinism which everyone admits to be in human life. As a result of these techniques developed by the naturalistic school, the novel today is able to present a truer picture of life. These are the techniques which Doña Emilia, with her unfailing common sense, accepts of Zola's naturalism, rejecting all the dross of his system—dross which posterity, too, has rejected.

IV

SIX NOVELS IN THE ZOLA FORMULA

While there are traces of Zola's influence to be found throughout the work of Emilia Pardo Bazán, certain titles stand out as
particularly good examples of naturalism. They might be called
the six experimental novels of Pardo Bazán.

La Tribuna (1883)

The milieu studied in *La Tribuna* is that of a tobacco factory
and its surroundings in La Coruña. The year is 1868, at the
time of the Revolution. The racial heritage is that of the working classes of Galicia. The plot is very simple: a daughter of
the people becomes enthusiastic over the coming Republic and
the equality which it will bring; possessed of a good reading
voice, she is delegated to read the newspapers to her fellow
cigar-makers, and thus she becomes their leader and a sort of
tribune of the people; filled with confidence in the coming eqality,
she allows herself to be seduced by a hard-hearted but handsome
señorito, and has a child by him which he quite realistically for-
gets all about. The Revolution ends in a Restoration, high hopes
are dashed, and honor is flown.

The critics seem unanimous in their verdict that this is a
novel naturalistic in every respect. Blanco-García says of it:

> No es tan indeterminado el carácter de *La Tribuna*; aquí sí
> que hay situaciones picantes, lenguaje atrevido y populachero,
> ambiente naturalista de verdad, denunciando a leguas su filiación y
> origen, que nadie puede desconocer.[1]

I have already mentioned how de Tannenberg calls this novel a
pastiche of Zola:

> Elle ne s'en tint pas a la théorie; elle se mit à écrire des
> romans. Comme il fallait s'y attendre, elle débuta par le pastiche
> de Zola. *La Femme tribun*—un curieux épisode de la Révolution
> dans une ville ouvrière—est le roman naturaliste selon la formule,
> avec l'abondance fastidieuse des détails techniques (toute une page
> pour décrire comment on fabrique un cigare!), la brutalité voulue
> des peintures, la scène inévitable d'accouchement. . . .[2]

And González-Blanco justifies his own classification of it as follows:

> Era naturalista por todos conceptos: por su modo de exposición,
> absolutamente impersonal y objetivo; por la elección de un asunto,
> escabroso, según el sentir común; humano, y, por lo tanto, digno
> del arte, al parecer de las personas juiciosas; por la introducción

> del lenguaje popular, aun siendo éste dialectal y bronco, de la
> más baja extracción. . . .[3]

The principal reasons given for the naturalistic classification
are, as usual, those noisy by-products of naturalism, frankness
as to sex and sordidness, and use of *lenguaje populachero*. To be
sure, de Tannenberg mentions the long technical descriptions,
and González-Blanco the impersonality of the style, but on the
whole it is the daring treatment of a daring theme that effectively
labels the book in the eyes of the critics.

The matter-of-fact telling of a vulgar seduction perpetrated
on a working girl was audacious; then to include the drama of
a difficult child-birth showed still more audacity; finally, the
natural way in which Pardo allowed her common people to talk
eliminated all doubt but what this was a frank imitation of
Zola's way with a novel. Just to make sure, however, Doña
Emilia occasionally shows the strength of her naturalistic stomach by throwing in a collection of smells like the following:

> Además, como sus pulmones estaban educados en la gimnasia
> del aire libre, se deja entender la opresión que experimentaron en
> los primeros tiempos de cautiverio en los talleres, donde la atmós-
> fera estaba saturada de olor ingrato y herbáceo del Virginia hu-
> medicido y de la hoja medio verde—mezclado con las emenaciones
> de tanto cuerpo humano y con el fétido vaho de las letrinas
> próximas.[4]

Or a collection of beggars like this:

> A pocos pasos de la gente que comía, mendigos asquerosos
> imploraban la caridad: un elefancíaco enseñaba su rostro bulboso,
> un herpético descubría el cráneo pelado y lleno de pústulas, éste
> tendía una mano seca, aquél señalaba a un muslo ulcerado, invo-
> cando a Santa Margarita para que nos libre de "males extraños."
> En un carretoncillo, un fenómeno sin piernas, sin brazos, con
> enorme cabezón envuelto en trapos viejos . . . exhalaba un grito
> ronco y suplicante. . . .[5]

Were it not for the scientific terminology, one would be inclined
to classify this last choice bit as Hugoesque rather than naturalistic in origin. It is all very well to give the complete environment, but must one go to such lengths to describe a group
of revolting beggars who appear just once in the narrative?

To continue with examples of the obvious naturalism to be
found in *La Tribuna,* here is a sample of how its people talk:

> —Pero, bruto—exclamó la Tribuna con bondadoso acento—
> estás sudando como un toro, y te plantas entre puertas, en este
> pasillo tan ventilado . . . para coger la muerte.
> —Boh . . . —y el mozo encogió de hombros.

—Si reparásemos a eso . . . Todo el día de Dios estamos aquí
saliendo y entrando, y las puertas abiertas, y el frío de allí . . .
Mira onde afilamos la cuchilla.

Y señaló una rueda . . .

—La calor y el abrigo, por dentro . . . Ya se sabe que en no
teniendo aquí una gota . . . —y se dió una palmada en el diafragma.

—Así apestas, maldito—observó Ana . . .

—Antes—pronunció sentenciosamente Amparo—sólo probabas
vino algún día de fiesta que otro . . . Pues aquí no tienes por qué
tomar vicios, que, gracias a Dios, la borrachera, a las cigarreras,
poco daño nos hace . . .

—Las de arriba bien habláis, bien habláis . . . Si os metieren
en estos trabajitos . . . Para lo que hacéis, que es labor de señoritas,
con agua basta . . . Quiérese decir, vamos . . . que un hombre no
ha de ponerse chispo; pero un rifigelio . . . un tentacá . . . Queréis
ver como bailo?

Volvió a manejar la cuchilla . . .[6]

Two of the last few nouns are not to be found in the Academy
Dictionary. The whole diologue carries the ring of everyday
speech and seems perfectly suited to the mentality and background of the speakers. As Pardo herself says, in a prologue
written two years later, it is all very well for the author to use
elegant diction when speaking on his own account, but "cuando
haga hablar a sus personajes, o analice su función cerebral y
traduzca sus pensamientos, respete la forma en que se producen,
y no enmienda la plana a la vida. Este método lo siguió Cervantes. . . ."[7]

As to her frankness in description as a whole, Pardo offers
this defense in her prologue to *La Tribuna*:

Tal vez no falte quien me acuse de haber pintado al pueblo con
crudeza naturalista. Responderé que si nuestro pueblo fuese igual
al que describen Goncourt y Zola, yo podría meditar profunda-
mente en la conveniencia o inconveniencia de retratarlo; pero
resuelta a ello, nunca seguiría la escuela idealista de Trueba y de
la insigne Fernán, que riñe con mis principios artísticos. Lícito
es callar, pero no fingir.[8]

This is in line with other statements of hers, quoted in the
previous chapter, to the effect that the limit should be beyond
that set by the idealists and short of that set up by Zola and
company. The reader will recall that in illustration of her point
she refers to the child-birth scene in *La Tribuna* in which the
whole drama is presented *"entre bastidores."* Nevertheless, as
has been seen, Pardo went quite far enough to convince the
critics of the naturalism she had been absorbing.

But it was not only through frankness of detail and audacious subject matter that the book proclaimed its origin. Many descriptions reveal careful and detailed documentation on the part of the author. Twelve pages into the book and the reader runs onto this technical description of the art of making *barquillos*— those thin wafer cakes, shaped like little cornucopias, which are hawked along the sidewalks and through the parks of Spanish cities.

> Instalóse el señor Rosendo en su alto trípode, de madera, ante la llama chisporroteadora y crepitante ya, y metiendo en el fuego las magnas tenazas, dió principio a la operación. Tenía a su derecha el barreno del amohado, en el cual mojaba el cargador, especie de palillo grueso; y extendiendo una leve capa de líquido sobre la cara interior de los candentes hierros, apresurábase a envolverla en el molde con su dedo pulgar, que a fuerza de repetir este acto se había convertido en una callosidad tostada, sin uña, sin yema y sin forma casi. Los barquillos dorados y tibios, caían en el regazo de la muchacha, que los iba introduciendo unos en otros a guisa de tubos de catalejo, y colocándolos simétricamente en el fondo del cañuto. . . .[9]

There is something wrong with that description. It is hard to say just what for the details seem to be there, but one does not really get the picture. Let us try another. Here is the page on how to make a cigar, of which de Tannenberg was complaining:

> No valía apresurarse. Primero era preciso extender con sumo cuidado, encima de la tabla de liar, la envoltura exterior, la epidermis del cigarro, y cortaria con el cuchillo semicircular trazando una curva de quince milímetros de inclinación sobre el centro de la hoja para que ciñese exactamente al cigarro; y esta capa requería una hoja seca, ancha y fina, de lo más selecto, así como la dermis del cigarro, el *capillo*, ya la admitía de inferior calidad, lo propio que la tripa o cañizo. Pero lo más esencial y difícil era rematar el puro, hacerle la punta con un hábil giro de la yema del pulgar y una espátula mojada en líquida goma, cercenandole después el rabo de un tijeretazo veloz. La punta aguda, espiral, la tripa no tan apretada que no deje aspirar el humo ni tan floja que el cigarro se arrugue al secarse, tales son las condiciones de una buena tagarnina. . . .[10]

Does the reader now feel he could roll his own cigars? Or did he decide it was too difficult and skip the instructions? Compare now, from the standpoint of interest, this picture from *Le Ventre de Paris* in which the skilful butcher's boy describes how to make black pudding. After all, there is some resemblance between stuffing a sausage and filling a cigar. The scene is the kitchen behind the shop; the whole family is in the room engaged in various pursuits.

> —Eh bien, aurons-nous de bon boudin? demanda Lisa.
>
> Il déposa ses deux brocs, et, lentement:
>
> —Je le crois, madame Quenu, oui, je le crois . . . Je vois d'abord ça à la facon dont le sang coule. Quand je retire le couteau, si le sang part trop doucement, ce n'est pas un bon signe, ça prouve qu'il est pauvre . . .
>
> —Mais, interrompit Quenu, c'est aussi selon comme le couteau a été enfoncé.
>
> La face blême d'Auguste eut un sourire.
>
> —Non, non, répondit-il, j'enfonce toujours quatre doigts du couteau: c'est la mesure . . . Mais, voyez-vous, le meilleur signe, c'est encore lorsque le sang coule et que je le reçois en le battant avec la main, dans le seau. Il faut qu'il soit d'une bonne chaleur, crémeux, sans être trop épais.
>
> Augustine avait laissé son aiguille. Les yeux levés, elle regardait Auguste. Sa figure rougeaude, aux durs cheveux châtains, prenait un air d'attention profonde. D'ailleurs, Lisa, et la petite Pauline elle-même, écoutaient également avec un grand intérêt.
>
> —Je bats, je bats, je bats, n'est-ce pas? continua le garçon, en faisant aller sa main dans le vide, comme s'il fouettait une crème. Eh bien, quand je retire ma main et je le regarde, il faut qu'elle soit comme graissée par le sang de façon à ce que le gant rouge soit bien du même rouge partout . . . Alors on peut dire sans se tromper:
>
> "Le boudin sera bon."[11]

While it is true that we get no more concrete an idea from Zola as to how to do the thing—perhaps not even as good an idea—as we do from Pardo's cigar-maker's manual, nevertheless there is no question which picture arouses the more interest, which has the more artistry in it. Zola does not care whether we learn how to make sausage; what he is doing is painting life in a butcher's household. Was it Doña Emilia who complained about the utilitarian ends of the experimental novel? Was it she who said: "Las descripciones de Zola . . . constituyen no escasa parte de su original mérito y el escollo más grave para sus infelices imitadores. . . ."[12]

But perhaps I am being unfair, for not all of her documentation produces such disappointing results. Consider this description of the dark lower room where the men were cutting up the tobacco:

> Dentro de una habitación . . . donde apenas filtraba luz al través de los vidrios sucios de alta ventana, vieron las dos muchachas hasta veinte hombres . . . saltando sin cesar. El tabaco los

rodeaba: habíalos metidos en él hasta media pierna: a todos les volaba por hombros, cuello y manos, y en la atmósfera flotaban remolinos de él. Los trabajadores estribaban en la pinuta de los pies, y lo que se movía para brincar era el resto del cuerpo merced a repetido y automático esfuerzo de los músculos; el punto de apoyo permanecía fijo. Cada dos hombres tenían ante sí una mesa o tablero, y mientras el uno, saltando con rapidez, subía y bajaba la cuchilla picando la hoja, el otro, con los brazos entrados en el **tabaco, lo revolvía para** que el ya picado fuese deslizándose y quedase sólo en la mesa el entero, operación que requería gran agilidad y tino, porque era fácil que al caer la cuchilla segase los dedos o la mano que encontrara a su alcance. . . .[13]

We find ourselves watching breathlessly with the two girls, fearing lest one of those falling knives will chop off a hand or finger.

Much can be gained by comparing Pardo Bazán's documentary descriptions with the one of Zola's from *Le Ventre de Paris*, which was quoted. It will be noted that Zola breaks up his technical details with conversation or with human interest, as when he inserts the paragraph about the close attention of Augustine. Does he wish to take us on a tour of the cellars under the Central Markets? Then he will have Marjolin steer *la belle Lisa* through them, and in the midst of the smells of the poultry and other unpleasantness is the personal interest, the sex interest, if you will, aroused by these two—man and woman —wandering around together by the light of one candle in the dark cellar. Pardo Bazán, too, succeeds better when she happens to chance on this happier procedure. The last quoted passage, about the chopping room in the tobacco factory, gained because we followed the two girls into it for the first time and shared their emotions. But in the passage on how to make a cigar the author lost her chance. She could have had someone trying to teach the girl Amparo how to make a cigar; instead, she gives us an impersonal sort of handbook description of the process and then goes on to say merely that Amparo tried all day to learn how to do it, without much success. An author can have an impersonal style and still make his descriptions personal, i.e., describe things and events only as seen through the eyes of some character in the story.

But quite frequently Doña Emilia becomes colorful and the interest revives in proportion to the vividness of the picture. Consider this study in browns; Amparo (la Tribuna) has just entered the cigar factory for the first time:

El colorido de los semblantes, el de las ropas y el de la

decoración se armonizaba y fundía en un tono general de madera
y tierra, tono a la vez crudo y apagado, combinación del castaño
mate de la hoja, del amarillo sucio de la vena . . . de la problemática blancura de las enyesadas paredes y de los tintos sordos,
mortecinos al par de discordantes, de los pañuelos de cotonía,
las sayas de percal, los casacos de paño, los mantones de lana y
los paraguas de algodón. Amparo se perecía por los colores
vivos. . . .[14]

This masterly handling of color recalls Pardo's admiration for
the de Goncourts as *coloristas*. Another vivid and interesting
scene is that of the factory girls relaxing on the edge of town
after they have had a picnic lunch:

Amparo y otras dos o tres del taller de cigarrillos, rendidas de
calor y ahitas de comida se habían tendido en una pequeña ex-
planada, que formaba el glacis de la fortificación, adoptando diversas posturas, más o menos cómodas. Unas, desabrochándose
el corpiño, se hacían aire con el pañuelo de seda doblado; otras
tumbadas boca abajo, sostenían el cuerpo en los codos y la barba en
las palmas de las manos; otras sentadas a la turca alzaban cuando
la pierna izquierda, cuando la derecha, para evitar los calambres.
Por la seca hierba andaban esparcidos tapones de botellas, papeles
engrasados, espinas de merluza, cascos de vaso roto, un pañuelo
de seda, una servilleta gorda.[15]

The picture is well drawn and, despite the naturalistic detailing
of the inevitable picnic rubbish, has a certain charm, especially
for the masculine reader. It is colorful and interesting enough
to be worthy of an artist's canvas.

Apropos of the picnic, one of the *cigarreras* had brought along
two of her four small brothers and sisters, all of whom were
afflicted with a hereditary disease. As the author had said some
pages before:

Guardiana era huérfana; su padre y madre murieron del pecho,
con diferencia de días, quedando a cargo de una muchacha, de dos
lustros de edad, cuatro hermanitos, todos marcados con la mano
de hierro de la enfermedad hereditaria: epiléctico el uno, escro-
fulosos y raquíticos dos, y la última, niña de tres años, sordomuda.[16]

And now at the picnic:

Allí también Guardiana, penetrada de alegría por otra causa
diversa: porque había traído consigo a dos de sus pequeños, el
escrofuloso y la sordomudita; en cuanto al mayor, ni se podía
soñar en llevarlo a sitio alguno donde hubiese gente, porque le
entraba en seguida la "aflición." La niña sordomuda miraba
alrededor, con ojos reflexivos, aquel mundo, del cual solo le llegaban
las imágenes visibles; por su parte el niño, que ya tendría unos
trece años, y que hubiera sido gracioso a no disfigurarle los lampa-

rones y la hipertrofía de los labios, gozaba mucho de la fiesta y se sonreía con la sonrisa inocente, semi-bestial, de los bobos de Velázquez.[17]

This family is, so far as I remember, the only case of heredity studied in the book, and it leaves one somewhat at a loss how to classify it—whether naturalistic because of the scientific interest and terminology, or romantic because of the grotesque effect produced by it. When one considers that the beggars, whose description I have already quoted, were also among those present at this same picnic, it would seem that Pardo was indulging in a desire for romanticism by emphasizing the contrast between the youth and comeliness of the cigar-makers and the repulsiveness of the beggars and the scrofulous child. This is further borne out by her reference to the "bobos" of Velazquez; perhaps Pardo thought that these ugly touches would set off the charm of the rest of her word picture as they did for the famous painter. However, as we shall see more and more, Pardo Bazán had the naturalist's interest in odd medical cases and liked to show off the knowledge she had picked up in this realm. Instead of making her main characters heredity cases, she introduced such cases on the side. This is not the only instance of a parallel to Zola which we will find tucked into one of her novels as a sort of afterthought or experiment in imitation. Also, we find trivial ugliness described with naturalistic candor, while she refuses to describe bedroom scenes and other amorous intimacies. The result is to keep what is repulsive in naturalism—such as mention of the smell of the latrines, or of the odious beggars on the outskirts of the picnic—and to discard what is attractive, namely, frankness with regard to sex. For instance, take the seduction scene in *La Tribuna*. The lovers are alone outside the city on a summer evening. Pardo carries us through the conversation necessary for him to get her to yield, and for her to secure his solemn oaths and promises of marriage. Then here is all that remains of the chapter, and remember they have not so much as embraced before:

Una cabeza pesada, cubierta de pelo copioso y rizo, descansaba ya sobre su pecho, y el balsámico olor de tabaco que impregnaba a la Tribuna le envolvía. Disiparonse sus escrúpulos y reiteró los juramentos y las promesas más solemnes.

Iba acabando de cerrar la noche, y un cuarto de amorosa luna hendía como un alfanje de plata los acumulados nubarrones. Por el camino real, mudo y sombrío, no pasaba nadie.[18]

So far, now, the reader has seen the sort of naturalistic candor which is to be found in *La Tribuna*—and that which is not to be found there. We have seen the evidence of conscientious, if often poorly handled, documentation, and the consequent unevenness in her description, sometimes vivid and colorful, sometimes dull and tiresome. We have also seen that the novel treats, incidentally, some heredity cases. But what of the chief characters? What of Amparo, the tribune of the people, herself? Consider what Leopoldo Alas says of her:

> Porque, no se piense que el autor se ha propuesto pintar la pasión tribunicia como puede ser en la mujer, arraigada, profunda, y haciendo cosas heróicas, no; Amparo es una muchacha vulgar, y nadie quiso otra cosa. . . .
> Un crítico ha dicho que Amparo, con su exaltación política, era poco verosímil. Yo he conocido muchas *tribunas* en los tiempos de la revolución . . . No hay nada de inverosímil en el carácter de Amparo. No era el ánimo del autor pintar un ser excepcional, un caso teratológico, que también cabría en su sistema, cuanto menos un tipo abstracto, inverosímil. El soplo de la vida está infundido en la heroína.[19]

And that Doña Emilia's main character should be such a person is logical in view of the unpleasant things she said of Zola's rectilinear personages and of his preference for exceptional cases of neurosis or abnormal heredity. Amparo is true to life and, according to Alas, a common type. It is not her character, surely, about which the story is built; she is much too ordinary. Is it then some other character or group? I do not think so. Amparo is really the only person one remembers after a certain lapse of time. The others are too pale for the most part. No, it is not the characters that recommend the book; as Alas says: "Lo principal en este libro no son las personas de dentro, sino su apariencia y las cosas que las rodean."[20] The book is a study of manners and customs among the working classes and especially among the *cigarreras*. The only unusual circumstance is the *moment* chosen—the glorious Revolution.

The novel of Zola's to which *La Tribuna* is most similar is *Le Ventre de Paris*. As in Zola's book everything centers about the Central Markets, so in Pardo's all centers about the tobacco factory. As in the French novel personages wander or are conducted through the markets as an excuse for describing the milieu, so in the Spanish book Amparo is shown about the factory and we go sightseeing behind her back. In *Le Ventre*, whatever plot there is centers around Florent and his political scheming; in *La Tribuna* all the action is conditioned by Amparo's political activities, her very seduction having been largely the result of false confidence in the social leveling to be accomplished by the Revolution. And by her excess zeal she meets her downfall—abandoned, dishonored, and with a fatherless child on her hands. Just so Florent pinned all his hopes on conspiracy, only to find himself once more headed for Cayenne. The conclusion of the two novels is much the same: the futility of placing too much trust in idealistic political enterprises. As Doña Emilia herself confesses in the prologue to her book:

> Al escribir *La Tribuna* no quise hacer sátira política; la sátira es género que admito sin poderlo cultivar; sirvo poco o nada para el caso. Pero así como neigo la intención satírica, no sé encubrir que en este libro, casi a pesar mío, entra un propósito que puede llamarse *docente*. Baste a disculparlo el declarar que nació del espectáculo mismo de las cosas; vino a mí, sin ser llamado, por su propio impulso. Al artista que sólo aspiraba a retratar el aspecto pintoresco y característico de una *capa social*, se le presentó por añadidura la moraleja, y sería tan sistemático rechazarla como haberla buscado. Porque no necessité agrupar sucesos, ni violentar sus consecuencias, ni desviarme de la realidad concreta y positiva, para tropezar con pruebas de que es absurdo el que un pueblo cifre sus esperanzas de redención y ventura en formas de gobierno que desconoce, y a las cuales por lo mismo atribuye prodigiosas virtudes y maravillosos efectos.[21]

Could anyone find a more perfect example of what Zola meant by the experimental novel? She, by her own admission, starts out merely to study and picture a certain *"capa social"*; in the course of documentation or composition she is driven to accept the general truth which is to become the inevitably suggested conclusion of her novel, without "grouping events, nor violating consequences, nor turning aside from concrete and positive reality." In other words, following always the general laws of human conduct and reaction, the result of her experiment is ever the same. Given the character of Amparo and her associates —all types taken from life—with their ignorance and enthusiasm, given the environment of a Galician city in time of revolution, given the tradition of *donjuanismo* prevalent among the *señorito* class, the reaction of all these forces upon one another will produce a novel like *La Tribuna* and its conclusion is inescapable. It is as inherent in the subject matter as the evil of alcoholism was inherent in the milieu of the Paris slums described by Zola in his *L'Assommoir*. Certainly the conclusion, similar as it is, is sustained as well in *La Tribuna* as in *Le Ventre de Paris*—perhaps even better sustained, for is not Amparo a more real protagonist than the dreamy visionary, Florent? In any case, it is apparent that *La Tribuna* is an experimental novel written and composed faithfully according to the Zola pattern.

Los Pazos de Ulloa (1886)

Far from being a mere *pastiche* of Zola, *Los Pazos de Ulloa* is nonetheless a naturalistic novel composed according to the formula. Its evolution must have been comparable to Balzac's *Cousine Bette*, the example which Zola uses to illustrate the principle of the experimental novel. The reader will recall that Zola said of his favorite Balzac novel:

> Le fait général observé par Balzac est le ravage que le tempérament amoureux d'un homme amène chez lui, dans sa famille et dans la société. Dès qu'il a eu choisi son sujet, il est parti des faits observés, puis il a institué son expérience en soumettant Hulot à une serie d'épreuves.[22]

The general observation behind *Las Pazos* is the decay of the old noble houses of Galicia, and the "Baron Hulot," the representative of this decadence or degeneracy of the nobility, is Don Pedro Moscoso, marqués de Ulloa. This is the key idea. Once having visualized the character of Don Pedro, the author had to put him in his proper setting and surround him with other types and characters to condition his responses. Finally, balancing the conflicting forces of the experiment, it remained to show that all led to the inevitable and logical conclusion. In the treatment of this book I propose to try to reconstruct the growth of the basic ideas and observations in Pardo's mind, and try to trace how she worked out the experiment which became this novel.

The possibilities of decadent nobility as a theme had been in the back of Pardo's mind for some time. Her story *Bucólica*, which appeared in a magazine in 1884, two years before *Los Pazos*, already contains the germ of the idea:

> Este señorito de Limioso no salió jamás de su concha, y creo que sus viajes se reducen a ir algún año a Pontevedra para ver *el fuego de la Peregrina*; no le dieron carrera, fuese por falta de medios o fuese por considerar más hidalga su ignorancia de mayorazgo pobre, y vive con su padre, chocho ya, y dos tías muy viejas y raras, en un caserón acribillado de goteras, que aquí llaman con gran respeto el *Pazo* (palacio) de Limioso.[23]

Limioso has only a minor part in *Bucólica*; his chief occupation is hunting and in that capacity—along with the Cura de Naya—he takes the tubercular protagonist of the story on country excursions. Now Limioso and the priest of Naya both reappear in minor proportions in *Los Pazos de Ulloa*. In fact, Don Pedro and his bride go to visit the *señorito* in his ruinous *Pazo* and are duly entertained by his aunts. However, here is the point: Pardo saw the possibilities for a deeper study of the degeneracy of Galician nobility. Limioso was too much of a comical figure, almost a caricature. Obviously she could not use him for the basis of her tragedy; but from some strange whim or desire to give connection to her regional novels she includes him—almost I would say she superimposes him—in *Los Pazos de Ulloa*. To one who reads that masterpiece alone he provides a comic note which relieves the strain of the more tragic main plot. To one who has read the author's work consecutively or followed the novels as they first appeared it is a pleasant reminder of the former story.

There is good psychology behind the principle of the serial. Many an author has capitalized on it. Balzac has characters reappear. Dumas wrote novels in series. Zola strung his novels together by the blood relations of his Rougon-Macquart family. And while Pardo does not have any family trees, still she does have old friends who constantly come back to greet us. After all, many of her novels are located in a comparatively small area in and around La Coruña, or *Marineda,* as she calls it; and it does add a touch of realism to find familiar faces coupled with familiar places. *La Tribuna* took place in Marineda; *Bucólica* happens in the country not far from the small town of *Cebre*; a short story, *Nieto del Cid,* contained in the collection called *La Dama joven* (1885), also happens in the neighborhood of Cebre, and it is in this tale that we are really introduced to the Cura del Boán, mentioned later in both *Los Pazos* and *La Madre Naturaleza.* His own story relates his prodigious defense against a band of robbers who besiege his house and finally kill him; *Los Pazos* presents him as a background character, friend of the Cura de Naya; and in *La Madre* his heroism is praised and his death lamented. *El Cisne de Vilamorta, Los Pazos,* and *La Madre* all take place in the near neighborhood of Cebre—somewhere between Santiago de Campostela and La Coruña (*Marineda*).

As to Pardo's documentation on the region and her delight in picturing it, we have this statement from her prologue to the *Dama joven*:

> *Bucólica* y también *Nieto del Cid* son apuntes de paisajes, tipos y costumbres de una comarca donde pasé floridos días de juventud y asistí a regocijadas partidas de caza, a vendimias, romerías y ferias; tierra original del interior de Galicia, que he recorrido a caballo y a pie, recibiendo el ardor de sol y la humedad de su lluvia, y ha dejado en mi mente tantos recuerdos pintorescos, que no cabían en el breve recinto de *Bucólica* y fué preciso dedicarles otro lienzo más ancho, al cual doy las últimas pinceladas. Han transcurrido dos lustros, y parece que era ayer cuando mi tordo, jadeante, con una gota de sudor en cada pelo, se detenía bajo la parra de algún *Pazo de Limioso*, después de vencer, a desatinado galope, las cuestas del camino real.[24]

The larger canvas she speaks of may refer to *El Cisne*, which appeared very shortly thereafter in the same year. But that still was not sufficient, and it took *Los Pazos* and *La Madre Naturaleza* to satisfy her taste for the regional—at least for the time being. Pardo Bazán knew well her native Galicia and those critics are not few who say that her distinctly regional novels constitute her best work.

Consider Pardo now with a mind full of memories of Galician country life, and the inclination to build a drama around "*algún Pazo de Limioso*." She visualizes Don Pedro Moscoso, a magnificent specimen of manhood, strong and hardy physically, accustomed to an outdoor life following the hounds, proud but not overly strong of will, giving free vent to his passions and enthusiasms—the heredity of a proud but uncultivated race, not given to self-discipline or introspection. Don Pedro is an extrovert, a country boy who has grown up in the woods and always had his own way. He has no head for books or figures, and will leave his management to the majordomo. . . . Ah! And that personage, what sort of man is he? The common scheming type of shrewd peasant no doubt. . . . And what of the other servants of the *Pazos*? Will there be women? A woman, perhaps? And with Don Pedro's hot blood. . . . No doubt Doña Emilia had heard many stories of master and pretty servant-maid in illicit but tolerated relationship. No doubt her feministic spirit had rebelled against the double standard in amorous dealings, a standard which gives the man entire freedom and regards a woman as tainted if she has even lightly flirted or had an unsuccessful courtship of the most conventional sort. Surely such a standard is not Christian! A sincere and devout Christian priest would not tolerate that a Don Pedro make a concubine of his kitchen maid. . . . A Saint Francis of Assisi would not stand for it. . . . A Serge Mouret would be disturbed by it. . . . How revoltingly bestial those peasants were with whom poor ineffectual Serge tried to deal in Zola's book! Spanish peasants are not like that. . . . L'Abbé Mouret should have been more firm with his people, but how could he be, poor innocent, fresh from the seminary! Zola doesn't have much talent for describing the things of the faith. . . . I could have drawn Serge more realistically. . . . I wonder what he would have done as chaplain to Don Pedro! What an idea! . . . A young priest with his Christianity still pure and uncompromising—but innocent and trusting, too. . . . I could describe his arrival at the *Pazos*, his first impressions. . . . It would take him some time to catch on to the state of affairs. . . . and when he did, have him condemn it, threaten to leave the house rather than tolerate it. . . . That way I can get someone to strike at this freely tolerated concubinage. . . . But my plot is too simple; there must be more characters. . . . A woman to tempt the chaplain, perhaps? If he could be tempted, the pure innocent! The kitchen maid would only be revolting to him. . . .

The plot is now well on its way, the character of Nucha will be found to correspond to Julián, the young priest. Don Pedro will have a little scamp of a son by Sabel, the maid. Complications will be added by having Sabel be the daughter of Primitivo, the majordomo. The latter becomes the villain of the story when Julián tries to right the immoral state of affairs by taking Don Pedro off to Santiago to get him a wife; for a wife will mean the wane of Sabel's power over the marquis and of Primitivo's power likewise. And in the choice of his wife Don Pedro will make a fatal mistake; he will be caught in the mesh of his own honor code which hitherto had been so easy with him; hear him as he reasons out the problem:

Además, no es lo mismo distraerse con una muchacha cualquiera que tomar esposa. La hembra destinada a llevar el nombre esclarecido de Moscoso y a perpetuarlo legítimamente, había de ser limpia como un espejo . . . Y Don Pedro figuraba entre los que no juzgan limpia ya a la que tuvo amorosos tratos, aun en la más honesta y lícita forma, con otro que su marido. Aun las ojeadas en calles y paseos eran pecados gordos. Entendía Don Pedro el

> honor conyugal a la manera calderoniana, española neta, indul-
> gentísima para el esposo e implacable para la esposa. Y a él
> que no le dijesen: Rita no estaba sin algún enredillo. . . .[25]

And so instead of following his inclination and choosing Rita—a
strong and spirited type who would have made a good match—
he follows the advice of Julián, who naturally selects the sister
who most appeals to his own ascetic temperament. Nucha is a
frail, nervous girl, entirely unsuited to Don Pedro, but no matter, she is pure, of that he may be certain. From this point on
the tragedy is inevitable and follows with fatal or naturalistic
determinism.

Perhaps the reader thinks my zeal for finding parallels to
Zola has carried me away when I trace the source of the character Julián to Serge Mouret, but I do not do so without some
evidence to back up the idea. Julián is the only character in
the book who does not seem to belong naturally there; the rest
are all good Galician types. Even Nucha, as the one mystic in
a city family of girls, is not an unusual Spanish type. But Julián
is something superimposed, as Lorenzo Benito said of him, in
his review of Los Pazos:

> . . . no interesa en tan alto grado la figura de Julián. Con ser
> simpática en extremo, no atrae. Choca, en primer lugar, con la
> creencia, bastante generalizada, de que si existe, constituye no
> sólo una excepción entre los de su clase, sino que es una excepción
> casi imposible en esa tierra gallega. . . .[26]

After his first night at the Pazos, the first thing the young priest
wants to do is say mass; he doesn't want to drink the chocolate
that Sabel brings him until he has tasted of the divine sustenance.
Great is his disappointment when told that the chapel is locked
and the key in the pocket of the late-snoozing abbot of Ulloa.

> Julián contuvo un suspiro. Dos días ya sin misar! Cabalmente
> desde que era presbítero se había redoblado su fervor religioso, y
> sentía el entusiasmo juvenil del nuevo misacantano, conmovido
> aun por la impresión de la augusta investidura; de suerte que
> celebraba el sacrificio esmerándose en perfilar la menor ceremonia,
> temblando cuando alzaba, anonadándose cuando consumía, siempre
> con recogimiento indecible. En fin, si no había remedio. . . .[27]

The reader will remember the scene from La Faute de l'Abbé
Mouret which I quoted at the beginning of the last chapter—the
picture of the young priest absorbed in his early morning mass,
unbothered by the invasion of the church by the sparrows, too
absorbed to worry about the empty benches. Like Julián, he is
fresh from the seminary, still filled with the "youthful enthusi-

asm of one new at saying mass." The old servant, La Teuse, tries in vain to get his attention as he leaves the House of God in the morning:

—Si vous croyez qu'il m'écoute! . . . Ça n'a pas vingt-six ans, et ça n'en fait qu'à sa tête. Bien sûr, il en remontrerait pour la sainteté à un homme de soixante ans; mais il n'a pas vécu, il ne sait rien, il n'a pas de peine à être sage comme un chérubin, ce mignon-là.[28]

And Julián too has not lived very much, else he would not have dwelt so long at the Pazos without catching on to the parentage of little Perucho. Both young men are sincere and innocent. Both are washed and comely to behold. Serge inspires the disdain of the brutal and unwashed Frère Archangias; Julián is nicknamed Mariquitas by the rough and ready Abad de Ulloa.[29] And if the reader still thinks the parallelism slight, let him withhold judgment until we come to treat *La Madre Naturaleza*, sequel to *Los Pazos*, in which the whole basic idea comes from *La Faute de l'Abbé Mouret*.

There are some good studies of the influence of heredity and environment in *Los Pazos*. On reviewing his first impressions of his host, before retiring on the night of his arrival

Julián recordaba unas palabras del señor de la Lage.
—Encontrará V. a mi sobrino bastante adocenado. . . . La aldea, cuando se cría uno en ella, y no sale de allí jamás, envilece, empobrece y embrutece.[30]

And as a matter of fact, Pardo seems to have satisfied a sort of scientific caprice in giving both Sr. de la Lage and his nephew Don Pedro the same hereditary manifestations. Then, by placing one in town and one in the country, she can produce an interesting study in the effect of environment; both seem to be better fitted for medieval champions than for life in the tame world of our time:

Viéndoles juntos, se observaba extraordinario parecido entre el señor de la Lage, y su sobrino carnal: la misma estatura prócer, las mismas proporciones amplias, la misma abundancia de hueso y fibra, la misma barba fuerte y copiosa; pero lo que en el sobrino era armonía de complexión titánica, fortalecida por el aire libre y los ejercicios corporales, en el tío era exuberancia y plétora: condenado a una vida sedentaria, se advertía que le sobraba sangre y carne, de la cual no sabía qué hacer; sin ser lo que se llama obeso, su humanidad se desbordaba por todos lados; cada pie suyo parecía una lancha, cada mano un mazo de carpintero.

Se ahogaba con los trajes de paseo; no cabía en las habitaciones reducidas; resoplaba en las butacas del teatro, y en misa repartía codazos para disponer de más sitio. Magnífico ejemplar de una raza apta para la vida guerrera y montés de las épocas feodales, se consumía miserablemente en el vil ocio de los pueblos, donde el que nada produce, nada enseña, ni nada aprende, de nada sirve y nada hace. ¡Oh dolor! Aquel castizo Pardo de la Lage, naciendo en el siglo XV, hubiera dado en qué entender a los arqueólogos e historiadores del XIX.[31]

Were I not speaking of heredity and environment, I might remark that this is an excellent specimen of Doña Emilia's *gallardía* breaking through her naturalistic impersonality, much as old Pardo de la Lage was choked by his civilized suit of clothes. There is apparent sympathy between Pardo Bazán herself and this beefy old inhabitant of Santiago; she too was troubled with overabundant flesh and *se ahogaba* within the restraints of fashionable dress. Her large spirit rebelled too against the unfair restrictions placed by society upon her sex. She obviously shares the doctor's view when he blames Nucha's difficulties in child-birth upon her unhygienic upbringing:

A las mujeres se les da en las ciudades la educación mas antihigiénica: corsé para reducir lo que debe ser vasto; encierro para producir la clorosis y la anemia, vida sedentaria, para ingurgitarlas y criar linfa a expensas de la sangre. . . . Mil veces mejor preparadas están las aldeanas para el gran combate de la gestación y alumbramiento, que al cabo es la verdadera función femenina.[32]

But the influence of heredity and environment is not confined to isolated cases in the book; it is the whole book. The principal reason for the general verdict that this novel is Pardo's masterpiece is the perfect balance of forces achieved in it. The various characters, clearly drawn and realistic all of them, react on one another just as one would expect them to. Each one is the product of his heredity and past environment; each one is consistent. The last half of the book follows from the mistake in choosing the wrong sister for wife, with the fatal certainty of a classic tragedy. Few critics have realized the perfect determinism here manifest better than Lorenzo Benito in his review of the book. He stages an argument with its author to prove to her that despite her condemnation of naturalistic determinism in *La Cuestión palpitante*, she has here given a perfect example of the application to literature of that same determinism.

Don Pedro Moscoso . . . es una figura valientemente dibujada, y con toda la entonación y el relieve necesario. Es una de esas figuras de las que puede decirse que salen del cuadro.

¿Y sabe V. por qué? Porque ese determinismo del que V.

> reniega, le ha guiado para vencer las dificultades de ejecución. D.
> Pedro Moscoso es un hombre de corteza ruda, de aficiones violentas,
> de pasiones no contenidas porque su voluntad, si alguna vez se
> rebela contra la imposición tiránica del medio en que vive, no tiene
> la energía suficiente para luchar con la tenacidad inflexible de
> Primitivo. . . . Alienta en D. Pedro Moscoso el buen deseo, el ansia
> de emancipación, pero este deseo, necesita un auxiliar más poderoso
> que Julián. Aun así, se agarra a él como el náufrago y . . . hace
> un viaje a Santiago. . . .[33]

There he finds a good wife for himself and comes back to the
Pazos resolved to live a good life and let Julián chase out the
concubine. But the young priest finds Primitivo too smooth for
him; promises are made but Sabel remains on the scene. Nevertheless, if Nucha should bear a son, things might yet come out
all right, but alas:

> Julián es vencido en su lucha con Primitivo; el heredero varón
> es reemplazado por una hembra, y D. Pedro vuelve a caer fatal-
> mente impulsado en brazos de Sabel.
> Su ruina es ya inevitable. Las escenas que se suceden son
> todas lógicas, y el desenlace natural dadas las premisas. ¿Puede
> pedirse un determinismo mayor que éste? ¿ni un efecto artístico
> mas completo? Confiese V. su pecado, déjese V. de escrúpulos
> monjiles, y ya que profesa V. el naturalismo, tenga V. el valor
> de proclamar las excelencias del procedimiento con todas sus
> exigencias necesarias. ¿Le asusta a V. la palabra determinismo?
> Paréceme que sí, y sin embargo, es V. de las que creen que el
> nombre no hace a la cosa, como dicen los franceses.[33]

Even the sinister and silent Primitivo, whom some might call a
rather romantic villain, Benito thinks to be a natural product of
his surroundings:

> ¿Quiere V. una prueba más palpable de ese inconsciente de-
> terminismo artístico que ha guiado su pluma de V.? Ahí está
> Primitivo, fruto espontáneo del medio ambiente, planta parásita
> que crecerá siempre entre las ruinas de los antiguos solares . . .
> Primitivo es la resultante del sistema de fuerzas que le engendra,
> y como la cosa más natural y lógica del mundo y con la impasibili-
> dad de la piedra que cae obedeciendo a las leyes de la gravitación,
> obligará a su hija a ser la barragana de su señor, a soportar sin
> lamentarse todas sus brutales exigencias, mientras él le roba
> descaradamente cuanto posee . . . y aguarda con toda calma y tran-
> quilidad el momento de poder poner a su amo el pie encima y
> aplastarle como un sapo, sin que se traduzca en su fisonomía la
> más ligera transformación. . . .[33]

But there is more involved than just the character of Primitivo and the others. In addition to the people there is the setting
in which they find themselves—in this case, the great stone

Pazos, gloomy and musty with age. Not for naught did the Countess name the book *Los Pazos de Ulloa,* for the house itself is the all-important milieu of this naturalistic novel. The successive reactions of those two nervous souls, Julian and Nucha, to the sinister old mansion is one of the best presented developments in the book. They build up their own atmosphere of portent and fear by their own worrying temperament and ineffectiveness in the face of the impassive Primitivo. The tragedy is developing from the wedding feast onward:

> . . . y Julián, que viendo colmados sus deseos y votos ardentísimos, triunfante su candidatura, sentía no obstante en el corazón un peso raro, como si algún presentimiento cruel se lo abrumase.[34]

Things go along fairly smoothly until that disastrous day when a girl child is so painfully brought into the world. Never very strong, Nucha's nervous system has received a profound shock. It is not helped any by the disgust of her husband both at her weakness and at her failure to gratify his wish for a son-and-heir. Then comes the discovery of the parentage of Perucho and all the horrible revelation accompanying it. The ascendancy of Primitivo now more and more makes his enmity to be feared. And all around is the gloomy old stone pile in which they live— with winter coming on with its storms and grey days.

One day Julián goes down the back stairs to the kitchen; he is arrested on the last few steps by the sight of a horrible old witch-like woman telling Sabel's fortune with an old pack of cards. The young priest stops and holds his breath, trying to catch any word the revolting creature may utter loud enough for him to hear. Finally the stairs creak and he has to come on down, the old woman gathering up her cards with a muttered apology. What could she have been telling Sabel? What evil ideas was she putting into her head? Were they not all plotting against Nucha and her baby?

> Volvió Julian a su cuarto agitadísimo. Ni él mismo sabía lo que le correteaba por el magín. Bien presumía antes a cuántos riesgos se exponían Nucha y su hija viviendo en los Pazos: ahora . . . ahora los divisaba clarísimos. ¡Tremenda situación! . . . A la niña la robarían para matarla de hambre; a Nucha le envenarían tal vez. . . .[35]

Much disturbed, he goes to his room and tries to read. But he cannot concentrate; the sad sounds of the Galician night come in the window to distract him; the wind moans in the trees. Did someone cry out? It couldn't be, but

. . . creyó escuchar de nuevo el *ay* tristísimo. ¿Serían los perros?
Asomóse a la ventana; la luna bogaba en el cielo nebuloso, allá a
lo lejos, se oía el aullar de un perro, ese aullar lúgubre que los
aldeanos llaman *ventar la muerte*, y juzgan anuncio seguro del
próximo fallecimiento de una persona. Julián cerró la ventana
estremeciéndose. No despuntaba por valentón, y sus temores in-
stintivos se aumentaban en la casa solariega, que le producía
nuevamente la dolorosa impresión de los primeros días. Su temperamento linfático no poesía el secreto de ciertas saludables reac-
ciones, con las cuales se desecha todo vano miedo, todo fantasma
de la imaginación. . . .[36]

One might charge Pardo with romanticism in making the
Pazos so sinister did she not so scientifically explain that all the
terror came from the lymphatic temperament of those who were
afraid.   Julion's halucination now continues.   He hears a real
scream; there can be no doubt this time.   He runs down the
dark corridors, candlestick in hand; he turns a corner:

. . . ¡Dios santo! Sí, era la escena misma, tal cual se la había
figurado él . . . Nucha de pie, pero arrimada a la pared, con el
rostro desencajado de espanto, los ojos no ya vagos, sino llenos de
extravío mortal, en frente su marido, blandiendo un arma
enorme . . . Julián se arrojó entre los dos . . . Nucha volvió a
chillar.
—¡Ay, ay! ¡Qué hace V.! ¡Que se escapa! . . . ¡Que se escapa!
Comprendió entonces el alucinado capellán lo que ocurría,
con no poca vergüenza y confusión suya . . . Por la pared trepaba
aceleradamente, deseando huir la luz, una araña de desmesurado
grandor, un monstruoso vientre columpiando en ocho velludos
zancos. . . .[36]

The chaplain had bad dreams that night and his nerves continued overwrought the following morning.   He goes out to say
mass and coming back to the Pazos:

. . . la gran huronera de piedra se le presentó imponente, ceñuda
y terrible, con aspecto de prisión, como el castillo que había visto
soñando. El edificio, bajo su toldo de negras nubes, con el ruido
temeroso del cierzo que lo fustigaba, era amenazador y sinies-
tro. . . .[37]

Julián enters the house, finds Nucha nursing the baby.   They
look out the window; it is a day of dark clouds and violent gusts
of wind.   Both exclaim at once:

—¡Qué día tan triste!
Julián reflexionaba en la rara coincidencia de los terrores de
Nucha y los suyos propios; y pensando alto prorrumpía:
—Señorita, también esta casa . . . vamos, no es por decir mal
de ella, pero . . . es un poco *miedosa* ¿no le parece?
Los ojos de Nucha se animaron, como si el capellán le hubiese

adivinado un sentimiento que no se atrevía a manifestar.

—Desde que ha venido el invierno—murmuró hablando consigo misma—no sé qué tiene ni qué trazas saca . . . que no me parece la misma. . . . Hasta las murallas se han vuelto más gordas y la piedra más oscura. . . . Será una tontería, ¡ya sé que lo será!, pero no me atrevo a salir de mi habitación, yo que antes . . . andaba por todas partes. . . .[38]

Nucha determines to overcome her fears and get Julián to accompany her on an errand to the cellar. All the while the thunderstorm is growing more violent. As they go, they talk of the cruelty of the former lords of the manor, the conversation having started that way when they passed an old pillar in the basement to which still clung a rusty iron ring. A Negro slave was once chained to it. Nucha gets to her storage room and back to her living quarters all right, and feels satisfied with herself because of her triumph over the fearful house, but

Nucha, de repente, se incorporaba lanzando un chillido, y corría al sofá, donde se reclinaba lanzando interrumpidas carcajadas histéricas, que sonaban a llanto. Sus manos crispadas arrancaban los corchetes de su traje, o comprimían sus sienes, o se clavaban en los almohadones del sofá, arañándolos con furor. . . . Aunque tan inexperto, Julián comprendía lo que ocurría: el espasmo inevitable, la explosión del terror reprimido, el pago del alarde de valentía de la pobre Nucha. . . .

¡Filomena, Filomena! Aquí, mujer, aquí. . . . Agua, vinagre . . . el frasquito aquel. . . . Aflójale el vestido. . . . Ya me vuelvo de espaldas, mujer, no necesitaba avisármelo. . . . ¿Ya está cubierta y floja? . . . Que respire bien el vinagre. . . .[39]

It took Nucha some time to recover from her fright. Then came the election and its disappointment to the candidate, Don Pedro. Nucha had hoped he would be elected and they could leave the fearful Pazos, but now

—No aguardo, no puedo aguardar más. Esperé a que acabasen las elecciones dichosas, porque, creía que saldríamos de aquí, y entonces se me pasaría el miedo. . . . Yo tengo miedo en esta casa, ya lo sabe V. Julián; miedo horrible. . . . Sobre todo de noche.[40]

And it is her fear of the house which brings on the dreadful denouement—Nucha and Julián caught alone together in the chapel and planning to travel to Santiago together, never thinking of possible scandal. The subsequent dismissal of Julián and the black despair and ultimate death of poor Nucha, left all alone in the sinister house, are now inevitable.

The whole work is a masterpiece of determinism; given those characters and that environment, one feels that the result could not have been otherwise. Very little is left to chance or coincidence. Even if Nucha's child had been a son, would Don Pedro have ever loved her, could he have loved that sort of woman? No, I think the reader will have to agree with Lorenzo Benito both as to the determinism and as to the artistic effect of *Los Pazos de Ulloa*. ". . . ¿Puede pedirse un determinismo mayor que éste? ¿ni un efecto artístico más completo? Confiiesa V. su pecado. . . ."[33] And I must add that it is also an experimental novel of the best. Starting from the initial assumption of the decay of Galician noble houses, the novel shows Don Pedro's attempt to lift himself from the domination of his majordomo, to raise his self-respect by taking an honorable wife, to preserve his lineage with a legitimate son. All his efforts fail and he falls lower than before. Why? Because of the final rottenness of the very ideals of his caste. The tradition of pride and of doing as one pleases is not likely to instill self-discipline in a young man. Rustic life further dulls him; riding to hounds makes a man hardy but not shrewd. And the old honor code, that sore point in Spanish society, plays its part. By its leniency he could live and co-habit with his kitchen maid; by its harshness he lost a clever, healthy wife who would have saved him, and took to himself a nervous, weak-spirited woman who was inevitably his undoing. And with the downfall of the house of Ulloa must fall a whole order in Spanish society; old ideals must make way for new. The novel goes deep. The hypothesis was shrewd and the experiment proves it conclusively.

There still remains the important question of naturalistic candor as found in *Las Pazos de Ulloa*. On this point the reviewer, Lorenzo Benito, has this say:

> Lo que no he de callar, porque me produjo una impresión desagradable que nada tiene de artística, es aquel prurito de pintar cuántas inmundicias había en el archivo de la casa de los Ulloa . . . Si ha sido como sospecho, muestra de su adhesión al naturalismo de Zola con todas sus exageraciones, entonces he de decir a V. que no ha sido todo lo fiel que debiera, porque se ha detenido V. discretamente en la boda de Nucha y D. Pedro en los umbrales de la cámera nupcial.[41]

And here, I take it, is what Benito disliked most about the library of Ulloa:

> . . . La tarea, en apariencia fácil, no dejaba de ser enfadosa para el aseado presbítero: le sofocaba una atmósfera de mohosa humedad; cuando alzaba un montón de papeles depositados desde tiempo

inmemorial en el suelo, caía a veces la mitad de los documentos hecha añicos por el diente menudo e incansable del ratón; las polillas, que parecen polvo organizado y volante, agitaban sus alas y se le metían por entre la ropa; las correderas, perseguidas en sus más secretos asilos, salían ciegas de furor o de miedo, obligándole, no sin gran repugnancia, a despachurrarlas con los tacones, tapándose los oídos para no percibir el ¡chac! estremecedor que produce el cuerpo estrujado del insecto; las arañas, columpiando su hidrópica panza sobre descomunales zancos, solían ser más listas y refugiarse prontísimamente en los rincones oscuros, adonde las guía misterioso instinto estratégico. De tanto asqueroso bicho, tal vez el que más repugnaba a Julián era una especie de lombriz o gusano de humedad, frío y negro, que se encontraba siempre inmóvil y hecho una rosca debajo de los papeles, y al tocarlo producía la sensación de un trozo de hielo blando y pegajoso.[42]

Admittedly it is a rather crawly page, to say the least—although it sounds to me more like a healthy young tomboy's delight at frightening her playmates, who might not be blessed with so strong a stomach, than like a piece of naturalistic documentation. For one thing, there is scarcely a single technical term in the passage. Perhaps, rather, she is just a bit amused at the distress of her dainty Julián among *"tanto asqueroso bicho."* And she will probably be still more amused at the protests of her dainty readers. Naturalism to Doña Emilia seems to be in one respect a license to describe freely what to people of weaker sensibilities is repulsive. It is Zolaism turned in a slightly different direction—for her prudishness still persists when it comes to bedroom scenes. Benito is quite right on this point. The only difficulty is that most readers prefer bedrooms to bugs; hence greater popularity is achieved by the author of *Nana*.

One of the best studies of erotic relations in Pardo Bazán —and more particularly in *Los Pazos*—comes from the pen of the French critic Vézinet, who has this to say of the scenes in which Sabel figures:

Il est néamoins un procédé dont abusent les naturalistes français et dont n'use guère Mme Pardo Bazán. Elle évite les peintures lubriques. Nous voyons don Pedro et Sabel en face l'un de l'autre, en tant que maître et servante; nous ne les voyons pas en tant qu'amant et maîtresse. Une fois pourtant le marquis agit en amoureux: de la crosse de son fusil il frappe Sabel, qu'il a surprise avec un paysan dans une attitude suspecte. Et la scène est pénible; mais un de nos auteurs aurait donné la scène sensuelle du raccomodement. Mme Pardo Bazán ne la donne pas.

Quelques tableaux sont audacieux; ils ne sont pas licencieux. Sabel cherche à séduire le bon Julián . . . Elle pénètre chez le prêtre "en camisole et en jupon, la chemise entre-baillée, Les cheveux denattés, un pied et une jambe nus." Et lui, il remarque en rugissant qu'elle n'a "ni la peau tannée ni les membres déformés." Un autre jour elle simule une crise nerveuse, se laisse tomber sur le lit, pousse des cris, se débat. Le chapelain accourt avec une serviette mouillée pour lui frictionner les tempes; mais en approchant, il devine, malgré son inexpérience, que la coquine joue la comédie. Les deux incidents, le second surtout, prêtaient aux descriptions scabreuses. Nous avons cité tout ce que contenait de suggestif le premier; nous n'avons rien cité du dernier parce qu'il n'y a rien à citer. En France, l'auteur n'aurait pas manqué de prodiguer des détails sur l'attaque de nerfs, sur ce que les mouvements saccadés de la servante laissaient distinguer de sa personne. . . . Mme Pardo Bazán nous apprend uniquement que Sabel . . . étendue sur le lit, lançait de pitoyables ah! et de profonds soupirs. Et sur le désordre de ses vêtements, elle ne dit pas un mot.[43]

I intimated that in writing *Los Pazos de Ulloa* Pardo Bazán was sounding out the rotten beams beneath Galician nobility, beneath the old order of things, the old honor code with its fast and loose qualities. But let no one think that this is a simple thesis novel—after the manner of Pereda's *El buey suelto,* for instance—for it is nothing of the sort. It is merely a good naturalistic or experimental novel. The conclusion is suggested by the facts; it is never preached. There is even some doubt as to just what position the author takes on the problems suggested. There cannot be said to be one altogether sympathetic character or *raisonneur* in the book. Julián means well, but he is such an ass at times that the author has us guessing. She has thus come extremely close to giving us a true picture of life, in which rarely is one individual always right. She sees all the points of view, balances all the forces, draws the story out to its perfectly logical conclusion—without distortion, without apparently taking sides, without breaking her impersonality. The illicit relations of Don Pedro and Sabel are treated frankly just as the countryside treats such things—and just as a French novelist would treat the theme. Vézinet makes a very interesting comparison in this respect between Pardo's book and those of Valera, Pereda, and Galdós:

Cette analyse cursive suffit à nous révéler un auteur intrépide que n'effraye pas une donnée hardie. Mme Pardo Bazán est naturaliste à la manière française. Chez les romanciers espagnols, chez Valera, chez Pereda, même chez Galdós, les adultères sont aussi rares qu'ils sont fréquents dans notre littérature. Et quand il s'en commet, on les étudie non en eux-mêmes, mais dans les problèmes de conscience qu'ils soulèvent. Valera passe très vite sur la liaison criminelle du Commandeur et de doña Blanca (*el Commendador Mendoza*). Une question angoissante l'intéresse: la fille née de cette union, volerait l'héritier légitime, si elle recevait la succession . . . comment empêcher ce crime? —Dans Pereda, doña Clara trompe son mari (*Pedro Sánchez*). Mais l'auteur défend une thèse . . .: on doit prendre sa femme dans son propre milieu . . . —Galdós touche à peine à l'amour coupable de Carlos Erault et de Lucrecia Richmond . . . (*El Abuelo*). Notre attention se concentre sur les deux filles de Lucrecia, l'une légitime, l'autre adultérine. . . .

Rien d'analogue chez Mme Pardo Bazán. Elle ne se préoccupe pas de ce que deviendra le petit Perucho. Nul problème ne la sollicite, du moins dans *los Pazos de Ulloa*. D'autre part, elle décrit, comme si c'était une situation courante, un adultère particulièrement corsé puisqu'il se reproduit continuellement sous le toit conjugal au vu et au su de tous. Qui s'en émeut? Le chapelain seul. La valetaille s'en amuse; les gens du village s'en amusent; les curés des environs s'en amusent; et ils choisissent comme candidat à la députation le triste sire, dont la conduit scandaleuse est un défi aux lois de la morale et de la religion. L'adultère! Quel villain mot pour désigner une peccadille! On n'enfle pas la voix pour une vétille; on sourit tout simplement, d'un air entendu; on cligne de l'oeil, malicieusement; rien de plus.[44]

In tracing what I thought was probably the growth of the cast of characters and plot in Pardo's mind, I indicated that Julián was included in the story in order to have someone who would object to Don Pedro's amours. How does this harmonize with what Vézinet says of Doña Emilia's frank treatment of a licentious theme? One would almost take it, from what he says, that she herself also winks at the lord of Ulloa's peccadillo. Certainly Julián is not always the author's mouthpiece, for was it not he who urged Nucha on Don Pedro at the expense of her sister Rita, thus bringing on the whole tragedy? Nevertheless, it still seems obvious that Julián voiced Pardo's own protest against Don Pedro's free and easy ways, however much they may be condoned by society. The evidence, I believe, will bear out this point of view. For one thing, does not the whole tragedy of *La Madre Naturaleza* stem from the *ménage à trois* in *Los Pazos*? The sins of the father are there visited upon the children. Furthermore, in a later novel, *Una Cristiana*, Pardo holds up as a heroine a girl who rather than countenance with her presence her father's amours with his pretty servant, decides to marry without love in order to get out from under the sin-sheltering roof. Is this not a direct parallel to Julián's situation in *Los Pazos*? Did he not protest that as a Christian chaplain he could not countenance such goings-on with his continued presence at the Pazos? It all comes back to the strange mixture —or rather the wonderful balance—that was an essential part of Pardo Bazán's personality. Her sincere Christianity led her to condemn Don Pedro's peccadillo, and her progressive feministic spirit rebels at the excessive strictness of the honor code as regards women. No wonder she could not have a *raisonneur* in her story; she would have to look far indeed to find a Spanish type who could see both sides of an issue and decide it as fairly as she herself. To find one who would condemn Don Pedro, she had to take an ascetic, a person who would also be very conservative in his standards of purity in women, and there Pardo's humanity cannot side with him. Her best *portavoz* in this novel is the tragic sequence of events—just as in Zola's *Germinal* the socialistic message is not voiced by any one personage but rather is to be found in the very facts of the story.

Much confusion has arisen around the figure of Pardo Bazán because scholars have tried to classify her by isolated statements of hers or even on the basis of *La Cuestión palpitante* alone. In the previous chapter we saw how in that book she protested against Zola's determinism—only to admit in a polemic shortly afterwards that a Catholic author could accept a strong partial determinism in human life. Now in analyzing *Los Pazos* we have seen what perfect determinism is there manifest. Even the Christian characters in the book—Nucha and Julián—do not succeed in turning aside this force, but rather succumb to it. It is nearer total determinism than partial. With regard to naturalistic frankness, we have seen how Pardo's taste draws the line at certain scenes. Yet she deliberately throws in repulsive descriptions, such as the insect-infested library, to show us that—scruples or no—she still believes in the naturalist's right to tell all. With regard to her frank treatment of a case of adultery, we have Vézinet's word for it that she approaches the subject in the French manner and not indirectly or purely for purposes of posing a moral problem, as other Spanish novelists did. Many critics have emphasized Pardo Bazán's international, non-provincial point of view—among them the Argentine, Manuel Gálvez.[45] Despite any protestations of the worthy Countess in her critical writings, I think we must conclude that, at the time of writing *Los Pazos de Ulloa* at least, she was a thorough-going naturalist.

La Madre Naturaleza (1887)

Was anyone ever better qualified to write a truly realistic novel than Emilia Pardo Bazán, with her unemotional common sense and balance? Unbiased by prejudice and not given to poetic exaggeration, her novels often seem more real than those of Zola himself—although they usually lack his power. However, in *Los Pazos,* and also in *La Madre Naturaleza* which follows, Pardo has incorporated enough of the poetry of old Galicia to add a necessary beauty, and the whole is so well conceived as to rival in power and artistry some of Zola's best work. In fact, in *La Madre Naturaleza* the events are more realistically accounted for than in Zola's *La Faute de l'Abbé Mouret,* the model from which she got the basic idea, and the power of her writing is surely as great as his.

The parallelism in plot between *La Faute* and *La Madre* is at once apparent. Both are a retelling in a modern setting of the old story of Adam and Eve. In the first, Serge Mouret is stricken by an attack of brain fever, and his uncle, Dr. Pascal Rougon, conceives the rather strange idea of putting his nephew in an old abandoned manor house, there to be nursed back to health by the caretaker's ward, Albine, a girl who had grown up on the great estate. Serge wakes with all memory of the past wiped away. He and Albine, like Adam and Eve, are left to their own devices there in the great walled garden, both perfectly innocent. There follows the delightful story of their love, led on gradually by the fullness of life all round them to more and more intimacy, until the day when they find the great tree in the heart of the garden, beneath whose protecting boughs they learn "what mothers whisper to their daughters on the eve of their wedding day." But now they have "eaten of the fruit of the tree of the knowledge of good and evil," their innocence is gone, they are suddenly afraid:

> Albine jurait qu'un pas, au loin, les cherchait.
> —Cachons-nous, cachons-nous, répétait-elle d'un ton suppliant.
> Et elle devenait toute rose. C'était une pudeur naissante. . . .
> —Ne vois-tu pas que nous sommes nus?[46]

Unexpectedly their way is blocked; it is the wall of the garden, the garden that had always seemed boundless before. They follow along the wall and suddenly there is a break in it; **Albine** knew of the opening but ". . . le trou semblait avoir été **agrandi** par quelque main furieuse." And suddenly:

> Un pas lourd, derrière la muraille, faisait rouler les cailloux. . . . Alors tout deux voulurent se cacher derrière une broussaille, pris d'un redoublement d'honte. Mais déjà, debout au seuil de la brèche, Frère Archangias les voyait. . . .
>
> —Je vous vois, je sais que vous êtes nus. . . .[47]

Through the break in the wall, there across the valley behind the accusing figure of Frère Archangias, Serge sees his church, the nestling houses of the village; memory returns; the idyl is over. Adam and Eve are ejected from their paradise.

Pardo's story, a sequel to *Los Pazos*, concerns itself with the love of Perucho for his half-sister, Manuela. They of course have not been told of their relationship, Perucho supposing that Sabel's husband, the present majordomo, is his father. The two young people run wild together in the bosom of mother nature. Sent away to school, Perucho longs to return to Manuela's side. The coming of Gabriel Pardo as a suitor to Manuela arouses Perucho's jealousy and stimulates his desire. One day the brother and sister wander far afield—farther than ever before. They cross a stream, wander along it, finally climb a mountainside. On top they are completely alone, miles from everywhere. The Pazos are just visible down in the valley below. The mountain top is flat, almost a hollow, and there in the midst grows a great tree. . . . Later, Gabriel suspects what has happened, worms it out of Perucho, and then reveals to the boy and girl the horrible truth of their relationship. With the approval of the priest, Julián, Manuela enters a convent, Perucho goes to Madrid. The paradise is lost, never to be regained.

Zola is frank in his intention to imitate the Bible story. Here we have his general idea in the *ébauche* or sketch which he always made before writing:

> . . . Puis ils sont lachés dans le parc, Eve et Adam s'éveillant *au printemps* dans le paradis terrestre . . . C'est la nature qui joue le rôle du Satan de la Bible; c'est elle qui tente Serge et Blanche (Albine) et qui les couche sous l'arbre du mal par une matinée splendide. . . . Je calque le drame de la Bible, et, à la fin, je montre sans doute Frère Archangias apparaissant comme le dieu de la Bible, et chassant du paradis les deux amoureux.[48]

And as Don Gabriel reasons with himself and worries over the prolonged absence of Perucho and Manuela, he muses:

> —Se me figura que la naturaleza se encara conmigo y me dice:

Necio pon a una pareja linda, salida apenas de la adolescencia, sola, sin protección, sin enseñanza, vagando libremente, como Adán y Eva en los días paradisíacos, por el seno de un valle amenísimo, en la estación apasionada del año, entre flores que huelen bien, y alfombras de mullida hierba capaces de tentar a un santo. ¿Qué barrera, qué valla los divide? Una enteramente ilusoria, ideal; valla que mis leyes, únicas a que ellos se sujetan, no reconocen, pues yo jamás he vedado a dos pájaros nacidos en el mismo nido que aniden juntos a su vez a la primavera próxima . . . y yo, única madre y doctora de esa pareja, soy su cómplice también, porque la palabra que les susurro y el himno que les canto, son la verdadera palabra y el himno verdadero . . . y para entenderlo, simple, ¿qué falta hacen libros ni filosofías?[49]

Compare now a few sentences from *La Faute*:

C'était le jardin qui avait voulu la faute. Pendant des semaines, il s'était prêté au lent apprentissage de leur tendresse. Puis, au dernier jour, il venait de les conduire dans l'alcôve verte. Maintenant, il était le tentateur, dont toutes les voix enseignaient l'amour.[50]

Mother Nature is the Serpent who leads both pairs of lovers to the tree of knowledge. Note the lyrical fashion in which Zola describes the tree:

C'était au centre, un arbre noyé d'une ombre si épaisse, qu'on ne pouvait en distinguer l'essence. Il avait une taille géante, un tronc qui respirait comme une poitrine, des branches qui étendaient au loin, pareilles à des membres protecteurs. Il semblait bon, robuste, puissant, fécond; il était le doyen du jardin, le père de la forêt, l'orgueil des herbes, l'ami du soleil qui se levait et se couchait chaque jour sur sa cime . . . Sa sève avait une telle force, qu'elle coulait de son écorce; elle le baignait d'une buée de fécondation; elle faisait de lui la virilité même de la terre . . . Par moments, les reins de l'arbre craquaient; ses membres se roidissaient comme ceux d'une femme en couches; la sueur de vie, qui coulait de son écorce, pleuvait plus largement sur les gazons d'alentour, exhalant la molesse d'un désir, noyant l'air d'abandon, palissant la clairière d'une jouissance. L'arbre alors défaillait avec son ombre, ses tapis d'herbe, sa ceinture d'épais taillis. Il n'était plus qu'une volupté.

Albine et Serge restaient ravis. Dès que l'arbre les eut pris sous la douceur de ses branches, ils se sentirent guéris de l'anxiété intolérable dont ils avaient souffert. . . .[51]

Pardo, now, is more naturalistic than Zola; hers is a plain, everyday oak tree—albeit the only one on the lonely mountaintop, site of an ancient Roman fortresse:

Acercáronse al roble, cuyo ramaje horizontal y follaje obscurísimo formaban bóveda casi impenetrable a los rayos del sol. Aquel natural pabellón no se estaba quieto, sino que la purísima y oxigenada brisa montañesa lo hacía palpitar blandamente, como

vela de esquife, obligando a sus recortadas hojas a que se acaricia-
sen y exhalasen un murmullo de seda crujidora. Al pie del roble,
el humus y las hojas y la sombra proyectada por las ramas, habían
contribuído a la formación de un pequeño ribazo, resto quizá de
uno de aquellos túmulos, así como el duro y vigoroso roble habría
chupado acaso la substancia de sus raíces en las vísceras del gue-
rrero acribillado de heridas y enterrado allí en épocas lejanas.
 —Ahí tienes un sitio precioso—dijo Perucho.
 Dejóse caer la montañesa, recostada más que sentada en el ten-
tador ribazo.[52]

It is typical of the difference between the two authors that in
imitation of Zola's exotic tree, Pardo should depict an oak, and
that as a symbol of overflowing fecundity she should present the
almost revolting idea that the tree obtained sustenance from the
decaying remains of a Roman soldier.   At any rate, the tree,
with its tempting greensward beneath, fulfils the same function
as that in the previous versions of Zola and Genesis.

No one realized better than Zola how poetically extravagant
he had been in *La Faute de l'Abbé Mouret*.   Looking back on it
from a distance, he attributes it to "un coup de soleil":

 Gustave Flaubert est le romancier qui jusqu'ici a employé la
 description avec le plus de mesure. Chez lui, le milieu intervient
 dans un sage équilibre. . . .

 Nous autres, pour la plupart, nous avons été moins sages, moins
 équilibrés. La passion de la nature nous a souvent emportés, et
 nous avons donné de mauvais exemples, par notre exubérance, par
 nos griseries de grand air. Rien ne détraque plus sûrement une
 cervelle de poète qu'un coup de soleil. On rêve alors toutes sortes
 de choses folles, on écrit des oeuvres où les ruisseaux se mettent à
 chanter, où les chênes causent entre eux, où les roches blanches
 soupirent comme des poitrines de femme à la chaleur du midi. Et
 ce sont des symphonies de feuillages, des rôles données aux brins
 d'herbe, des poèmes de clarté et de parfums. S'il y a une excuse
 possible pour de tels écarts, c'est que nous avons rêvé d'élargir
 l'humanité et nous l'avons mise jusque dans les pierres des che-
 mins.[53]

Here is an example of what Zola is speaking of.   The garden has
just decided to show Serge and Albine the way to the *tree*:

 . . . Le jardin, en les voyant, avait comme un rire prolongé, un
 murmure satisfait volant de feuille en feuille, jusqu'au bout des
 avenues les plus profondes. Depuis des journées, il devait les
 attendre, ainsi liée à la taille, reconciliés avec les arbres, cherchant
 sur les couches d'herbe leur amour perdu. Un chut solennel courut
 sous les branches. Le ciel de deux heures avait un assoupissement
 de brasier. Des plantes se haussaient pour les regarder passer.
 —Les entends-tu? demandait Albine à demi-voix. Elles se

taisent quand nous approchons. Mais, au loin, elles nous attendent, elles so confient de l'une à l'autre le chemin qu'elles doivent nous indiquer. . . .⁵⁴

And when the fatal moment arrives, all the birds, beasts, and insects join in one grand copulation.

Doña Emilia again takes her lovers as far as the first kiss. Certainly no one can accuse the Countess of undue sensuality, but neither can they accuse her of poetic exaggeration. Zola's tree with its steaming and oozing sap, its bursting vitality, is like something out of the *Arabian Nights*; Pardo's is just a great spreading oak on a breezy Galician mountaintop. Zola's garden is exotic, picture-bookish, blurred, while the Spanish landscape is clear, definitely in focus. The topography of the Paradou garden is as vague as that described in Genesis. Why were the lovers unable to find the tree until the appointed day if it was larger than any other, and if the sun rose and set in its crest? Why did they never see the wall until the last fatal day? Why were all the flowers still grouped in the garden after years and years of non-cultivation? Well, did not Zola say it was a *coup de soleil*?

But let us not give the impression that Pardo Bazán's book is all very matter-of-fact and uninteresting. On the contrary, it is full of some of the best word-pictures that ever fell from the pen of a prolific author. Here is a description of a threshing-scene on a hot summer's day. The sunlight is dazzling, the colors vivid; the heat almost makes you perspire from sympathy.

> The sun, implacable, metallic, drank up the sweat of the workers almost before it issued from their dilated pores; and, nevertheless, the task went on and on, for to sustain energy were ever at hand, between each bedding-down, the earthen jugs of wine passing from hand to hand. The women workers, dressed in narrow skirts of faded chintz which revealed their sturdy muscles, shake the straw, place it in great piles, prepare the new bedding-down of grain, and meanwhile the man, standing and leaning on his flail, drunken with sunlight, open-throated with his coarse shirt sticking to his body, dispatches quickly his bit of cigar, and now he is spitting on his hands, preparing to flourish again his instrument when the hour of combat sounds. Terrble hour in which are spent energy and vigor enough for a month! The light dazzles and blinds; the atmosphere is like the blast from a furnace; there is not stirring the breath of air required to bend the weakest of grasses: the leaves of the fig trees, surrounding the threshing floor at the Pazos rest motionless, as if cut out of tin, and the green figs, stiff as metallic cactus leaves; at times a little bird will fall

to the ground in an agony of suffocation, with his bill desperately
open and his plumage ruffled; in the immediate surroundings the
viper raises his flat-nosed head, and his little jet eyes burn, he
glides through the angry grass, and the bumblebees, in a daze, do
not succeed in coming forth from the heart of the flower in which
they have sunken their beaks. . . . And amid the general swoon
of nature perishing and expiring in the heat, only man recognizes
his servile condition and fulfils the prophecy of Genesis, beating
out the sheaves which are to give him sustenance![55]

The reader will note the photographic reality of the first part
of the description, a reality which later shades off into the poetic
when the author starts to speak of the birds, bees, and vipers.
The latter part especially—with its reference to Genesis, too—
recalls Zola's book. The whole is a very good sample of many
vivid pictures in the novel. Practice has done much to perfect
the touch of her brush since *La Tribuna,* four years before.

In *La Madre Naturaleza,* Doña Emilia continues her study of
two men with the same heredity living in different environments.
The reader will remember her comparison of the young marquis,
Don Pedro, with his city uncle, Don Manuel Pardo de la Lage.
Here we have the picture of Don Pedro grown old:

Sentado en el banquillo . . . estaba otro hombre más corpu-
lento, más obeso, más entrado en edad o más combatido por ella,
con barba aborrascada y ya canosa, y vientre potente, que re-
saltaba por la posición que le imponía la poca altura del banco.
A Gabriel le pasó por los ojos una niebla; creyó ver a su padre,
don Manuel Pardo, tal cual era hacía unos quince o veinte años,
y con mayor cordialidad de la que traía premeditada, se fué derecho
a saludar al marqués de Ulloa.[56]

The decay of Don Pedro has been quick, a mere matter of some
fifteen or twenty years since last we saw him in *Los Pazos.*
Gabriel and he are first cousins but they do not appear to be of
the same generation. Apparently his outdoor life has been excessively hard on him:

El abandono da le persona, las incesantes fatigas de la caza,
la absorbción de humedad, de sol, de viento frío, la nutrición
excesiva, la bebida destemplada, el sueño a pierna suelta, el
exceso, en suma, de vida animal, habían arruinado rápidamente la
torre de aquella un tiempo robustísima y arrogante persona, de
distinta manera, pero tan por completo como lo harían las luchas
morales y las emociones febriles de la vida cortesana.[57]

And Pardo Bazán cannot resist telling us what would have been
the effect of a different environment upon that given heredity
and physical development:

Tal vez parecía mayor la ruina por la falta de artificio en

ocultarla y remediarla. Ceñido aquel mismo abdomen por una faja, bajo un patalón negro habilmente cortado; desmochada aquella misma cabeza por un diestro peluquero; raídas aquellas mejillas con afiladísima navaja, y suavizada aquella barba con brillantina; añadido a todo ello cierto aire entre galante y grave, que caracteriza a las personas respetables en un salón, es seguro que más de cuatro damas dirían, al ver pasar al marqués de Ulloa: —¡Qué bien conservado! Cuarenta años es lo más que representa.[57]

Turning now to the country-bred daughter of the weak and nervous heroine of *Los Pazos,* our author gives us another study of the effects of differing environment upon a given heredity:

La montañesa echó delante, ágil y airosa como una cabrita montés. . . . La cintura de Manolita, en vez de ser de forma cilíndrica, tenía las dos planicies, delante y detrás, que suelen delatar la inocencia del cuerpo . . . su andar era andar de cervatilla, sin languidez alguna.[58]

To the wasp-waisted eighties, the spectacle of a girl with a flat, natural waist instead of a round, constricted one was no doubt somewhat of an unusual phenomenon. Don Gabriel admires the ease and straightforwardness of the mountain girl but still thinks a little civilizing would not do her any harm:

—¡Cuánto tengo aguí que enmendar, que enseñar, que formar! —reflexionaba Gabriel . . . —¡La han descuidado tanto! Lo que exista aquí de bueno ha de ser bueno de ley, por deberse exclusivamente a la fuerza e influjo del natural, a la rectitud del instinto. Más fácil es habérselas con esta niña, entregada a sí misma desde que nació, que con esas chicas criadas en una atmósfera artificial, y a quienes la solicitud y los sabios . . . o hipócritas consejos de las mamás, tías y amiguitas han cubierto de un barniz tan espeso y compacto que el demonio que sepa lo que hay debajo de él.[58]

But if polished Don Gabriel objects to the false veneer of the average city girl, listen to Don Pedro vent his spleen on the subject:

—¡Allá en los pueblos se educa a las muchachas de un modo y por aquí las educamos por otro! . . . Allá queréis unas mojigatas, unas *mírame y no me toques*, que estén siempre haciendo remilgos, que no sirvan para nada, que se pongan a morir en cuanto un pie de aquí a la escalera de la cocina . . . y luego mucho de sí señor, de gran virtud y de gran aquel, y luego sabe Dios lo que hay por dentro, que detrás de la cruz anda el diablo, y las que parecen unas santas . . . más vale callar. Y luego, al primer hijo, se emplastan, se acoquinan, y luego ¡revientan de puro maulas! . . .[59]

Of course, Pardo has good reason for these comparisons between city and country women. *Los Pazos de Ulloa* was the story of Nucha, the city señorita, whose weakness brought on the tragedy of that first drama; *La Madre Naturaleza* illustrates that it may be equally bad to let a girl run wild in the bosom of Mother Nature. For the Countess does not seem to reach the same conclusions as did Zola in *La Faute*; the latter presents religion as an unnatural and tragic artificiality that separates the two lovers, while in Pardo Bazán's version it is presented more sympathetically—albeit at times we wonder if Don Gabriel is not in part her *raisonneur* as much as the priest, Julián. Here is an argument between them toward the end of the book:

> —Por una desdicha que ha tenido, por una falta que todo disculpa, cuyo alcance ella no ha podido comprender, y cuya raíz y origen están, al fin y al cabo, en lo más sagrado y respetable que existe . . . ¡en la naturaleza!
>
> —Señor de Pardo—respondió el cura, que ya había recobrado su apacibilidad de costumbre—lo que la naturaleza yerra, lo enmienda la gracia; y el advenimiento de Cristo y los méritos de su sangre preciosa fueron cabalmente para eso; para remediar la falta de nuestros primeros padres y sanar la naturaleza enferma. La ley de la naturaleza, aislada, sola, invóquenla las bestias; nosotros invocamos otra más alta . . . Para eso somos hombres, hijos de Dios y redimidos por él.[60]

And from the last sentences of the book it would seem that Don Gabriel had been won over to the priest's way of thinking—at least far enough to question the pure goodness of Mother Nature:

> Gabriel Pardo se volvió hacia los Pazos por última vez, y sepultó la mirada en el valle, con una extraña mezcla de atracción y rencor, mientras pensaba:
>
> —Naturaleza, te llaman madre . . . Deberían llamarte madrastra.[61]

The basic hypothesis behind this experimental novel is the same as that of *La Faute de l'Abbé Mouret*, i.e., put a pair of healthy young human animals in the bosom of nature with no restraints but their innocence, and sooner or later, inevitably, they will go the way of all flesh. Zola had to force reality a little in order to secure a pair of innocents and a secluded spot in this busy world of ours; Serge has to lose his memory and the Paradou garden has to be imagined. Pardo brings about the test quite naturally. Perucho had never known he was half-brother to Manuela; so he did not need to lose his memory. As for the necessary wilderness, there was plenty all about. The curious thing is that neither Zola nor Pardo Bazán follows Genesis exactly as to the conclusion. Zola has Albine die, while Serge continues his career as village priest. Pardo has Manuela go to a convent, while Perucho continues his life as before. Both authors interpret the casting of the lovers out of the Garden as a separation, whereas in the Bible they are not separated. This should serve to emphasize further that Pardo Bazán was imitating Zola's version of Adam and Eve, rather than that of Moses. A further parallel between these two modern renderings, as opposed to the Biblical one, is that both pairs of innocents are quite unaware that any social prohibition stands in the way of their union. No one had told them not to eat of the forbidden fruit; both are the innocent victims of Mother Nature, the temptress.

Insolación (1889)

When Pardo Bazán published the delightful little story, *Insolación,* in 1889, the scene described was contemporary to her. Unfortunately it is no longer so to us, and from the point of view of the modern reader the *moment* of this novel is important. In order to appreciate properly the effects of the sun on the heroine one must know something of the fashions then prevailing in women's dress. The modes of the 1880's called for a long hour-glass silhouette. Corsets extended from just under the armpits to well below the hips and were drawn very tight over waist and lower ribs. Dresses were fitted closely over this foundation from the high neck to well below the waist, at least in front. Hoops were no longer worn; the ornate and heavy skirts were swept smoothly over a straight front and were extended behind by a bustle. The whole impression was one of stiffness, artificiality, and restriction—restriction especially of the breath —and thereby hangs a tale, for this was the weak point in a lady's armor.

Having found Don Gabriel Pardo useful as an occasional mouthpiece for her ideas in *La Madre Naturaleza,* our author has him reappear in *Insolación.* As the story opens, the heroine, a young and vivacious widow, is at a fashionable *tertulia* in Madrid listening to the fantastic ideas of Don Gabriel. The latter maintains that all Iberians are especially susceptible to the intoxicating effects of the flaming Spanish sun—witness the bullfights as a case in point. But yes, he goes on, even the ladies are not immune to the sun, even one from cloudy Galicia like la señora viuda de Andrade:

> Aquí está nuestra amiga Asís, que a pesar de haber nacido en el Noroeste, donde las mujeres son reposadas, dulces y cariñosas, sería capaz, al darle un rayo de sol en la mollera, de las mismas

> atrocidades que cualquier hija del barrio de Triana o del Ava-
> piés. . . .[62]

Other peoples, such as the English, must have alcohol to get
tipsy, but not the Spaniards, who can do it 'con el aire, el agua,
el ruido, la música y la luz del cielo."

Having thus laid down her hypothesis as to Spanish heredity,
Doña Emilia proceeds to work out the literary experiment by
subjecting the young widow from Galicia to a strong dose of
Castillian sunshine. The very next day turns out to be a beautiful Sunday and we find our friend Asís on her way to mass:

> Cerca de Cibeles me fijé en la hermosura del día. Nunca he
> visto aire más ligero, ni cielo más claro; la flor de las acacias del
> paseo de Recoletos olía a gloria, y los árboles parecía que estrena-
> ban vestido nuevo de tafetán verde. Ganas me entraron de correr
> y brincar como a los quince, y hasta se me figuraba que en mis
> tiempos de chiquilla no había sentido nunca tal exceso de vitali-
> dad, tales impulsos de hacer extravagancias, de arrancar ramas
> de árbol y de chupazarme en el pilón presidido por aquella buena
> señora de los leones. . . . Nada menos . . . me estaba pidiendo
> el cuerpo a mí. . . .[63]

A few steps farther on she comes upon the Andalusian, Pacheco,
a gentleman whose acquaintance she had just made the day before. It must have been the clear sunny day that made them
greet each other so informally. Indeed, what else could have
induced her to accept before she knew it Pacheco's invitation
to ride with him to the Feria de San Isidro on the banks of the
Manzanares outside Madrid? The lady goes home to change
clothes and freshen up while the gentleman hunts up her carriage and has the coachman bring it around to her door. She
had assuaged her conscience by saying that after all she could
hear mass as well at the chapel of San Isidro but

> El campo de San Isidro es una serie de cerros pelados, un desierto
> de polvo, invadido por un tropel de gente entre la cual no se ve un
> solo campesino, sino soldados, mujerzuelas, chisperos, ralea api-
> carada y soez; y en lugar de vegetación, miles de tinglados y
> puestos donde se venden cachivaches que, pasado el día del Santo,
> no vuelven a verse en parte alguna. . . .
>
> Aparte del sol que le derrite a uno la sesera y del polvo que se
> masca, bastan para marear tantos colores vivos y metálicos. Si
> sigo mirando van a dolerme los ojos. Las naranjas . . . parecen
> de fuego; los dátiles relucen . . . no se ven sino claveles amarillos,
> sangre de toro . . . el olor a aceite frito de los buñuelos, que se
> pega a la garganta y produce un cosquilleo inaguantable. . . . Y
> luego la música, el rasgueo de las guitarras, el tecleo insufrible de
> los pianos mecánicos. . . .[64]

Of course we must remember that inasmuch as Doña Asís is telling us the story herself, she naturally will make out as good a case as possible, blaming her undue familiarity with Pacheco on the strange environment in which she finds herself:

> Ahora que reflexiono a sangre fría, caigo en la cuenta de que era bastante raro y muy inconveniente que a los tres cuartos de hora de pasearnos juntos por San Isidro, nos hablásemos don Diego y yo con tanta broma y llaneza. Es posible, bien mirado, que mi paisano tenga razón; que aquel sol, aquel barullo y aquella atmósfera popular obren sobre el cuerpo y el alma como un licor o vino de los que más se suben a la cabeza, y rompan desde el primer momento la valla de reserva que trabajosamente levantamos las señoras un día y otro contra peligrosas osadías. De cualquier índole que fuese, yo sentía ya un principio de mareo cuando exclamé:
> —En la cárcel estaría a gusto con tal que no hiciese sol . . . Me encuentro así . . . no sé cómo . . . parece que me desvanezco.
> —¿Pero se siente V. mala? ¿mala?—preguntó Pacheco seriamente, con vivo interés.
> —Lo que se dice mala, no: es una fatiga, una sofocación . . . Se me nubla la vista.[65]

Pacheco convinces her that her trouble is hunger and insists that they eat lunch together in a *fonda* at the fair. This seems to her highly improper but finally he persuades her. She even allows him to send her carriage home, with instructions to return in late afternoon. Meanwhile:

> El sol campeaba en mitad del cielo, y vertía llamas y echaba chiribitas. El aire faltaba por completo; no se respiraba sino polvo arcilloso. Yo registraba el horizonte tratando de descubrir la prometida fonda, que siempre sería un techo, preservativo contra aquel calor del Senegal. Mas no se veía rastro de edificio grande en toda la extensión del cerro.[66]

And instead of a *fonda* they find a booth whose canvas roof does little more than filter the sunlight. Asís, feeling thirsty enough to drink up "el Manzanares entero," seizes upon the only liquid available:

> ¡manzanilla superior! ¡A cualquier cosa llaman *superior* aquí! La manzanilla dichosa sabía a esparto, a piedra alumbre y a demonios coronados. . . .[67]

And the effect of this supposed thirst quencher was:

> Sólo que en vez de refrescarme, se me figuró que un rayo de sol, disuelto en polvo, se me introducía en las venas y me salía en chispas por los ojos y en arreboles por la faz. Miré a Pacheco muy risueña, y luego me volví confusa, porque el me pagó la mirada con otra más larga de lo debido.

—¡Qué bonitos ojos azules tiene este perdiz!—pensaba yo para mí.[67]

The wine, it seems, was a faithful ally of the sun, and before long the lady found herself quite happy in the midst of the hoi pelloi and quite forgetful of her social position. However, upon leaving the *merendero* around four in the afternoon she did not feel so well. The heat was at its height and it seemed as though three times as many people had found their way to the fair and all were twenty times as noisy. What with the sun, the heat, the wine, the excitement, fear of the crowds, and the general lack of air, the poor lady was in a bad way:

> Al punto que nos metimos en aquel bureo, se me puso en la cabeza que me había caído en el mar: mar caliente, que hervía a borbotones, y en el cual flotaba yo dentro de un botecillo chico como una cáscara de nuez: golpe va y golpe viene, ola arriba y ola abajo. ¡Sí, era el mar; no cabía duda! ¡El mar, con toda la angustia del mareo que empieza![68]

And a few pages farther on: ". . . me latían las sienes, se me encogía el corazón y se me nublaban los ojos: no sabía lo que me pasaba: un sudor frío bañaba mi frente."[69]

Pacheco, meanwhile, had been leading the widow away from the fairgrounds and along the Manzanares to a tavern, where poor Asís lay down on a couch in the back room. But let us let her tell it the way it seemed to her:

> Cesé de ver la bahía, el mar verde . . . Sin duda ya me habían depositado en tierra firme, pues noté un consuelo grandísimo, y luego una sensación inexplicable de desahogo, como si una manaza gigantesca rompiese un aro de hierro que me estaba comprimiendo las costillas y dificultando la respiración. Dí un suspiro y abrí los ojos. . . .
>
> Fué un intervalo lúcido, de esos que se tienen aun en medio del síncope o del acceso de locura, y en que comprendí claramente todo cuanto me sucedía. No había mar, ni barco, ni tales carneros . . . La tierra firme era el camastro de la taberna, el aro de hierro el corsé que acababan de aflojarme; y no me quedé muerta de sonrojo allí mismo, porque no ví en el cuarto a Pacheco.[70]

After this lucid moment Asís slips back into her nautical hallucination, believing herself to be reclining in a comfortable stateroom aboard ship. Before long she feels better and opens her eyes to look directly into those of Pacheco. He is most gentle and respectful but it *was* an odd situation. And shortly she finds herself calling him *tú* and "con el mayor recato y comedimiento" Pacheco was helping her hook up her bodice. Always the perfect gentleman, he also found her hat, gloves, hat-pin, and other accessories. As they leave the tavern:

> La calma de la noche y el aire exterior me produjeron el efecto de una ducha fría. Sentí que la cabeza se me despejaba y que así como se va la espuma por el cuello de una botella de champaña, se escapaban de mi mollera en burbujas el sol abrasador y los espíritus alcohólicos del endiablado vino compuesto.[71]

There can be no doubt that Pacheco was a seducer of no mean ability. By taking the lady to San Isidro's fair he enlisted the strong aid of sun, wine, heat, and the infectious gaiety of the lower classes. Even the lady's costume worked in his favor, making her more dependent on his masculine strength. It was very skillful of Pardo Bazán to have the young widow tell this part of the story in the first person; for being herself a woman, Pardo can do it most convincingly, perhaps drawing upon her own memory of an experience with the sun and crowds of Madrid. Once through the episode at the fair, Doña Emilia shifts the story into the third person. This, too, has obvious advantages, for what is to ensue would be rather embarrassing for the young widow to relate herself. Indeed, even the author professes a certain reticence concerning some of the events.

Starting with her hypothesis about the hereditary susceptibility of Spaniards to the sun, Pardo has proceeded to subject her protagonist to a very strong dose of *insolación*; the consequences are logical and can be left pretty much to the skill of the beseiger, Pacheco. It is obvious that after the incident of the fair, Asís would have difficulty in placing that gentleman again at arm's length. Indeed, she herself seems to think that the only solution is to take the train and escape to Galicia. But that proved harder than it seemed, and at the end of four days' ardent seige, the widow was destined to yield and spend the night with her lover.

There can be little doubt of the naturalistic determinism underlying this novel. The forces of heredity and environment prove far too strong for Doña Asís. There remains for discussion, however, the interesting question of naturalistic candor. Doña Emilia is still feeling certain scruples, although this is the frankest novel so far. One chapter, for instance, begins thus:

> Doloroso es tener que reconocer y consignar ciertas cosas; sin embargo, la sinceridad obliga a no eliminarlas de la narración. Queda, eso sí, el recurso de presentarlas en forma indirecta, procurando con maña que no lastimen tanto como si apariciesen de

> frente, insolentonas y descaradas, metiéndose por los ojos. Así la implícita desaprobación del novelista se disfraza de habilidad.[72]

And then she goes on to describe the defeat of the lady's plan to avoid keeping her appointment with Pacheco by driving off in her carriage ahead of time. All Doña Emilia tells us is that the coachman arrived promptly at five o'clock before his mistress' door, only to wait disconsolately and in vain until seven, when a masculine figure emerged from the house and walked briskly off in the direction of Recoletos. When Pardo Bazán describes the drooping figure of the coachman sitting there over his drooping horse as the last rays of the sun climb the sides of the buildings and fade away, one is reminded of the episode from *Madame Bovary* where Flaubert describes the wanderings of a coach containing Emma and Léon as it rolls over the streets of Rouen. But in both authors it is merely playfulness, a desire to tantalize the reader a little before giving him the real thing. For upon the following day Asís and Pacheco are spending the summer evening together in the lady's apartment and Doña Emilia lets us come right into the parlor and see this:

> Pacheco arrastró un sillón hacia la ventana y se sentó en él.
> —¡Desatento!—exclamó riendo la señora. —¿Pues no decías que era para mí?
> —Para ti es—respondió el amante cogiéndola por la cintura y obligándola quieras o no quieras a que se acomodase en sus rodillas. Se resistió algo la dama, y al fin tuvo que acceder. Pacheco la meció como se mece a las criaturas, sin permitirse ningún agasajo distinto de los que pueden prodigarse a un niño inocente. Por forzosa exigencia de la postura, Asís le echó el brazo al cuello, y después de los primeros momentos, reposó la cabeza en el hombro del andaluz.[73]

And a few pages further on we are even permitted to follow the widow into her dark bedroom:

> Saltó Asis de brazos de su adorador, muerta de risa, y al saltar perdió una de sus bonitas chinelas, que por ser sin talón, a cada rato se le escurrían del pie. Recogióla Pacheco, calzándosela con mil extremos y zalamerías. La dama entro en su alcoba, y abriendo el armario de luna empezó a buscar a tientas una toquilla de encaje para ponérsela y que no la marease aquel pesado. Vuelta estaba de espaldas a la poca luz que venía del saloncito, cuando sintió que dos brazos la ceñían el cuerpo. En medio de la lluvia de caricias delirantes que acompaño a demostración tan atrevida, Asís entreoyó una voz alterada, que repetía con acento serio y trágico:
> —¡Te adoro . . . ¡Me muero, me muero por ti![74]

But nothing was to happen that night. That was only Wednesday, and Pacheco left at midnight before the maid came back from her night off.

Next day Pacheco interrupts the widow's packing to take her to lunch and when he comes again in the evening, plans for the trip to Galicia have merged with marriage plans. As a preliminary, they spend the night together. This time we are excluded—until next morning, when both lovers lean out the window to greet the morning sun:

> Diríase que los futuros esposos deseaban cantar un himno a su numen titular, el sol, y ofrecerle la primera plegaria matutina.[75]

Despite the pleasant sort of frankness already cited, the French critic, Vézinet, again points out Pardo's tendency to be frank as to certain repulsive details:

> Doña Francesca (Insolación) possède une salle de bain. Mais n'attendez pas la description d'une installation féerique comme il y en a dans les romans, comme il n'y en a pas "dans les appartements loués." Figurez-vous prosaiquement "une pièce sombre qu'éclaire une lampe a pétrole et une baignoire en cette sorte de zinc recouvert de porcelaine, qui rappelle une casserole."[76]

As a matter of fact, there are few examples of repulsive ugliness in the book, and nothing to compare with the library of Ulloa.

Certain Spanish critics doubted the *vraisemblance* of such a whirlwind seduction's ending in marriage, but Pardo makes it clear that Pacheco was not entirely altruistic in marrying a well-to-do widow with good political connections. In any case, it seems to me that the happy denouement is quite in keeping with the air of lightness and gaiety which pervades the book throughout. Just as Emile Zola delighted in surprising the public with a small, mild, and intimate novel after one of his broad and scandalous studies of a wider environment—after *L'Assommoir* he published *Une Page d'Amour*—so Pardo Bazán followed the broad canvas of *La Madre Naturleza* with this little story of love in the capital of Spain. And again, just as in his *Aux Bonheur des Dames* Zola surprised his public by having the heroine—a poor working girl—marry the big boss of the department store, so *Insolación* breaks the precedent of several tragic novels by ending happily in marriage. At the same time the book is a perfect example of naturalism, and one of the most entertaining to come from the busy pen of Pardo Bazán.

Morriña (1889)

Another Zola technique which Pardo Bazán successfully imi-

tates is the art of choosing a title which will at the same time
arouse curiosity and embody the whole theme of the naturalistic
study presented. *La Tribuna* arouses our curiosity as to just
what a feminine tribune-of-the-people might be. *Los Pazos de
Ulloa* sounds grandiloquent and yet by the use of the regional
and somewhat archaic-sounding term, *Pazos,* suggests the underlying theme of decaying nobility. And certainly the title *Insolación* foreshadows well the quick action and gay treatment of
this naturalistic investigation into the effects of the sun upon a
lady's defenses. Published the same year as *Insolación,* the small
novel, *Morriña,* is the next to be considered in our series. It,
too, has a title which bespeaks the mood and action of the story.
If *Insolación* presents a study in sunshine, *Morriña* is by contrast a study in melancholy; the one is *sol,* the other *sombra.*

To translate *morriña* merely as "homesickness" is to convey
only part of its meaning. It goes deeper and indeed, as described by Pardo Bazán, seems to be a serious sort of melancholia, almost a racial fault to be found in many *gallegos.* The
protagonist of the story describes her symptoms as follows:

> . . . Pegó conmigo la moriña, y si no salgo creo que se me revuelve
> la cabeza o me voy derecha a la sepultura. Yo no comía. Yo me
> metía a cavilar por los rincones. Yo me fuí quedando morena,
> morena, y tan flaca, que la ropa se me cae. Yo de noche tenía
> unos aflictos como si me atasen una soga al pescuezo tirando
> mucho. . . .[77]

Aside from the Galician servant girl, who has the *morriña,*
all the characters are quite ordinary. Indeed, Don Juan Valera,
in commenting on the book, is at pains to point out just how ordinary they are. One senses his disapproval of Pardo Bazán's
effort to describe photographically a group of people so little
worthy of her interest:

> Rogelio, que así se llama el muchacho, estudia leyes en la
> Universidad Central; no es ni tonto, ni discreto, ni feo, ni bonito,
> ni alto, ni bajo, ni malo, ni bueno. Es un ser totalmente vulgar;
> menos que adocenado. Individualmente no hay razón para que nos
> interese y para que se escriba su historia. Su madre, Doña
> Aurora, buena mujer, interesa algo más, por el amor de madre
> que llena su alma. Tampoco, sin embargo, es Doña Aurora sujeto
> muy distinguido por estilo ninguno. Su casa, situada casi enfrente
> a la Universidad; sus tertulianos, viejos amigos de su marido
> **difunto, todo está copiado** de la realidad, sin idealización, adornos
> ni añadiduras. Se diría que la pluma de la novelista, al copiarlo,
> es como el rayo de luz que graba la imagen fotográfica en el
> vidrio preparado al efecto.[78]

Even though Valera may disapprove of it, the practice of describing ordinary people realistically and of placing them in a common and realistically described setting is certainly good naturalism. But this is not all that Don Juan finds objectionable; he is distressed by the all-pervading determinism which brings on the suicide of the young protagonist:

> ¿Por qué se enamora tan perdidamente Esclavitud? Si su temperamento amoroso, transmitido por herencia, la lleva a ese amor, ¿por qué ese amor es tan exclusivo, que sin él no le queda más recurso que la muerte? ¿Es tan invencible su pasión que no vale nada contra el libre albedrío, o no hay libre alberdrío, sino fatal determinismo? ¿Cómo la que tiene tanto valor para morir, no tiene ninguno para luchar con sus inclinaciones? Aunque el cura hubiera sido un pecador, ¿no había sido cristiano, no había educado cristianamente a Esclavitud? [The reference is to the priest, who was Esclavitud's father.] ¿Por qué, pues, la moral cristiana y el santo temor de Dios no retienen a Esclavitud al borde del abismo? Su pasividad, su rendimiento, la entereza y el sacrificio completo que hace Esclavitud de su cuerpo y de su alma, parecen obra, no del diablo . . . ni del pecado original, contra quien la religión da medios en los Sacramentos, . . . sino de un poder más grande, inexorable, inflexible, tremendo, inconsciente, contra el cual no valen plegarias, ni súplicas, ni bautismos, ni penetencias, ni nada: poder que se actúa, y cuyo efecto se cumple como cualquiera ley mecánica, física o química; como un eclipse, como la caída de un cuerpo, que busca su centro de gravedad, como la combinación de dos substancias, a las que la afinidad obliga a combinarse . . . Este escrúpulo del determinismo fatal nos acibara el deleite estético que la lectura de *Morriña* de otra suerte produciría sin mezcla de acíbar.[79]

So we see that Valera joins with Lorenzo Benito and Blanco García in remarking the inconsistency existing between Pardo's condemnation of determinism in *La Cuestión* and the way she follows its principles in her novels.[80] Neither Catholic nor naturalist himself, Don Juan thoroughly enjoys pointing out how disloyal Pardo has been both to her professed Christianity and to her expressed disapproval of such absolute determinism in literature. Indeed, he seems to think her more naturalistic than she cares to admit. However, his enthusiasm may have carried him away to a certain extent, for he has started his analysis on a wrong assumption. Pardo did not indicate anywhere in her book that Esclavitud had inherited a "temperamento amoroso" from her mother. Valera has forgotten the title and with it the key to the book. He recognized the determinism but failed to put his finger on the source. Naturalistic determinism—as Zola is at pains to explain—is not fatalism; the causes must be accounted for. And Doña Emilia does account for them: it is the *morriña* that makes the comfort of religion of no avail, for from beneath its clouds of melancholy Esclavitud sees herself an outcast even from the love of God. Socially undesirable on earth because of her illegitimate birth, she imagines herself also outside the pale of celestial society, or as she says herself:

—¡Ay! ¡No sé! Desde el primer día dije yo entre mí: si aquí no te quieren, Esclava, es que estás de sobra en el mundo. Ya viniste a él contra la voluntad de Nuestro Señor . . . Ya Dios te miró siempre con malos ojos . . . ¿No lo sabe, señorito? . . .

—¡Si viese como me trabajaba *eso* allá dentro! . . . —articuló con vehemencia la muchacha, abriendo el corazón como si, próxima a desmayarse, desabrochase el corpiño para respirar. —Siempre estoy imaginando: "Esclava, a ti Dios no te puede querer bien. Nunca buena suerte has de tener, nunca. Ya desde que naciste estás en poder del enemigo, y buena gana tiene el enemigo de soltar lo que agarra. Por mucho que te empeñes en ser un ángel, estarás eternamente en pecado mortal. Ya lo tienes de obligación. Para ti no hay padre, ni madre, ni nada menos que vergüenza cuando te pregunten por ellos. Y así, todo lo que hagas te tiene que salir del reves, y si te encariñas con una persona, peor, que Dios te ha de quitar aquel cariño."[81]

The key to the novel is there. Esclavitud's God is an avenger, a visitor of the sins of the fathers upon the children, and she visualizes him as angry with her. Religion offers no comfort. Finding herself alone and among strangers in Madrid, she almost dies of the *morriña*. Transfering to a Galician household, she hopes to find people who will love her a little. Once there, she torments herself because the *señorito* doesn't seem to like her, never speaks to her. Finally, when Doña Aurora, discovering the cause of the servant's melancholy, speaks to her son and gets him to be friendly with the girl, poor Esclava sees the heavens open.

—Sí señor. Cavilando en eso me vinieron unas melancolías muy hondas. Se me metió en la cabeza el *verme*. . . .

—¿El *verme*?

—Le decimos allí así a uno . . . como un bicho, vamos, un gusano, una cavilación, para hablar verdad. Toda la santa noche pasaba a devanar la madeja . . . ¿Qué haré para que me pierda la tema el señorito? ¿Cómo me valdré para darle gusto?

Ello sería . . . o no sería: pero no se puede negar que, después de firmadas las paces con Rogelio, el aspecto exterior de Esclavitud empezó a modificarse completamente. Sus ojos se reanimaron, sus mejillas florecieron, su voz perdió aquel tono dolorido, su conversación fué mas expansiva; y sin alterar en nada sus ocupaciones, varió tanto su manera de desempeñarlas, que si antes parecía víctima resignada del deber, y su silueta tenía algo de aflictivo al proyectarse sobre las paredes de la casa, ahora su ir y venir, su resuelta actividad, la llenaban y regocijaban toda.[82]

Her need for affection makes her yield willingly to the attentions of the *señorito* but when it comes to talk of going to Galicia for the summer, her pessimism returns; she will never see the homeland again, of that she feels sure. In the depths of her despair she can but let Rogelio take everything his brutal young instinct impels him to. And when the last glimpse of his train fades away, the *morriña* claims its victim. Unwanted by God and all the world, she has nothing left to live for and resolves to take her own life that very night.

Doña Emilia has built a story about a certain Galician trait which no doubt she had observed many times. As Doña Aurora soliloquizes after trying unsuccessfully to make the girl reveal the cause of her melancholy:

. . . La muchacha tiene las buenas cualidades de nuestro país, pero no le faltan los defectos. Es humilde, modosa y callada, pero también es algo zorrita, y no hay modo de saber lo que piensa ni lo que le pasa. Las chulapas de por aquí son unas caridelanteras y unas raídas, pero al menos son toros claros. . . .[83]

While the basic general observation which this experimental novel illustrates is the disastrous results of the Galician *morriña,* there is opportunity also for an extremely interesting study of the awakening of sex in an adolescent boy. As Doña Emilia describes it, it is almost exclusively a physical and instinctive thing. Rogelio is a perfect example of a *bête humaine* after the manner of Zola. Few qualms of conscience does he suffer; seldom does he stop to reason with himself. The story of his first love affair is probably the nearest thing to Zola to be found in Pardo Bazán's many treatments of the amorous relationships. By a series of selected quotations I am going to illustrate this point, but first, in order to appreciate Rogelio's temptation, let us have a closer look at the girl:

. . . En señal de contento . . . habíase quitado el pañuelo negro de la cabeza, dejándolo caer negligentemente sobre el cuello, cuya blancura extraordinaria realzaba el contraste con la negra seda. Su cutis era ahora el cutis de las gallegas jóvenes, una tez fresca que parece conservar el brillo de la humedad del suelo nativo, y afrenta, con las nacaradas tintas de las mejillas, la enfermiza palidez de las hijas de Madrid. Sus interesantes ojos verdes, con reflejos amarillentos, acentuaban el carácter primaveral y tierno de

la hermosura de Esclavitud. . . . Pero el adorno que verdaderamente agraciaba a la muchacha era su cabellera rubia, de un
rubio algo tostado, con reflejos de oro que rielaban en lo más
saliente de las simétricas ondulaciones . . . que fluían a uno y otro
lado de la raya, como orla magnífica de la estrecha frente y delicada
sien. . . . Si por la mañana parecía lisa . . . por la mucha agua . . .
al ir corriendo el día y el trajín doméstico, se rebelaba, y fosca y
suave a la vez, formaba al rostro un nimbo, parecido al de las
santas de los retablos viejos. Y es que el tipo de Esclavitud, con
aquel peinado sencillo y aldeano, recordaba las creaciones de la
inconografía mística, . . . a lo cual contribuía su aire modesto,
sus ojos bajos. . . . Cuando miraba de frente, sonriendo, se notaba
la fisonomía de la campesina bajo el anguloso diseño de la virgen.[84]

Although old enough to be in the university, Rogelio is still
very girl shy:

. . . las señoritas eran su meurte: siempre creía que se burlaban
de él . . . que no hacían sino tomarle el pelo, gozarse de su confusión y comentarle luego a solas, con maliciosa . . . ironía. . . .[85]

He is first attracted to Esclavitud "porque le parecía incapaz de
burlarse de nadie." But he is dreadfully insulted when the girl
refuses to classify him among the men she fears:

—Pero y entonces ¿cómo pretende V. mi casa? ¿No ha visto
V. que en ella hay un hombre?
Señaló a Rogelio. . . .
—¿Este señorito es su hijo? . . . Este no es de los hombres que
yo decía. Por ahora es un rapaz.
Demudóse Rogelio como si le hubiesen dirigido el más atroz
insulto. . . .[86]

Now we have the first intimate scene between the boy and girl;
Rogelio has been primed by his mother to make friends with the
servant:

. . . Entró Esclavitud, llevando en una batea de mimbres hasta
media docena de camisas planchadas. Por efecto de la carga, que
le obligaba a levantar los brazos, la muchacha lucía su fino talle y
su andar compasado y armonioso. . . .[87]

A very Zolaesque detail, that, and one which the boy would be
sure to notice. When he pretends to threaten her, note that the
girl's emotions are described by their physical manifestations:

—Vamos a ver cómo están planchaditos estos puños. ¡Si les
encuentro un solo candil!
Al oír la voz del señorito, Esclavitud se había sobresaltado,
figurándose en el primer instante que le regañaban de veras; pero
al levantar los ojos y fijarlos en la cara de Rogelio, comprendió
que se trataba de una broma. Radió en su mirada tan sincera
alegría; se dilató tan visiblemente su pecho; se esponjó de tal
modo, en fin, que las excelentes entrañas del estudiante se con-
movieron. . . .[87]

But it is in their second scene together that Pardo comes the closest to Zola. Rogelio has popped a button off his shirt collar and calls the girl to sew it on for him. He makes a great joke of it, laughing and warning her not to stab him in the jugular vein with the needle. Then, the button all sewed on again, he asks the young servant to tie his necktie for him.

La muchacha tomó la chalina de seda y al rodearla al cuello del señorito, se tropezaron las miradas de los dos. Mientras duraban las otras operaciones no había sucedido semejante cosa, porque Rogelio volvía la cabeza todo cuanto se lo permitían los accesos de risa que le entraban: ahora sí tenía que suceder, pues Esclavitud levantaba el rostro, y Rogelio, más alto, veía por fuerza, tan cerca que le mareaban, las dos pupilas verdes sembradas de puntitas de oro, y la raya del pelo, derecha, angosta y limpia, como surco que parte un campo de madura mies, y la concava frente, tersa y suave, y las venitas azules de las sienes y párpados. El aliento puro de la muchacha subía hasta la boca del estudiante, causándole un principio de embriaguez, como si hubiesen destapado una botella de oxígeno.

Fué asunto de un instante, pero instante en que por la intensidad de la sensación, Rogelio creyó vivir un año. La infancia, con su ligereza de mariposa, sus vagos horizontes de plata y azul, se quedó atrás; y la golosa juventud, la de insaciables labios, surgió tendiéndolos con afán a la copa eterna. La sangre de Rogelio, hasta entonces lenta, enfriada por el clorosis, saltó en las venas con impetuoso hervor, y refluyendo al corazón de golpe, volvió a derramarse por el organismo. Un velo rojo, el que nubla las pupilas del criminal en el momento decisivo, cubrió también los ojos del estudiante, mientras le asaltaba la tentación brutal y furiosa de cerrar los brazos, comerse a besos la linda cabeza y deshacer a achuchones el cuerpo . . . La misma violencia del deseo paralizó su acción, y como Esclavitud había terminado el arreglo de la corbata, cuando Rogelio iba a ceder a la sugestión culpable, la muchacha se desviaba ya, colocándose a distancia conveniente para jugar del efecto del lazo.

Fué como si se interrumpiese la comunicación del alambre con la pila. Rogelio volvió en sí, tan sobrecogido de terror considerando lo que había estado a punto de hacer que sentía enfriarse las manos. "¡Qué atrocidad, Dios mío! . . . ¡qué disgustazo para mi madre!"[88]

That scene speaks for itself, I think; for a few moments there the human beast was in complete control. The whole incident is physical—the girl's pretty blonde head and face so close, the sweetness of her breath, the sudden awakening of desire, only to be broken off by the girl's finishing her task and stepping back. It is a scene worthy of the master of naturalism himself.

The inevitable conflict between desire and decency—or timidity—now follows the initial temptation:

> . . . y en cambio de noche . . . creía tener una obligación . . . de realizar lo que por el día consideraba un atentado y un acto de locura. "Después sí,—pensaba,—que nadie podrá llamarme chiquillo; y yo mismo me convenceré de que no lo soy." . . . Después de dos o tres días de huir de la Esclavitud, ideaba un pretexto para ir a sorprenderla en el cuchitril donde planchaba . . . y una vez allí, no se le ocurrió más que sentarse . . . y engañar a su violento capricho contemplando a la chica que, encendida y sudorosa, encorvado el brazo derecho en arco rígido, hincaba con esfuerzo la plancha en las pecheras o los puños de las camisas. Cuando el ímpetu de abrazarla le acudía muy fuerte, Rogelio se levantaba y refugiábase en su despachito. . . .[89]

Rogelio doesn't argue with himself or engage in battles of conscience, after the manner of a romantic or classic hero. No, it is mainly a question of awakening instincts realistically stronger at night than by sober light of day. There is, too, the desire to appear older warring with the inevitable timidity of an adolescent—a battle of sensations, after all, and that is good naturalism.

Now the hand of chance steps in and makes the mother, Doña Aurora, have a bad fall on the steps. As a result she is quite ill from shock and must keep to her bed for several days under the doctor's care. Esclavitud is obliged to sit up and keep vigil over her mistress. Rogelio, frightened, brings his own mattress into his mother's room, where the pretty servant helps him make up his bed on the floor. The boy goes to sleep, then wakes during the night to find Esclavitud's eyes fixed on him. Whispers ensue and Rogelio persuades her to lie down beside him; they go on conversing in that position. The scene has its possibilities.

> . . . El aliento virginal y fresco de la muchacha se mezcló por segunda vez con el del estudiante; pero le produjo una impresión muy diferente de la primera. Sea que el sustazo de la caída de su madre . . . sea que el lugar . . . no permitiese malas tentaciones, ello es que al tener tan próxima a Esclavitud y tan fácil cualquier desmán, ni se le pasó por las mientes intentarlo, y sólo notó una especie de efusión rara y cariñosa, un movimiento de ternura inexplicable, mientras sus ojos se llenaban de lágrimas. Alargando la mano y apretando con violencia la de la chica, murmuró:
> —Esclava ¡por poco se muere hoy mamá![90]

But the author has fooled us. Although Rogelio is feeling tenderly expansive, the circumstances are not conducive to passion. Instead, he tells the poor girl that if he should lose his mother, she would be all he had left in the world. The boy is in one of those spells of sentimentality so common to adolescence. He doesn't fully realize what he is saying or what his words mean to the young girl, hungry as she is for affection.

> . . . No se encontraba en estado de medir la trascendencia y efecto de sus palabras, ni menos sospechaba que la sensibilidad y la bondad pueden ser en determinadas ocasiones más funestas que la cólera y el odio. En su emoción había mucho de nervioso, y las frases salían de sus labios provocadas por una reacción del susto de la mañana. . . .
>
> . . . Viendo que no le producía Esclavitud las malas tentaciones de otras veces, pensaba que su cariño, se había depurado, y que aquel juego anómalo era lo más inocente del mundo. O para decir toda verdad: estaba en una crisis de sentimiento, y ni pensaba ni medía sus promesas y afirmaciones. . . .[91]

Doña Aurora regains her health and soon discovers what is afoot in her house. Arrangements are made and steps taken. Esclavitud is to work elsewhere during the summer; Rogelio and mother are going to Galicia. It is in a mood of despairing, dumb devotion that the poor girl goes to the boy's room on the last night. Rogelio tries to cheer her up; then,

> Con el movimiento de un niño que pide halagos, acercó su mejilla a la boca de Esclavitud, y ésta, sin protesta alguna, como el que ejecuta una acción hija de la costumbre, puso en ella los labios. Estaban como las palmas, secos y ardientes, y a Rogelio le pareció que le arrancaban la piel . . . Corrió bastante tiempo—y el mismo no acertaría a explicar el por qué de esta tardanza, anómala si se examina bien lo incitante de la hora y sitio y la ceguera de los pocos años—antes que se le despertase una sed criminal y ardiente. Cuando la embriaguez le ofuscó, saltó de la cama y fué a dar vuelta a la llave de la lámpara, sin conseguir por eso oscuridad completa, pues un rayo de luna primaveral, entrando por la vidriera del despacho, lo bañaba en luz fantástica, azulada y soñadora. Al recobrar, entre la pálida penumbra, los labios donde la fuerza de la ilusión juvenil le movía a creer que se dejaba presa el alma a cada respiración del aliento, ya no los soltó, ni acaso los soltaría aunque viese allí a su madre, que representaba para él el Deber. . . .[92]

Surely, of all the books analyzed so far, it is in *Morriña* that Doña Emilia comes nearest to imitating the all-pervading *volupté* to be found in Zola's pages. The descriptions are more sensuous and the love scenes more frankly portrayed. The girl is the victim of her *morriña* and both she and the boy respond to their instincts like the unthinking young human animals they are.

Morriña is one of those *drames intimes*, such as *Une Page d'Amour, Le Rêve,* or *La Joie de vivre,* which Zola was wont to sandwich in between his bolder works dedicated to larger environments. *Morriña* is not therefore any the less a true experimental novel. The general truth observed concerns the tragic effect of the peculiar Galician melancholia on a young girl. The author's documentation also included the study of awakening sex life in a young man. The characters of the second plan are interesting as types but only serve as background, despite their intense reality, remarked by Don Juan Valera. All the forces that enter the book are well balanced and accounted for. The determinism, as Valera observed, is strong and there is present the naturalistic tendency to place more emphasis on the physical as a motive force than upon reason or free will. The little novel is naturalistic from cover to cover.

La Piedra Angular (1891)

La Piedra Angular is a novel built around the problems of an executioner named Juan Rojo. In true naturalistic fashion Pardo Bazán recounts the determining forces which have combined to produce this central character. The development of these background forces could have constituted the whole body and meat of the novel. Instead, Doña Emilia has preferred to let Juan Rojo tell his own story in the space of twenty pages. His autobiography begins with the startling revelation that he originally studied for the priesthood. Although he was a good student at the seminary, we learn that the bishop refused him a chaplainship upon graduation. Disappointed in this respect, he then turns his education to use and becomes a schoolmaster. The school is forced to close, and soon after, Rojo is drafted into the army, where he serves three years, rising by virtue of intelligence and obedience to the rank of sergeant. His term of service completed, he turns again to school teaching. All would have been well, relates Juan Rojo, had he not fallen in love—completely so, as a man does who has never had much to do with women. Once married, he not only found the pay insufficient but there was even difficulty in collecting what pay was due him. In these dire straits, he accepts a position as a sort of constable used by the victorious Republicans to brutalize and sack the dwellings of the Carlist priests and other opposition sympathizers. Rojo was always very careful to get his orders in writing, so that he could rest assured of not being responsible for his acts. Later he was made tax gatherer or extortioner of political contributions by the Restoration. By then he had two children to support, so he could not afford to be too particular as to his occupations. Furthermore, all was perfectly legal and honorable. Rojo does not believe he has ever done anything at all censurable; he is as honest as the next man:

> Pero yo no sería comisionado de apremios si fuese una mala acción. . . . Yo, ni en ésa ni en las demás acciones de vida he faltado, porque sé muy bien qué es delito y qué no es delito, y podría ahora mismo someter a un juez todos mis actos, seguro de que no tendría por qué avergonzarme. Yo soy honrado a carta cabal; yo, si encuentro en la calle millones, los devuelvo a su dueño; yo respeto como el que más lo que debe respetarse; pero era cuestión de dar de comer a la familia . . . y serví al Estado, lo mismo que lo servía, pongo por caso, el Delegado de Hacienda. . . .[93]

Trained in the army to obey unquestioningly and forced by economic necessity to accept whatever work offered itself, Rojo not unnaturally came to believe that anything commanded legally is justifiable in the agent. Nevertheless he shrank at the suggestion he become an executioner and claimed to have been tricked into it. Out of work and with a hungry family on his hands, the position offered a steady income until he could find something else; meanwhile, they assured him, he would probably never have to discharge his duties—murders were very rare. . . . But the time did come and, faced with the threat of torture for refusing to obey, he considered that he had no choice but to go through with the odious business. Then began the social ostracism, the estrangement with his wife, her desertion, the habit of drinking *caña* to forget, and the consequent liver trouble and consultation with Dr. Moragas, to whom he tells his life story.

Plainly this brief biographical sketch could form the nucleus for a whole novel. The mystery is why Pardo crams all these interesting facts into a twenty-page conversation between Juan and the doctor, instead of expanding them in accord with their possibilities. Zola would have jotted down this much merely as a preliminary sketch and then by utilizing his documentary notes—taken in the course of mingling with men like Rojo—he would have given us a complete picture of the forces which produced and enslaved the executioner of Marineda. But perhaps the mystery is not so great when we consider that as an aristocrat and a pillar of society it would have been most difficult for Pardo Bazán to obtain her documentation in the true Zola man-

ner. Could a nineteenth-century lady of her social standing rub
shoulders with the local executioner, a man shunned and ab-
horred by the lowest of the low? Plainly it would be more practical to obtain his life story from one of her lawyer friends, and
this is precisely what she seems to have done. Indeed, to prove
that her documentation was largely bookish we need go no further than her own admission: "Para *La Piedra angular,* repito,
solicité datos y libros de personas que cultivan la antropología
jurídica; tuvieron la bondad de facilitármelos, yo procuré ser-
virme de ellos como Dios me dió a entender para fines artísticos."[94]

Instead, then, of building her novel about Juan Rojo's past,
she prefers to limit her story to a crisis in his life. Already as
the story opens Rojo's wife has left him and his only child,
Telmo, is in trouble. The boy is already feeling the ostracism
surrounding his father. None of the city's schools will admit
him and the other children are reluctant to have anything to do
with him. One day as he stands on the edge of a group of boys
mutely hoping they will let him join their play, the leader of the
group has a bright idea. He offers to let Telmo come with them
to the beach on condition that he is to obey like a soldier and do
what they tell him bravely. Once there it develops that Telmo
is to defend a ruined castle on the seashore against the stoning
assault of the gang of boys. Telmo welcomes the chance to show
his courage and worthiness to be accepted as an equal. The ad-
vantage is first of all with the defender as several of the be-
siegers are hit in the shins by the sure aim of the executioner's
son. But they dare him to stop dodging behind the parapets and
stand out in the open. Telmo had loyally observed the stone-
thrower's code of aiming only at the legs, but the attackers had
no such scruples with respect to this pariah's son. They aim for
the head and Telmo falls wounded from the wall. Finding him
pale, bleeding, and unconscious, the boys are afraid and run off.
Fear of the boy's father and of the police prevents their report-
ing the incident. The neighbors, however, discover the boy and
relay the news by Rojo's servant. The executioner goes and
brings his boy home in his arms. Being a mother herself, Doña
Emilia understands children and the siege on the beach is one
of the most effectively presented incidents in *La Piedra Angular.*

The aristocratic world of Doña Emilia makes contact with
Juan Rojo through the person of idealistic Dr. Moragas. With-

out revealing who he was, the executioner had already consulted the doctor about his liver trouble on the morning before Telmo's injury. Realizing too late that he had just taken money from the *verdugo*, Moragas had thrown the silver *duros* out the window, vowing to have no further dealings with Rojo. Imagine his chagrin, then, upon being summoned to the latter's house to care for the injured youngster. At first he refuses; it is only by much pleading that they persuade him to have a look at the boy. Later his deep-seated quixotism leads him to take an interest in Rojo as a *caso moral.* It is to him, then, as we have seen, that the executioner tells his life story.

Dr. Moragas seems to have been a real person whom Pardo Bazán knew. Indeed, she has evidently put a number of her *contertulianos* into the story. Her contemporary, Leopoldo Pedreira, upon reviewing the book thinks it a veritable *roman à clef* :

> El Dr. Moragas . . . este doctor existe y es un muy venerable y querido pariente del autor de estas líneas.
> Nené lleva en sus venas algunas gotas de mi misma sangre. En Cáñamo creo reconocer un antiguo contertuliano de la Señora Pardo Bazán.
> Sepa, pues, el curioso que los personajes de *La Piedra Angular*, como los de la famosa novela *Pequeñeces* andan aun por el mundo. . . .[95]

No doubt the pros and cons of capital punishment had been discussed and argued vigorously in the lady's own *tertulia* and so she put the same people with the same arguments into her book. There was no documentary problem as long as she stayed on this level of society.

But when it came to Juan Rojo's drinking companions, what to do? It seems obvious that here again her documentation is bookish. There are at least two cases of alcoholism which seem to have come directly out of Zola's *L'Assommoir*. There is a parallel to Coupeau, whom drink made good-natured and easygoing to the point of tolerating a *ménage à trois,* and there is also a parallel to *le père Bijart,* who was so brutalized by drink that he beat his little daughter, Lalie. Here we see Juan Rojo comfortably playing cards with his only three friends, friends low enough in the social scale to pardon whatever a man may have to do *por el pan* :

> Los cuatro jugadores de brisca eran cuatro ejemplares del alcoholismo muy diferentes entre sí. Casi deberíamos descontar uno, el especiero tabanero Rufiano. Este no bebía más caña de la necesaria para impulsar a los otros . . . —Marcos Leira era el

> ser abyecto conducido por la bebida a la atrofia del sentimento
> del honor popular (tan enérgico como el caballeresco) . . . y capaz
> ya hasta de soltar un chiste cuando, no recatándose de él, garraba
> el teniente a la hojalatera por la talle. Antiojos el beodo brutal,
> en quien el alcohol despertaba el sordo impulso de la locura
> sanguinaria . . . En cuanto a Juan Rojo . . . el no le pedía sino
> olvido. . . .[96]

And if the reader is not yet convinced of the parallelism, let him
look closer:

> A Marcos Leira, el hojalatero, le daba el vino por distinto
> lado: por el buen humor y la sandunga. Si a la mañanita, antes
> de matar al gusano, solía vérsele alicaído, con una murria siniestra,
> en diciendo que se echaba al cuerpo el primer vasito de caña rubia
> y melosa . . . ya estaba el honrado Marcos lo mismo que unas
> pascuas de alegre, y suave como el terciopelo con su esposa y sus
> chiquitines . . . Entonces no sólo se mostraba decidor, cariñoso,
> galante, sino que se tumbaba en la cama o salía, dejando en paz
> a Concha y al oficial, que trabajaban mucho más solos. Las malas
> lenguas se despachaban a su gusto comentando la inclinación de la
> bella hojalatera a zafarse de su esposo; pero tal vez fuese exceso
> de malicia el roer los zancajos a la mujer del borrachín, puesto
> que su tienda y tráfico andaban lucidísimos, dirigidos por ella,
> que, siempre limpia y repeinada, semejaba una reina entre tanta
> alcuza, regadera, colador, reverbero, linterna, y palangana, ful-
> gentes como la plata bruñida. . . .[97]

Does not this picture recall Gervaise, cheerful and efficient in
the midst of her laundry shop, while Coupeau is out boozing and
Lentier sits in the sun reading the paper—and not above taking
his share in the *ménage à trois* from time to time? And Coupeau
also was cheerful and obliging to Lentier; indeed, was it not he
who suggested that his wife's old flame move in with them?

> . . . Si on conservait de la rancune après des neuf ans et des dix
> ans, on finirait par ne plus voir personne. Non, non, il avait le
> coeur sur la main, lui! D'abord il savait à qui il avait affaire, à
> une brave femme et à un brave homme à deux amis, quoi! Il était
> tranquille, il connaissait leur honnêteté. . . .
> —Faut rester ici, ma vieille, si le coeur t'en dit . . . On s'ar-
> rangera. . . .
> Et il expliqua que la chambre du linge sale, nettoyée, ferait
> une jolie pièce. . . .
> —Non, non, dit Lentier. . . .[98]

Now as for the child-beater, Antiojos, while not as brutal as *le
père Bijart* in *L'Assommoir*, still by his blows he finally accounts
for the death of his daughter. Here is the first mention of this
case of alcoholism:

> . . . La hija menor, raquítica, que no había conseguido aun el

suspirado ingreso en la Granera, se dedicaba a "preparar labor" a su respetable papá, cuyo taller consistía en una de las barracas que a manera de rojos hongos pululan a la sombra del Cuartel de Infantería. . . . Allí se pasaba la vida la mísera segundona de Antiojos, esperando la problemática llegada de un parroquiano para correr a avisar al remendón, que solía recibirla con malas palabras, y mucho peores obras. Mientras no aparecía el parroquiano, la muchacha, que, por tener desgracia en todo hasta había recibido en la pila el feo nombre de Orosia, no estaba ciertamente mano sobre mano o dándose aire con el abanico. Ella remojaba la suela; ella la batía sobre la chata piedra, estropeándose las rodillas; ella señalaba con el punzón las distancias del clavillo; ella cosía el material; ella enceraba el hilo y recortaba y engrudaba las plantillas; ella abría los ojales, y cuando Antiojos llegaba despidiendo rayos por la inflamada nariz y los encandilados ojos, apenas tenía ya que hacer sino lo indispensable para no perder la dignidad del *maestro*, la cual se cifraba especialmente *en la forma*, es decir en la hormaza de madera donde encajaba la bota o zapato que debía restaurar.

—¡Cabra, vaca sucia, malditona!—solía decir a Orosia en su pintoresco lenguaje.

—¡Como me toques a la forma . . . te estripo!

Y la sin ventura Orosia lo ejecutaba todo . . . menos tocar a la forma, que era por lo visto la misteriosa clave del arte zapateril.[99]

To be sure, Pardo seems to have documented herself on the shoemaker's art and enjoys showing off her knowledge of technical terms; but it seems to have been love's labor lost, for she does not again mention the drunken shoemaker or his daughter until some two hundred and thirty pages farther on, when we witness the death of Orosia:

"Venga, venga aquí, don Pelayo," detuvieron, mal de su grado, al médico, que pretendía escurrirse. —Llegóse, y rompiendo por entre la multitud, vió en el suelo a una muchacha probremente vestida, fea, desmedrada, raquítica, de rostro azulado mejor que pálido: la sostenían dos caritativas mujeres, y ella, con los ojos cerrados y sumidos, entreabierta la boca, hundida la nariz, respiraba congojosamente, o más bien arqueaba; Moragas reconoció desde el primer instante el estertor preagónico.

—Es Orosia, la hija del borrachón de Antiojos, un zapatero de viejo que trabaja en esa barraca que V. ve; mejor dicho, quien trabajaba era la chica; el padre no hace más que andar empalmando curdas . . . La hija tuvo ayer por la mañana un vómito de sangre, y—(aquí guiñó un ojo el agente) debió de ser de algún golpe *mal dado* que el bruto del padre le pegaría en el estómago con la *forma*, porque lo tenía de costumbre . . . Y dice que esta madrugada la oyeron quejarse mucho las vecinas, porque

el padre la hizo venir por fuerza al trabajo, y la infeliz no podía
con su alma. . . . Ahora la encontramos así . . . ¿Qué hacemos?[100]

It is obvious that these exemplary cases of alcoholism were, if
not directly lifted from Zola, at least based very closely on the
more extensive studies portrayed by him in *L'Assommoir*. She
seems to have taken out of Zola the two incidents—the drunkard
as complacent cuckold and the drunkard as child-beater—and
transplanted them into her book without caring much whether
or not they took root there. The incidents are very short and
seem superimposed. There is not even a conversation recorded
between Juan Rojo and any of these people. They are merely
backdrops, ready-made stage props, as it were, borrowed from
another production to lend atmosphere to her play.

The story of an executioner could hardly be brought to a
climax without a murder in Marineda—and so Doña Emilia introduces one. Dr. Moragas witnesses the odd procession as a
calm, slight little female figure is led through the streets to jail.
Later he learns from the newspapers that she and her lover had
conspired to kill her husband. Apparently they had killed him
in his sleep, then carted the corpse to a woods near town and
split his head open with an ax. All of this remains second-hand
and impersonal. We never know the principals of the crime at
close quarters. We just hear the friends of Moragas (and of
Pardo) argue the pros and cons of capital punishment in the
local Casino. Moragas serves as *raisonneur* for the author in
being opposed to the supreme penalty. Finally the boring arguments of the Casino friends come to an end, the girl is condemned to die by the *garrote,* and Moragas goes to see her in
jail. The good doctor lets his kindness run away with him and
succeeds in cheering up the girl by promising her that she will
be pardoned. Time passes. Even the most rabid upholders of
capital punishment finally telegraph Madrid beseeching pardon
for the murderess, but none is forthcoming. The doctor's daughter, Nené, is sick and recovers. Finally, Telmo, the executioner's
son, appears one day in the fall and Moragas remembers his
promise to get the boy into a school. He also remembers his
promise to the poor girl in jail. The upshot is another visit to
Juan Rojo in which Moragas seeks to strike a bargain with the
verdugo. He will adopt Telmo and educate him if Rojo will re-
fuse to execute the woman prisoner.

This is quite an effective scene. Telmo is all Rojo has left in the world. He loves him and does not want to lose him. But the doctor easily shows him that the boy himself is enchanted at the prospect of going to live with Dr. Moragas. Rojo gives his word that he will not execute and lets Telmo go with the doctor. But he cannot face the ordeal of holding out against all the forces of justice which, he feels, really have a claim on his services. The good doctor thought he was saving Rojo too from a life of degradation. Instead, the executioner commits suicide by jumping off a high cliff into the sea, taking with him the instruments of his trade.

The deterministic forces which produced Juan Rojo have worked out to their logical conclusion, for no doubt drink, despair, ostracism, and the break-up of his family would ultimately have led him to suicide even had there been no Dr. Moragas to attempt an intervention. *La Piedra Angular* could have been a first-rate novel in the hands of a more able author, who undoubtedly would not have devoted fifty per cent of the novel to Dr. Moragas and his friends. Instead he would have given us greater documentation in the lives of *les basses classes*. The principals of the murder trial would have been real people with motivation well worked out, and the result would have been far more convincing as to the injustice and barbarism of executions. While Doña Emilia's novel is basically naturalistic, it suffers so much from inadequate documentation that most readers no doubt will consider the book a mere thesis novel. Rather than go so far as that, I would call it a naturalistic novel suffering from two defects: namely, insufficient documentation and a superabundance of uninteresting upper-class personages drawn from the author's own circle of friends. *La Piedra Angular* emphasizes the comment of Leopoldo Alas that Pardo Bazán would find it difficult to be a thorough-going naturalist *por ser quien era*. Nevertheless, this novel deserves a place in the list of books written according to the Zola formula and we can perhaps forgive its imperfections in view of the superlative success achieved by the Countess in other more thorough-going naturalistic studies such as *Loz Pazos de Ulloa, La Madre Naturaleza,* and *Morriña.*

V

OTHER PARALLELS TO ZOLA IN PARDO BAZÁN

I have analyzed the six most perfectly naturalistic novels that Pardo Bazán wrote. She published others which are partially naturalistic, and in practically all of them one may find at least traces of naturalism. But to analyze the degree of influence exercised by Zola's formula on each of Doña Emilia's many other novels would be endless and unneccessary. That she followed the formula of the experimental novel so closely in six of her works would in itself be enough to establish influence. But it was not only in literary theory that the Spanish author was influenced by her French master. From him she took ideas for sub-plots, such as the cases of alcoholism in *La Piedra Angular,* and ideas for main plots, as in *La Madre Naturaleza.* It is with this latter form of direct influence that this chapter will largely concern itself. I wish to show that, while Emilia Pardo wrote only six novels in complete conformity to Zola's ideas, his influence may be seen in her work as late as *La Quimera* (1905) —fourteen years after *La Piedra Angular,* her last experimental novel.

Furthermore, a point which I wish to emphasize throughout is the essential realism of Pardo's temperament. This realism or truth-worship is manifest in all her work. It is undoubtedly what first attracted her to naturalism, and it is the key by which we may reveal the basic unity of a novelistic work which to the superficial observer appears most varied, even eclectic, in character. To show further parallels to Zola and to show the qualities in the great Spanish novelist which made her appreciate him will be the purpose of this chapter. Often the parallels themselves reveal these qualities.

In my discussion of *La Madre Naturaleza* I established its debt to Zola's book, *La Faute de l'Abbé Mouret.* That is one of the most poetic and romantic books the French author ever wrote. The mere fact that Pardo admired it shows she had the capacity to appreciate poetry. But when she came to imitate it, did she preserve the poetry? Only partially. Her tree of knowledge is a lonesome oak, drawing its strength from the bones of long departed Roman soldiers. That is a poetic idea, but anyone will admit that her tree is far more realistic than

Zola's forest giant with its bursting sap and tropical growth. Six years before she wrote *La Madre,* Pardo had already attempted an imitation of one of the descriptions in *La Faute.* This occurs in *Un Viaje de novios* (1881). There is a beautiful love scene in *La Faute* which Zola places in a rose garden. He lyrically compares the roses of various shapes and ages to beautiful women of all types and experience. Albine herself is like a fresh young rose. The scene struck a responsive chord in Doña Emilia, but we shall see what happens to it in passing through her hands. Here is Zola's passage:

> ... Les roses avaient leur façon d'aimer. Les uns ne consentaient qu'à entre-bailler leur bouton, très timides, le coeur rougissant, pendant que d'autres, le corset délacé, pantelantes, grandes ouvertes, semblaient chiffonées, folles de leurs corps au point d'en mourir. Il y en avait de petites, alertes, gaies, ... d'énormes ... avec des rondeurs de sultanes engraissées, ... d'honnêtes, décolletées en bourgeoises correctes; d'aristocrates, d'une élégance souple, d'une originalité permise, inventant des déshabillés. Les roses épanouies en coupe offraient leur parfum comme dans un cristal précieux; les roses renversées en forme d'urne le laissaient couler goute à goute . . .; les roses en bouton serraient leurs feuilles, ne livraient encore que le soupir vague de leur virginité.
> —Je t'aime, je t'aime, répétait Serge à voix basse.
> Et Albine était une grande rose, une des roses pales, ouvertes du matin ... Elle sentait bon, elle tendait des lèvres qui offraient dans une coupe de corail leur parfum faible encore. . . .[1]

Here is Pardo's adaptation:

> ... El jardinete que formaba el peristilo era una gentil confusión de rosas de todos tonos y tamaños. Las *Malmaison* decollaban rosadas y turgentes, como un hermoso seno; las té se deshacían, dejando pender sus desmayados pétalos; las de Alejandría, erguidas y elegantes, vertían su copa de esencia embriagadora; las musgosas reían irónicas con sus labios de carmín, al través de una barba tupida y verde; las albas desafiaban a la nieve con su fría y cándida belleza, con su rigidez púdica de flores de batista. Y entre sus lindas hermanas, la exótica viridiflora ocultaba sus capullos glaucos, como avergonzándose del extraño color alagartado de sus flores, de su fealdad de planta rara, interesante tan sólo para el botánico.[2]

To complete the parallel, as Zola had compared Albine to a freshly opened rose, so Pardo earlier in her book had referred to her heroine thus:

> ... La imagen más adecuada para representar a Lucía era la de un capullo de rosa muy cerrado, muy gallardo, defendido por pomposas hojas verdes; erguido sobre recio tronco.[3]

Now notice this difference. In the first place, Pardo is not describing a love scene among the roses. The garden is merely part of the setting to the house which the newlyweds are to rent in Vichy. And to be truly naturalistic the Spanish author shows off her documentation by giving us all the technical names of the roses. The parallel continues in the personification of the roses. But, here again, which is the more realistic, which the least poetic? Pardo's version, obviously. Much of the original's lyricism was lost in the imitation through a lack of personal interest. There was no one in the rose garden when Pardo described it. She succeeds better when she puts Lucía on the balcony to smell the roses:

> En el jardín, las rosas, embriagadas del calor bebido durante la mañana entera, se deshacían en perfumes; hasta las frías rosas blancas tenían mátices rancios, como de carne pálida, pero carne al fin. De todo el coro de aromas se formaba uno solo, penetrante, fuertísimo, que se subía a la cabeza, como si fuera la fragancia de una rosa no más, pero rosa enorme, encendida, que exhalaba de su boca de púrpura hálito fascinador y mortal. . . .[4]

This passage approaches Zola in sensuousness, but still the imitation remains less poetic and more matter-of-fact than the original.

Now what qualities of the Countess' character can we deduce from this parallel alone? For one thing, she was enthusiastic enough over Zola's beautiful scene to attempt an imitation. This shows poetic appreciation. But when she did imitate, her picture was closer to what a camera would have seen. It is the old quality of common sense balance which made her *Cuestión palpitante* a masterpiece, the same clear, unwarped sense of the real which often makes her novels seem more realistic than those of Zola himself. It was the essentially realistic temperament of Pardo Bazán which responded to the literary tenets of naturalism, and it was that same balanced temperament which prevented her achieving the lyrical flights of the master of Médan— much as she admired them.

After *Un Viaje* came *La Tribuna*, and after that, in 1885, appeared *El Cisne de Vilamorta*. This work owes so little to Zola that I did not include it in my list of experimental novels to be analyzed. Nevertheless, the book is essentially realistic, if not naturalistic in the Zola sense, and the prologue has some interesting material for our study:

> Parece que no necesita refutación el error de los que parten en dos mitades la realidad sensible e inteligible, con la misma frescura

que si partiesen una naranja, y ponen en la una mitad todo lo
grosero, obsceno y sucio, escribiendo encima *naturalismo*, y en la
otra, y bajo el título de *idealismo*, agrupan lo delicado, suave y
poético. Pues tan errónea idea pertenece al número de las insidu-
osas vulgaridades que podemos calificar de telarañas del juicio,
que no hay escoba que consiga barrerlas bien, ni nunca se destie-
rran por completo. Es probable que hasta el fin del mundo dure
esta telaraña espesa y artificiosa, y se juzgue muy *idealista* la
descripción de una noche de luna y muy *naturalista* la de una
fábrica; muy *idealista* el estudio de la agonía de un ser humano
(sobre todo si muere de tisis como *La Dama de las Camelias*) y
muy *naturalista* el nacimiento del mismo ser![5]

The Swan of Vilamorta is himself a young poet of somewhat
romantic turn of mind and the novel deals with a certain brief
section of his life. In her prologue Doña Emilia tries to circum-
vent any possible criticism to the effect that she is offering the
public a more "idealistic" book in order to atone for her sins
in writing such a crudely frank novel as *La Tribuna*. In the
passage quoted she ironically pokes fun at the popular tendency
to classify the beautiful as idealistic and the ugly as naturalistic.
Doña Emilia implies, however, that merely because her subject
matter in the *Swan of Vilamorta* may be prettier, it is not any
the less real. All levels of reality are available to the artist for
portrayal. The essential is that the portrayal be a true one,
regardless of subject matter.

Lorenzo Benito, in commenting on this novel, maintains that
all of Pardo's remarks in the prologue might just as well have
been left unsaid, for even the novel's chief protagonist does not
seem to him to be a romantic type at all.[6] On the contrary, he
finds the Swan to be quite a prosaic person, as are most of the
other personages in the book. Being convinced of the realism
with which these pseudo-romantic characters are portrayed, he
goes on to assert that this novel of Pardo's is as naturalistic as
the others. But I believe Benito is mistaken. At least, the book
is not naturalistic after the manner of Zola. If it is an experiment, it proves nothing. If there is a theme, it is merely the
character of the Swan himself. Zola's novels prove something
and are never based on the study of one character. However,
the novels of those other naturalists, the de Goncourts, usually
study a section of the life of one person, and perhaps this one
work of Pardo's owes more to their influence than to Zola. Be
that as it may, we see that in *El Cisne* Pardo continues to maintain her right to portray reality on all levels. It may have been

her own matter-of-factness which made the romantic figure of the Swan of Vilamorta turn prosaic in her hands.

In the same year in which *El Cisne* appeared, 1885, a collection of short stories was published under the title of *La Dama joven.* Some of the tales were definitely naturalistic; others, of Catholic inspiration, were mystical and idealistic. In the prologue to the collection Pardo says in defense of this variety:

> . . . Yo sé que todas son *verdad,* con la diferencia de darse en la esfera práctica, que llamamos de los hechos, o en otra no menos real, la del alma. Vida es la vida orgánica, y vida también la psíquica, y tan cierta la impresión que me produce un Nazareno o una Virgen, como los crudos detalles de *La Tribuna,* o las rusticidades de *Bucólica.* Reclamo todo para el arte, pido que no se destaque su vasto reino, que no se mutile su cuerpo sagrado, que sea lícito pintar la materia, el espíritu, la tierra y el cielo.
>
> Para explicar como esta teoría no es un eclecticismo de ancha manga . . . necesitaría yo ahora doblar el tamaño del prólogo. . . .[7]

She here puts into words what she implied in the prologue to *El Cisne*—anything is admissible so long as it is true and is not distorted or idealized in the sense of exaggeration.

After the *Swan of Vilamorta* come four experimental novels —already analyzed—bringing us up to 1890 and the publication of the sequel novels, *Una Cristiana* and *La Prueba.* These are products of the Catholic or mystic side of Pardo's nature, which contributed its share to the collection, *La Dama joven.* The use of the first person would exclude them from classification as experimental novels a la Zola. They seem to represent a temporary reaction against naturalism and are often classed as psychological novels. There has been much adverse comment on their merits as literature, and with most of this criticism I am in entire sympathy. Some critics profess to see in them the beginnings of Pardo's later manner as typified in *La Quimera* (1905) and *La Sirena negra* (1908). Inasmuch as the latter two novels both end in the conversion of the protagonist, there may be some basis for this belief. In any case, these novels of 1890, being inferior in quality and mystical in tendency, can have little significance for our study.

After *La Piedra Angular* (1891), last of the novels in the true Zola formula, came *Doña Milagros* (1894) and *Memorias de un solterón* (1896). They are sequel novels and would have been better examples of naturalism had not Pardo elected to write in the first person. They have a theme which suggests elements in

Zola's work. The two novels are built around the social downfall of an old Galician family from nobility to middle class to
working class. The cause of this downfall is to be found in the
great number of daughters in the family. The books have therefore a feministic tendency, for we have the picture of a little
old widower in reduced circumstances, with eleven daughters
on his hands—every one of them a liability! Spanish society
has no place for them except as wives to suitable husbands. The
latter are nowhere to be found. To work would be to break
caste and become of the common people. Dilemma! One of the
girls is independent, a modern woman. She finally gets tutoring
work about town. In the end all the daughters go to work and
everyone is happy. The two novels are feministic and progressive. They preach the gospel of work, and in doing so, reflect at
least one of the tendencies to be found in Zola, especially in his
later novels.

After 1896, Pardo amused herself with *novelas novelescas*
such as *El Tesoro de Gastón, Saludo de las brujas,* and others,
until 1905 and *La Quimera.* This is a work which will bear
much scrutiny, from the standpoint of literary merit and of the
amount of Zola's influence thereon. The basic idea unquestion-
ably came from Zola's *L'Oeuvre,* i.e., to write ostensibly the
story of an artist's struggles and actually to set forth beneath
that cover one's own literary and aesthetic ideals and conflicts.
And just as the French author personified himself in the character, Sandoz, so in Minia Dumbria the Countess of Pardo Bazán enters her own story. The novel moves in three different
milieux. There is the country place in the interior of Galicia,
the gay society life of Madrid, and the life of the Spanish colony
in Paris—exactly the three *milieux* among which Pardo Bazán
divided her year. Minia's Galician estate, the *Alborada,* is none
other than Doña Emilia's *Meirás;* even the gruesome incident in
which Minia shows Silvio Lago her empty sepulchre is autobiographic; as her intimate friend, Blanca de los Ríos remarks:

En la capilla de su Castillo de Meirás hizo construir su sepulcro; aquel sepulcro *vacío,* cuya contemplación me escalofrió,
como a *Silvio Lago,* dictó a la que ha de ocuparlo pronto una de
las más vibrantes páginas de *La Quimera,* y es otro testimonio
palpable de aquella constante memoria de *La Intrusa,* que inspiró
tantas páginas de *La Sirena negra, La Quimera* y los cuentos de
la gloriosa escritora.[8]

And that Minia, like Sandoz in Zola's book, is often the author's *raisonneur* is clearly recognized by Doña Blanca:

> No, no conozco escritor—al menos de los nuestros—que, sin un solo alarde de *virtuosismo*—ya lo dice ella por boca de Minia Dumbria, que expresa su credo estético en todo—, haya dado tan viviente y completa impresión de la realidad y tan alta sensación del misterio de belleza del Arte.[9]

But the autobiographical material in the book is not confined to the one character, Minia Dumbria; as Blanca de los Ríos goes on to say:

> Quien, iniciado en la intimidad espiritual y estética de Emilia, y empapado en su magna obra, leyese *La Quimera*, sentiríase como anegado en el triple existencia de la autora: entre la Naturaleza, la vida social y el ensueño estético; entre la vida inquieta, vanidosa, frívola de la alta sociedad de Madrid . . .; y contrastando con este tumultuoso vivir . . . el otro pleno y sano vivir de Emilia en su *Alborada*, en su Meirás, en su Galicia, cuya húmeda tierra . . . cuyo ambiente neblinoso . . . cuyo bravo mar . . . se paladean y aspiran en estas páginas en que la autora que, como Minia, supo *apoderarse de la región*, se volcó entera; y uniendo a estas dos vidas hallamos la otra, la del Arte, tan intensamente vivida por Emilia, simbolizada en *Silvio Lago*, "el mal de aspirar," y en *Minia Dumbria*, "la aspiración lograda"; sin que falte la personificación del amor humano romántico y exaltado hasta la inmolación, que, herido por el desengaño, se vuelve a Dios y se trueca en amor místico: la *Ayamonte*. . . .[10]

The hint that Pardo might have been disappointed in love is interesting. One wishes Doña Blanca had given us more details. In any case, we have her authority that there is much of the autobiographic in Silvio Lago, the young artist who chases the Chimera. Silvio is Pardo young and Minia is Pardo old. Of the two, Minia is the closer picture, for Silvio after all is a character in his own right. In the same way Zola, while putting himself bodily in the character of Sandoz, still put much of himself into the struggles of Claude to attain artistic perfection.

That great picture of the Isle de la Cité, which was to have been Claude's masterpiece, is symbolic of Zola's work itself. There was the clear reality of the banks of the Seine, of Notre Dame in the background, of the busy life of Paris all around— and yet in the middle of the river, poised on her shallop's bow as if to dive, is that nude female form, spoiling the realistic effect, and symbolizing the lust and desire of the great metropolis. And through all of Zola's novels—coloring, warming, poeticizing his carefully documented reality—runs the strong undercurrent of sensuality, of sexual desire and passion. As Claude soon tired of his flesh-and-blood mistress and went back to caressing with his brushes the nude figures of his imagination, so Zola was content to live an ostensibly respectable life, satisfying his sex more and more completely by drawing caressingly voluptuous word pictures of the buxom females who fill his novels. And ever his passion would carry him into poetic exaggeration, marring the clear-cut picture of reality that was his ideal; never did he quite attain that style like *"Un beau marbre"*—destined to present a dispassionate picture, beautiful in its truth alone.

Similarly, Silvio, starting out as a realist wanting to paint nature and people as they are, and yearning ever for the time when he will no longer have to paint idealized portraits for a living, finally finds that pure reality is not for him. The difference lies in the fact that Zola's Claude never became reconciled to the way in which he idealized reality. In a moment of lucidity he is horrified by the work of his hands; the girl in the boat, instead of becoming more real, has grown into a sort of heathen idol:

> Qui donc venait de peindre cette idole d'une religion inconnue? Qui l'avait faite de métaux, de marbres, et de gemmes, épanouissant la rose de son sexe, entre les colonnes précieuses des cuisses, sous la voûte sacrée du ventre? Etait-ce lui qui, sans le savoir, était l'ouvrier de ce symbole du désir insatiable, de cette image extra-humaine de la chair, devenue de l'or et du diamant entre ses doigts, dans son vain effort d'en faire de la vie? Et, béant, il avait peur de son oeuvre, tremblant de ce brusque saut dans l'au delà, comprenant bien que la réalité elle-même ne lui était plus possible, au bout de sa longue lutte pour la vaincre et la repétrir plus réelle, de ses mains d'homme.[11]

Claude's despair at his inability to portray reality leads him finally to commit suicide. Not so Silvio Lago; Pardo's artist comes to see the error of his early realism and finds himself when he recognizes the admissibility of idealization in art:

> —Parece que se me han caído de los ojos unas escamas—declaró Silvio. —Yo antes fuí esclavo de la naturaleza en su aspecto material. Ahora sin salir de ella misma, encuentro tesoros de emoción. Se acuerda usted de mi *Recolección de la patata?* Aquello era sencillamente una vulgaridad, un rasgo de ordinariez. El asunto, el modo de tratarlo, el colorido. . . . Compárelo con esto que tenemos delante, tan majestuoso, tan sereno. . . . ¡Y pensar que ahora, que veo claro lo mejor, se ma caen de las manos paleta y pinceles![12]

The last sentence is a reference to the tuberculosis of which

Silvio was destined to die just as he was beginning to get well oriented in the way he wished to go. This seems a rather cruel thing for the author to do to him. But he dies a convert to Christianity, realizing the futility of chasing the Chimera of art. This pessimistic mysticism is one of the themes of the book but not the all-important one. The primary question which arises in the reader's mind is how far the author shares Silvio's conversion from realism to idealism in art. May we assume that the following selection is a formulation of her new standards of aesthetics?

> Ahora era un idealista, un moderno, y lo que perduraba de sus devociones antiguas, lo que practicaba con mayor fanatismo si cabe, era ese culto del dibujo firme, concienzudo, ahondado, que cada día prestaba mayor seguridad a su mano y mayores vuelos a su imaginación misma, en la cual la forma sensible de las cosas, lo concreto del espectáculo natural, se enriquecía y extendía, pronto a servir a la concepción ideal del poeta que siempre había existido en Silvio, y que se revelaba lleno de sentimiento y de efusión interior. Un Silvio nuevo surgía . . . Ya no aspiraba a la obra fuerte, al trozo de realidad: quería en esa realidad, realizarse él también, derramar su propia escencia, dominar con su yo lo externo, penetrándolo.[13]

There is ample evidence that this represents Pardo's new viewpoint. Taking her points in reverse order, we find (1) that she certainly has put much of her own "yo" in this novel, dividing herself between the two characters, Silvio and Minia; (2) that there is an appreciable poetic element in this story; and (3) that Pardo is still maintaining her firm drawing in the portrayal of the basic reality behind the book. For some time— ten or fifteen years—naturalism had been in disfavor with the public. People had grown tired of realistic pictures of all walks of life; as Gómez de Baquero aptly put it (1908):

> El señor Todo el mundo ha sido retratado en todas las posturas y de todas las maneras. Las mismas causas que trajeron el naturalismo se lo han llevado, mas no sin que dejara en la novela honda huella y definitivos progresos. Hasta ahora, la novela moderna no debe a ninguna escuela tanto como al naturalismo, y es, en gran parte, obra de él. Las flores que brotan en el futuro, en el huerto novelesco, habrán sido posibles por el naturalismo, que fecundó el terreno.[14]

And as to Doña Emilia's position in the general evolution of things novelistic, he adds:

> La evolución de la Sra. Pardo Bazán es la evolución de la novela, o una de las fases de la evolución de la novela, el tránsito

del naturalismo a un espiritualismo revestido de formas realistas, pero cuya finalidad es exterior a lo físico, al mundo de la Naturaleza.[15]

Fully realizing the trend of the times away from naturalism, Doña Emilia tried her hand first at the novel in popular style, e.g., *El Tesoro de Gastón*.   Finding that not overly successful, she finally turned away from the more natural world of regional or middle class settings, to the artificial world of high society in Madrid.   This was a sphere which the Countess knew intimately.   It was her own world.   But it was also a small world and Doña Emilia was distressed at the prospect of scandal after the manner of that stirred up by Padre Coloma with his *Pequeñeces*.   That consideration, and her tendency as a naturalist to choose simpler people for her subjects, were no doubt reason enough for her not having previously attempted a society novel. Nevertheless, she did finally decide to picture a corner of her own world and to avoid satire as much as possible.   Satire, as she says in her prologue, distorts reality.[16]   The novel is sympathetically written.   One senses that Doña Emilia is perfectly at home in its atmosphere.   For a heroine she visualizes a completely artificial woman, and the result is pleasing in every respect.   By having Silvio fall in love with this vision of the couturier's art, she can have him come to see the advantages of the artificial over the natural; hence arises the conflict between his realism and the idealization of which Espina herself is the living—and adorable—example.   Here is the lyrical way in which Silvio describes her:

> Su ropa sólo se diferencia de la que gastan las demás señoras que me visitan, en que parece inseparable del cuerpo. Se enrosca, y ciñe con tal esbeltez a él, que en cualquier postura que adopte, los pliegues hacen olvidar la tela. Lleva las faldas muy largas, pero ni tropieza ni se atasca en ellas; las maneja con soberana maestría. Son tan blandos los tejidos y van tan fundidos en la tela los adornos, tan difumadas las degradaciones del color, que el gentil bulto parece terminar en una bruma, en la molicie de un jirón de niebla pronta a borrarse.[17]

There is a certain sensuous appeal about this description of a woman who knew so well how to identify herself with her clothes.   Her long skirts in which she moves so miraculously without ever a false step are but a further source of enticement to her male admirer.   And the lady herself is well aware of this:

> —¡Pchs!   ¡Desnudos!   Hay desnudos infinitamente más correctos que el vestido. El desnudo no inquieta; ¿verdad?

> La miro y compruebo la exactitud de su observación. Los maestros de las decadencias y las afeminaciones voluptuosas del arte consiguen sus efectos con ropajes y paños. Ahí están los artistas del siglo XVIII, que no me dejarán mentir. El desnudo estorba para la picardía.[18]

This rejection of the worship of nudity undoubtedly represents one of the few negative reactions of Pardo Bazán to Zola. The master of Médan was not too skilful at describing a woman's clothes. Like his artist hero, Claude, he preferred them nude. When his protagonists move in high society, as they do in *Son Excellence Eugène Rougon,* it is the bared bosoms or comely arms of the ladies in evening dress that attract the admiring glances of the stronger sex. Zola indicates his contempt for those mirrors of fashion, such as Espina, who seem to have been poured into their clothes, remarking that they doubtless would be disappointing *au naturel.* His is the unsophisticated masculine viewpoint *par excellence.* Doña Emilia, on the other hand, being a woman, realizes the important role of dress in attracting and holding the interest of a man. In Silvio she has given us one of those rare males who are sufficiently sophisticated to realize that nature can be improved upon. Nevertheless, it took his acquaintance with Espina to make him fully aware of the fact. Let us hear him as he tells of a dream he had one night:

> Una mujer viene a mi encuentro. —¡Espina, Espina!— Arrastra un traje de gasa . . . lo más atrevido que he visto nunca. Porque bajo la gasa, Espina lleva un viso de tela sedeña, nacarada, de transparencias misteriosas. . . .
>
> "—¿De dónde saca usted que lo natural, por ser natural, ya es bello? Al contrario, tonto, al contrario. Lo bello es . . . lo artificial.
>
> "¿No soy bella yo?
>
> "Pues en mí lo natural no existe.
>
> "Soy una civilización entera, que ha infundido a lo raro, a lo ficticio, la vibración del arte.
>
> "Mi pelo es tintura, mi húmeda boca es pintura, mi atractivo no es la exhibición de mi cuerpo, sino el saber recatarlo, cual se recatan los misterios de los santuarios."[19]

It was the lesson of Espina that turned him from the limitations of realism to a wider artistic technique:

> Sin embargo—reconocía Silvio,—esta mujer, su aparición en hora dada de mi camino, fué el cambio de mi credo. Estoy divorciado para siempre del verismo servil, de la sugestión de la naturaleza inerte, de la tiranía de los sentidos. Soy libre y dueño de

crearme mi mundo; ya no venero a los que se limitan a copiar; ya no tengo fetiches; si imitase, sería para dar muerte.[20]

Certainly no one can say that Pardo has made a servile imitation, in *La Quimera,* of Zola's *L'Oeuvre*; in fact, in many respects she seems deliberately to have tried to make her work an opposite to it—exalting the artificial rather than the natural. This is true, too, of the *milieux* in which the two stories move. Silvio Lago, although an artist, is not a Bohemian and does not move in that world. As Gómez de Baquero says:

Al pintarnos a Silvio Lago avanzando fácilmente por el camino de la forma, retratista mimado de damas hermosas, en vís de hacer fortuna, la Sra. Pardo Bazán ha querido separar la lucha con la Quimera de todos los demás estímulos, dejar al personaje frente a frente con el adorable y temible monstruo. A diferencia de los bohemios de *L'Oeuvre*, de Zola, que luchan por la vida al par que por el ideal, este enamorado de la Quimera se agita en una esfera más distinguida; su lucha es más espiritual, más noble. . . .[21]

But Gómez must have forgotten that Claude had a pension that relieved him of financial worries throughout most of Zola's story and that he followed his artist's chimera just about as devotedly as Silvio, not caring for money but only to accomplish his ideal, an ideal which, like Silvio, he never attained: ". . . et il préférait l'illusion de son art, cette poursuite à la beauté jamais atteinte, ce désir fou que rien ne contentait. . . ."[22] Both artists pursued their unattainable ideals—their chimeras—although there was some difference in what each set up as an ideal.

Although Silvio did not move in Bohemian circles, he made some incidental contact with that world and the story presents some minor characters who are definitely Bohemian. One such is Solano, an artist who perhaps echoes Zola's Claude even closer than Silvio, and this despite the fact that Pardo has one of her personages deny the parallel:

—No vayas a estar soñando algo parecido a lo que cuenta Zola en *La Obra,* y que Solano tiene una chispa genial. . . .

—¿Quién sabe?

—No seas así . . . Tu comprendes que ese haría mejor en empuñar la lezna . . . ¡Se le ha puesto en el moño pintar; no puede, y odia de muerte a los que pudieron! Esta vez decía que se jugaba la carta última, la decisiva. Si el imbécil público no comprendiese lo sublime de su cuadrángulo, entonces, ¡ya sabe él lo que le resta!

—¿Sería capaz de un acto de desesperación?[23]

A few pages farther on, when Solano jumps off a viaduct, Silvio looks down at him and meditates:

> . . . aun yace el cuerpo del suicida. Nadie entre la multitud le reconoce; es su destino que no le conozcan, pues le faltaban puños para violentar a la Fama; pero como tiene la cara hacia arriba, y sus ojos . . . se han posado tantas veces en mí con insultante ironía . . . , yo le reconozco, y me quedo pegado a la barandilla, fascinado. . . .
>
> ¡Ese era, hace minutos, uno que anhelaba lo mismo que yo anhelo! Y siempre más valiente que yo; lo mismo cuando embadurnaba sus tablitas mendicantes y las enviaba a vender en los cafés, que ahora cuando reposa en el suelo con los miembros rotos, convencido de lo imposible de su Quimera.[24]

Here Silvio is like Fagerolles, the artist who compromises his principles to supply popular demand and please the public. Silvio was making a success of his idealized pastels of the society world but the true artist, living in his Bohemian poverty, looks on him with eyes full of "insulting irony." Again Pardo seems to have used an echo from Zola to give a bit of almost superfluous background to her book.

The instance just mentioned is not the only one of its kind in *La Quimera* either. There is an even closer parallel between the old artist, Bongrand, in *L'Oeuvre* and the Parisian artist, Marbley, described by Pardo. I leave the reader to draw his own conclusions from the following selections, first from *L'Oeuvre*:

> —Alors, si le peintre de *La Noce au village* ne compte pas!
>
> Mais Bongrand s'emportait, debout, le sang aux joues.
>
> —Fichez-moi la paix, hein! avec *La Noce*. Elle commence à m'embêter, *La Noce*, je vous en avertis. . . . Vraiment, elle tourne pour moi au cauchmar, depuis qu'on l'a mise au musée du Luxembourg. . . .
>
> Eux, connaissant bien le bruit courant, ils partageaient l'opinion que le peintre, depuis sa *Noce au village*, n'avait rien fait qui valût ce tableau fameux. Même, après s'être maintenu dans quelques toiles, il glissait désormais à une facture plus savante et plus sèche. L'éclat s'en allait, chaque oeuvre semblait déchoir.[25]

And now from *La Quimera*:

> . . . ¿Que pensará de mí el ilustre autor del "Harem turco"?
>
> No podía caer peor la reminiscencia. Para desazonar a Marbley, bastaba recordarle el "Harem," lo único verdaderamente sentido y franco que su pincel produjo. ¡Tema! ¡Todos habían de ensalzar el dichoso "Harem"! La singular rivalidad de un artista consigo mismo, el despecho furioso de haber tenido talento un solo día de la vida, podían tanto con el belga, que había momentos en que, no acertando a repetir o superar su obra, sentía deseos de quemarla.[26]

What is still more curious about this particular parallel is that Pardo quite evidently has understood that in the person of Bongrand, Zola was really referring to Gustave Flaubert—*La Noce au village* representing *Madame Bovary,* followed as it was by works *d'une facture plus savante et plus sèche*—and so in her imitation she refers to Marbley's great work as the *Harem turco,* a title which might suggest Flaubert's other masterpiece, *Salammbô.*

Finally, the parallels among minor characters in *La Quimera* are not all confined to links between that book and *L'Oeuvre;* Dr. Pascal also enters the story under the pseudonym of Dr. Luz, guardian to Clara Ayamonte, the other woman in Silvio's life. Clara is a romantic young widow who, finding her love for Silvio spurned, finds solace in mysticism. In her difficulty she sends for her former guardian and mentor, Dr. Luz, and upon his arrival he tries to distract her thoughts from love and religion to science. She questions him:

> —¿Qué será lo desconocido, dime? ¿Te formas tú idea de lo que podría ser, después de tanto estudiar y tantas mecánicas? . . .
> El Doctor respondió con su leve e indulgente ironía de científico:
> —Para mí lo desconocido es . . . lo que todavía no hemos tenido tiempo de estudiar. Lo desconocido de hace diez años se llama ahora el telégrafo sin hilos . . . los rayos X . . .
> De pie ante la máquina, Clara sentía, en vez de la admiración . . . una reacción invencible de desdén, y porfiaba, sonriendo con sonrisa de mártir:
> —¡Lástima no haber nacido dentro de dos mil años! Entonces tú sabrías curar a las enfermas como yo, que no presentan ninguna lesión cardíaca.
> Luz apreció la significación de la frase. El menosprecio de aquel alma lírica por las realidades científicas, lo había notado en más de una ocasión, pero nunca tan glacial y total como ahora. . . .[27]

And this is what Dr. Pascal's niece says to him in Zola's novel:

> C'est toi, maître, qui es un entêté, quand tu ne veux pas admettre qu'il y a, là bas, un inconnu où tu n'entreras jamais. Oh! je sais, tu es trop intelligent pour ignorer cela. Seulement tu ne veux pas en tenir compte, tu mets l'inconnu à part, parce qu'il te gênerait dans tes recherches. . . . Tu as beau me dire d'écarter le mystère, de partir du connu à la conquête de l'inconnu, je ne puis pas, moi! le mystère tout de suite me réclame et m'inquiète.[28]

The only difference between this minor plot in *La Quimera* and the main plot in *Docteur Pascal* is in the solution of the argument. This varies, of course, according to the outlook of the respective authors, science and the doctor winning out in Zola's version, while in Pardo's the girl's mysticism is sustained and she enters a convent. The reader will remember Pardo Bazán's first reaction to *Docteur Pascal* as quoted at the end of Chapter Three. There it was apparent that all her sympathies were on the side of the doctor's niece. Now, some twelve years after her book review, we find our Countess taking the liberty of rewriting *Docteur Pascal* to suit herself!

The influence of Zola on Pardo Bazán was not wholly in the realm of literary theory. We have seen how she borrowed ideas for character study from him, and even the basic plot for a whole novel (*La Madre Naturaleza*). Yet such was the genius of the Spanish author that she could take this borrowed foreign material, thoroughly hispanize it, add to it ideas and experiences of her own, and amalgamate the whole into a creation of artistic merit and even originality. *La Quimera* is, of all her novels, one of the richest in Zola influence, yet significantly enough to a large extent it is negative influence. The book is a sort of contra to Zola's *L'Oeuvre*. It would seem that even though Doña Emilia never accepted Zola's theories completely and even though by 1905 she considered herself to have outgrown naturalism altogether, she still could not free herself from the fascination of the master of Médan, and still had to imitate his characters and argue with his *esthétique*.

VI

CONFLICTING VOICES

Few authors have elicited so much contradictory and on the whole erroneous comment as the Countess of Pardo Bazán. First, there are those who misunderstand and condemn naturalism in all its forms and hence condemn the Countess, too, for having defended so reprehensible a school of writers. Second, there is a larger group made up of those who like and esteem Pardo Bazán even though they can see no good in naturalism. These well-meaning friends of Doña Emilia seek to minimize or explain away her connection with Zola's theory and practice. One man has written a book to prove that Pardo Bazán, despite all her efforts and protestations to the contrary, is merely a regionalist. Practically the only voice of true comprehension comes from outside Spain. I refer to the Argentine novelist, Manuel Gálvez, whose own literary philosophy is closely akin to that of the Countess.

A typical representative of those who condemn naturalism and Pardo Bazán along with it, is that distinguished historian of Spanish literature, Cejador y Frauca. His attitude is well expressed by one sentence. Here is how he starts a paragraph in his section on our authoress: "En *La Cuestión palpitante* (1883) trató con este feo título el feo naturalismo de Zola."[1] A few pages farther on he gives us a clearer view of what he considers naturalism to be, while at the same time admitting that Pardo Bazán is not quite so bad as Zola:

> . . . Pero la verdad es que la autora jamás se atrevió a traer el naturalismo en crudo, la novela documental, determinista, de solas fealdades sociales y hediondas porquerías, de negrura pesimista y mal humor. . . .[2]

Surely there is no need to refute so prejudiced a critic. But let us let him finish talking himself into an impossible position:

> La crítica de Pardo Bazán es poco honda y a veces algo parcial; es obra de aficionada, que en todo pica, y tiene talento para salir en todo airosamente . . . el naturalismo, que fué su tema principal, no parece bien comprendido por la autora. . . .[2]

Cejador's failure to comprehend either naturalism or Pardo Bazán would be merely ridiculous if he were alone in his incomprehension. The tragic thing is that some Spanish critics who are friendly to Pardo Bazán as a person and author, are equally prejudiced against naturalism. The writers of this second group seem still to share Cejador's opinion that the novels of Zola are "de solas fealdades sociales y hediondas porquerías." Such being the case, to admit that their noble friend, the Countess, could have been influenced seriously by the French master of naturalism would be to besmirch her fair name. "Don't speak ill of the dead" seems to have been the thought of Araujo-Costa when he wrote in 1921:

> No la comparemos nunca con Zola, que queda por lo que tuvo do romántico, y que es el reverso de nuestra eminente pensadora. Ni ella misma le tributa elogios admirativos en este tomo III (*El Naturalismo*), que es, en conjunto, el mejor hecho, el mejor pensado, el más rigurosamente científico y maduro.[3]

To say that Zola stands today only on the basis of what was romantic in his work is, of course, patently absurd. No less absurd, in view of the evidence, is it to say that Pardo Bazán's technique is "the reverse" of Zola's. Did she not write at least six novels in close conformity to his literary formula? And if Araujo-Costa found no "elogios admirativos" in Pardo's volume on *El Naturalismo* (1914), he must not have seen the passage, already quoted in my first chapter, where she is enthusiastic over Zola's ability to make the scene of a novel come alive,[4] or the passages where she speaks out in praise of *L'Assommoir,* thereby reversing her previous adverse judgments of the book.[5]

José Balseiro, author of *Novelistas españoles modernos* (1933), seems to write from much the same viewpoint as Araujo-Costa when he says:

> Pardo Bazán, pese a su refinamiento aristocrático que se alquitara más y más a lo largo de su vida y de su obra, por rendir tributo en *La Tribuna* a ciertos aspectos del naturalismo en boga, describió algún cuadro apestoso, sin llegar a las monstruosidades de un Zola.[6]

To him, it appears, Zola is an author of monstrosities and his influence is purely bad, producing such pages as that in *La Tribuna* where Pardo describes the smells of the factory, proceeding from so much perspiring humanity as well as from the nearby latrines.

The same author says of *La Cuestión palpitante*:

> . . . Quienes leyeron la obra vendados los ojos de pasión, o aquellos sentenciadores de oídas que no faltan nunca, dieron la impresión injusta de que la autora era apologista incondicional del credo estético de Zola. Pensar así era olvidar lo que ya leímos en el Prefacio de *Un viaje de novios,* o desconocer la independencia de

carácter, la arrogancia y firmeza que iban revelándose en los juicios de esta mujer extraordinaria.[7]

This is all very well except for the reference to the preface to *Un Viaje de novios*. I showed in Chapter III how this preface was in many respects just a first reaction on Doña Emilia's part, many statements in it being superseded by views more favorable to Zola both in *La Cuestión* and in other and later works. Balseiro, however, quotes the preface at length, selecting the parts most uncomplimentary to naturalism. Worst of all, he would have us believe that this immature work expresses, in definitive form, Pardo's unalterable literary creed: "En el ya nombrado Prefacio de *Un viaje de novios* expone Pardo Bazán su credo literario."[8] Moreover, when he comes to cite *La Cuestión palpitante*, he introduces his selections thus: "Entresaquemos, de *La Cuestión palpitante*, algunos de los numerosos reparos al naturalismo francés. Sólo así se apreciará la amplitud de miras de Pardo Bazán. . . ."[9] He proceeds then to quote only the fault she found with naturalism. We wonder how we are to judge her "breadth of vision" by so one-sided a glimpse at her book. Instead of reading *La Cuestión* with his "eyes blindfolded by passion," Balseiro has used friendship for an eye-bandage; from beneath it he can see only what the lady condemned of naturalism. Hating Zola and admiring the Countess, he cannot bear to see any sympathy between them.

But it is perhaps not Zola alone whom he hates. Balseiro is patriotic. He likes to think that Spanish literature can be self-sufficient with no need of help from foreign models. He gladly accepts the tactful praise that Pardo throws out for the traditional Spanish realism of Cervantes' time, as opposed to the exaggerations of French naturalism:

> Pardo Bazán prestó a su patria doble servicio con *La cuestión palpitante*: Enterarla, con precisión e imparcialidad, del movimiento que tomaba entonces la novela en Francia e Inglaterra, y recordarla que en sus producciones de anteayer—*La Celestina*, la picaresca, el *Quijote*—tuvo España un realismo literario—más artístico y humano a la vez que el naturalismo predicado por Zola—al que era menester volver los ojos, enriquecidos ya con las mejores aportaciones del clasicismo, del romanticismo y de la novela experimental prestigiada . . . por su campeón, el disecador de *Les Rougon Macquart*.[10]

Gómez de Baquero is more skeptical of Pardo's sincerity at this point. In an article appearing in 1908 he reacted somewhat differently than Balseiro:

> . . . Al relacionar con nuestro realismo castizo el naturalismo
> francés, la Sra. Pardo Bazán hacía lo que hicieron Martínez
> Marina y los pensadores de las Cortes de Cádiz al pretender en-
> troncar en nuestra tradición castiza española las novedades po-
> líticas del nuevo régimen. Buscar antecedentes indígenas a las
> novedades importadas, para hacernos ver que no son cosas ex-
> trañas, podía no ser del todo exacto, pero es política y conducta
> discreta de innovadores.[11]

Later, in his book, *De Gallardo a Unamuno* (1926), the same
critic really gets to the heart of the matter:

> Lo que ocurre es que los españoles tenemos el pavor de la in-
> vasión extranjera. Sentimos un miedo atroz de que nos conquisten
> el alma, como si no estuviésemos muy seguros de ella ni nos
> fiásemos de su independencia. En nuestro carácter y en nuestras
> costumbres hay cierta *endogamía* de ideas. Queremos casarnos
> exclusivamente con nuestras propias ideas castizas, y cuando por
> casualidad nos desposamos con alguna de fuera, la buscamos en
> seguida antecedentes indígenas para disculparnos de aquella in-
> fidelidad a la tradición.[12]

Gómez de Baquero's thought is that in her *Cuestión* Pardo was
merely throwing out a sop to the over-patriotic when she extoled the native realism of Cervantes and the rogue novel writers.
We have seen how eagerly José Balseiro picked up the sop, showing that this disease of literary chauvinism is still prevalent today.   No one, however, knew better than Doña Emilia herself
the tyranny and narrowness of this Spanish hatred for outside
influences.   In her famous lecture on the Spain of yesterday and
that of today—a discourse of whose French she was so proud—
she bitterly remarks:

> Un écrivain était bon et sympatique lorsqu'il se faisait l'apolo-
> giste de l'immobilité espagnole contre le mouvement européen;
> renier la culture étrangère, faire parade d'un espagnolisme ombra-
> geux et exclusif, ouvrait les foyers, les salons et les portes de l'in-
> stitut; j'ai entendu venter, chez un romancier qui a certainement
> d'autres mérites, le mérite d'ignorer les langues étrangères et de
> ne pas avoir touché de sa vie un seul roman français. Certes on
> lisait parfois des livres étrangers lorsqu'ils faisaient du bruit;
> certes on s'en inspirait, on imitait, on traduisait, on arrangeait,
> on puisait aux sources maudites; mais il ne fallait pas l'avouer.[13]

Thus Doña Emilia herself acknowledges that foreign influence
was widespread among the Spanish authors of her time.   Certainly she did her own share of imitating, and resented the
opinions of those who said she should not do so.

Returning to Balseiro's book we find that, not content with
quoting only her adverse comments on naturalism, he even tries

to prove that she was too independent ever to take up with any
foreign literary school whatever. To do this he has found an
apparently perfect quotation from the lady herself. He introduces it thus:

> . . . Lo cual habla del eclecticismo estético de la Pardo, expresa-
> mente declarado en su para el lector familiar estudio acerca de
> Alarcón:
> "Todo el que lea mis ensayos críticos comprenderá que ni soy
> idealista, ni realista, ni naturalista, sino ecléctica. Mi cerebro es
> *redondo*, y debo a Dios la suerte de poder recrearme con todo lo
> bueno y bello de todas épocas y estilos."[14]

What a beautiful declaration of independence that seems to be!
But let us look a little at what went before and after this quotation taken out of context. A few lines farther up the page Pardo
had said:

> . . . Quede, pues, a cargo del porvenir el juicio definitivo sobre
> el puesto que corresponde, en las gloriosas milicias de la novela
> española, a esos tres libros, de los cuales voy a hablar como se
> habla de un adversario que tal vez inspire, a los que le combatimos,
> mayor suma de admiración que a sus propios aliados egoístas.[15]

If Pardo Bazán was such an eclectic, why does she admit to having been an adversary of Alarcón's who was engaged in combatting him? But here is the next paragraph:

> Y cuenta que al apuntarme en el número de los adversarios de
> Alarcón, me parece que estampo una inexactitud, o que, por lo
> menos, necesito, para que se me entienda, añadir aclaraciones. No
> soy adversario de Alarcón por prevención contra la escuela a que
> se afiló tan resueltamente, ni por apego a la contraria. Todo el
> que lea mis ensayos críticos comprenderá que ni soy idealista, ni
> naturalista, sino ecléctica. Mi cerebro es *redondo*, y debo a Dios
> la suerte de poder recrearme con todo lo bueno y bello de todas
> épocas y estilos.[15]

Balseiro would certainly appear to have a very good case from
that paragraph; but the question remains in our minds as to
why Pardo nevertheless considered herself the adversary of
Alarcón. Perhaps we need to read a bit farther:

> Conozco, eso sí, que no todo estilo es de todo tiempo y que si
> hay leyes estables de hermosura, la más fija es la que impone a
> la producción artística el carácter supremo del *momento humano*—
> perdónese la frase—en que fué concebida y ejecutada. —Ni otra
> cosa dije en *La cuestión palpitante*, ni otra cosa diré en el caso
> muy improbable de que cien años viva. . . .
>
> Lo que me obligó a caminar en sentido contrario a Alarcón, no
> fué su escuela, sino la *ocasión* y *modo* que de abogar por esa
> escuela tuvo el ilustre guadijeño. La primera me pareció inopor-

tuna; el segundo, inconsiderado; y más semejante a declamación que a alegato literario franco y serio. . . .[15]

In other words, the 1880's did not seem to Pardo Bazán an opportune time to defend romanticism, nor did she enjoy the belligerent way in which Alarcón did it. Obviously, she thought it better to keep in style and be a naturalist in the eighties. What then did she mean by her statement that she was neither idealist, realist, nor naturalist, but eclectic? The answer lies in the very next sentence: "Debo a Dios la suerte de poder recrearme con todo lo bueno y bello de todas épocas y estilos."[15] She can enjoy the good and the beautiful of all epochs and styles. And from what she goes on to say we infer that Alarcón was out of his epoch; he defended romanticism in the era of naturalism. Pardo was eclectic in her appreciation of literature. Her wonderful balance kept her from swinging to extremes. We have seen that all along. But she believed in being abreast of her time. The essay on Alarcón appeared first in her *Nuevo teatro crítico* in 1891,[16] and the same year she had written the experimental novel, *La Piedra Angular*. Later on we have seen her trying to catch the new spirit of the times, first with *novelas novelescas* and then in the idealistic later works, *La Quimera*, and *La Sirena negra*. She was an eclectic in literary appreciation but never as a novelist, in which capacity she believed in following the style. Nevertheless, she was certainly at her best as a naturalist, for her chief talent lay in that wonderful *sens du réel* and her ability to portray that reality with *un dibujo firme*.

I think we must find Balseiro guilty on three counts: (1) presenting an early preface as an unalterable literary creed, (2) quoting only those sections of *La Cuestión palpitante* which are adverse to Zola, and (3) taking a text out of its context to prove something which the author did not mean.

A more difficult critic to refute than Balseiro is Emilio González López, author of a book called *Emilia Pardo Bazán, novelista de Galicia*. González, a Galician himself, is chiefly interested in Pardo Bazán's pictures of life in his native province. All would be well had he limited himself to this, but at the same time he seeks to prove that the Countess was primarily a regionalist author. The crux of this critic's argument rests on the undoubted superiority of Pardo's two novels of country life in Galicia, *Los Pazos de Ulloa* and *La Madre Naturaleza*. By them Doña Emilia gave birth to the regional novel of Galicia and on them rests her chief claim to fame. It is rather ironic, thinks González López, that Pardo should have criticized so bitterly the regionalism of Pereda, only to end up owing her place in Spain's hall of fame to her own mastery of the regional novel. This, he goes on to say, was primarily the result of her naturalistic system, which succeeded best when the novelist was describing a region or environment with which she was very intimately familiar.

There is considerable truth in that last statement, for undoubtedly the superiority of such novels as *Los Pazos* rests upon Pardo's thorough documentary knowledge of that part of Galicia. However, there is a fundamental difference between the regional work of Pereda and that of Pardo Bazán. It is, I think, that the Galician Countess was truly an international spirit who viewed her native province almost with the objectivity of an outsider. Thus she was able to portray it in such a way as to make it understandable and interesting to non-Galicians. Not so Pereda, as the Argentine, Manuel Gálvez remarks:

Y no sólo fué doña Emilia de su tiempo, sino que fué un escritor europeo. El más grave defecto de la literatura española, tomada en su conjunto, es su "provincialismo." Son raros los escritores españoles que concilian lo español y lo universal. Hay en ellos un excesivo apego a la terruña, antipático para los extraños. Aunque no lo digan, revelan un desprecio a lo extranjero, un orgullo sin fundamento, una suerte de "no conformismo" con la civilización y la modernidad. Pereda nos resulta inaguantable, y apenas si podemos leer a Valera. Los escritores españoles, por su falta de internacionalidad, son intraductibles. Nadie los comprendería fuera de España. El mismo Galdós, con ser tan grande, es excesivamente regional; y sino siempre por sus asuntos, sí por la manera de componer, de sentir y de ver.[17]

But there are some Spanish authors who have universal appeal, according to Gálvez:

Ello es que en España los únicos escritores universales, traducidos con éxito al francés, al inglés, al alemán y a otras lenguas, son aquellos que han recibido la poderosa influencia inglesa o francesa: Palacio Valdés, Valle-Inclán, Blasco Ibáñez, Emilia Pardo Bazán, Jacinto Benavente. Cierto que las mejores novelas de la gran escritora gallega son regionales. Pero también es cierto que hay en ellas algunas influencias francesas; si no en cuanto a los asuntos ni a los caracteres ni al ambiente, sí en cuanto a la manera de seleccionarlos, de distribuir sus materiales y de exponerlos. Los casticistas de la derecha, que creen alabarse llamándose a sí mismos españolísimos y rancios, condenan a doña Emilia por su curiosidad universal, por su espíritu europeizante,

> por su admiración de la literatura francesa, tan superior sin em-
> bargo tan infinitamente superior a la española.[18]

Gálvez sounds somewhat excessively francophile but his essential point is well taken: that it was the influence of French literature which lifted the work of Emilia Pardo Bazán above the level of the merely regional. I will even say that it is Zola's method applied to the Spanish regional scene which distinguishes Pardo Bazán from Pereda and gives to such novels as *Los Pazos* their universal interest and appeal.

González López is of the opinion that Doña Emilia wrote books about life outside of Galicia merely to avoid being classified as a provincial, and that if she did take up with naturalism a la Zola, it was only out of a typically feminine desire to keep in style:

> Muchos de sus actos nos producen la impresión de que para
> deshacer semejante sospecha ponía especial interés en vestirse
> a la moda del último figurín literario recién llegado de la capital
> francesa, emperifollándose con lazos extranjeros, con cualquier
> cosa que revelara a las claras su origen afrancesado; y es así
> como unas veces aparece como entusiasta exegeta del naturalismo
> zolesco . . . y en otras toma la tierra francesa como lugar para
> tratar la trama de sus obras . . . Pero en ella estos adornos eran
> accesorios, ornamentales; pues bajo el traje parisino se escondía
> "el mantelo" y "el dengue," las ropas típicas de la mujer gallega.[19]

It is true that Doña Emilia tried to keep in style, literarily speaking, but we have seen repeatedly how deeply realistic was her natural temperament and how it was Zola's idea of a novel as a study of a certain milieu which first attracted her to him and led her to imitate him. We have also seen how she never let her enthusiasm for Zola carry beyond a certain point. She never was more than a partial determinist. Essentially, Pardo Bazán remained much the same throughout her life, and her following of different literary styles did not prevent her from holding to certain fundamental beliefs through thick and thin. Indeed, Zola's idea of the novel as a study of certain segments or aspects of human life seems to have stayed with Pardo Bazán all her life. She merely extended the field of reality to include spiritual and religious experience, which she maintained was equally real and worthy of study. The point I wish to make is that what Pardo accepted of naturalism was incorporated into her fundamental concept and philosophy of life and was not merely a passing fancy or fad. To say, as González does, that naturalism was just a foreign gewgaw which she donned for a time over

top of her native garb is to make a most unfortunate and mis-
leading analogy. Rather is she the type of provincial girl who
goes abroad to be educated and upon her return in later life is
able to look upon her native heath with a new and educated eye.

When González López finally gets down to analyzing the truly
regional novels of Pardo Bazán, he finds his work considerably
simplified. He starts out by eliminating five novels from his discussion because they have nothing whatever to do with Galicia.
Then he narrows the field still more by setting aside most of the
novels and tales having to do with Marineda (La Coruña) :

> . . . en las que se pierde el colorido local hasta tal punto, que si no
> fuera por ciertas referencias anecdóticas y accesorias, que sitúan
> la narración en el espacio gallego, seria sumamente difícil saber
> si la acción tiene lugar en La Coruña o en cualquier otra ciudad
> no gallega del norte de España.[20]

The upshot of this process of elimination is that González finds
only four novels and sundry *cuentos* of Pardo's on which to base
most of his proof of her regionalism. The four chosen titles are
Pascual López (1879), *El Cisne de Vilamorta* (1885), *Los Pazos
de Ulloa* (1886), and *La Madre Naturaleza* (1887). There is a
whole chapter devoted to *Pascual López*, that fantastic youthful
novel about student life in Santiago de Compostela, a book which
Pardo did not include in her complete works and which can
scarcely be found today. No one could object to his choice of
Los Pazos and *La Madre* as representative of country life in
Galicia, nor of *El Cisne* as a picture of life in a small Galician
town, but apparently there have not been enough ardent disciples of *lo gallego* to keep *Pascual López* in print even inter-
mittently. González chose this novel because of its pictures
of the distinctly regional urban life in Santiago in contrast to
the more cosmopolitan life of Marineda. In proportion as the
four or five mature novels about La Coruña are greater than
Pascual López, just so much is the argument for Pardo Bazán's
essential regionalism reduced in strength.

González López concludes his study rather lamely with a look
at *Insolación* and *Morriña,* where he hopes to find Galician psychology, if not scenery. However, upon looking closer he cannot find much but naturalism in *Insolación* and the psychology
of the Galician lady protagonist seems to him more universal
than regional. Of *Morriña* he has this to say :

> *Morriña* es una novela eminentemente psicológica, y no sola-
> mente de psicología gallega: predomina en ella sobre la descrip-

ción de los detalles exteriores el concienzudo estudio de los caracteres de sus personajes. Es una novela que, a pesar de ser urbana, no es un documento social, sino pintura de figuras individuales. Obra que responde totalmente al mas legítimo realismo español que ahonda más en los rasgos morales de sus personajes que en la descripción detallada del medio ambiente; y se separa radicalmente del realismo afrancesado de *Insolación*. . . .[21]

If *Morriña* is chiefly a conscientious study of character, it seems odd that the two protagonists are essentially so simple. Rogelio is a bashful youth who finds in Esclavitud a girl sufficiently modest not to make fun of him and sufficiently lonely to appreciate his affection. We have already seen in the pages devoted to *Morriña* the skilful way in which Pardo traces the awakening and quite elemental passions of young Rogelio. His *medio ambiente* was his mother's house and Pardo did not need to go farther afield to make a thoroughly naturalistic study of the influence of environment, i.e., the pretty servant girl, upon Rogelio. To say that this novel with "true Spanish realism digs deep into the moral traits of its protagonists" seems to me quite absurd. The combination of homesickness, despair, loneliness, and fatalism wihch afflicts the soul of Esclavitud is not difficult to explain in terms of her background. There are no undue complications. No, it would seem that González López, like Balseiro, has been led astray by that same blind Spanish patriotism which is ever reluctant to admit that anything good can enter Spain from without and ever eager to prove that Spanish authors are at their best when least influenced from abroad and when following in the old tradition of "la inmobilidad española"—an ideal which Pardo Bazán devoted most of her life to combatting.

Doña Emilia was essentially a truth-worshipper. This is what undoubtedly first attracted her to Zola's naturalism. It was a school that made of the novel a study, something more than a mere piece of entertainment. And she has a gift for seeing the truth. She is not easily swayed by prejudice or enthusiasm. A firm equilibrium and a clear penetration are her two outstanding qualities. These are the elements that made of her so excellent a critic, able to voice in the present the judgment of posterity. She also has the critic's quality of broad appreciation. She can see another point of view and respect it, without necessarily accepting it. In like manner she could appreciate Zola's epic genius and lyricism, although in attempting to imitate them she was unsuccessful. Her pictures always came out as clear and real as her own matter-of-fact way of seeing the world around her. And it is this inevitable realism of her temperament that gives unity to her work.

The influence of Zola upon Pardo Bazán was great, long-continued, and entirely beneficial. Under it she wrote her best novels. Ostensibly regional many of them, they yet have a cosmopolitan, modern spirit which will make them last and which makes them intensely readable even to foreigners—a quality which is not always present in her contemporaries.

Pardo Bazán was a great and a large spirit, too big oftentimes for her Iberian home. She was cosmopolitan, modern, progressive without radicalism. She was blessed with a particularly sane and penetrating judgment. She did not readily lose her balance and yet she was capable of sincere enthusiasm. She could be enthusiastic about both Zola and Tolstoy, although she disliked the irreligion of the one, and condemned the excessive mysticism of the other. She was a great independent spirit and yet sufficiently humble to follow where her judgment recognized a worthy leader.

She was a naturalist, adopting most of that school's stylistic techniques; yet her own common sense, her profound *sens du réel*, kept her from going to the exaggerated extremes of a Zola. She saw the extent to which man's life is determined by his material surroundings and yet, good Catholic to the end, she never ceased to maintain that religion, too, is part of reality and deserves a place in any artistic portrayal of the complete environment of man.

NOTES TO CHAPTER I

1. Pierre Martino: *Le naturalisme français*, Paris, 1923, p. 2.
2. *Ibid.*, p. 3.
3. P. 5.
4. Emile Zola: *Le roman expérimental*, ed. François Bernouard, Paris, 1927, p. 81.
5. Martino, p. 10.
6. *La Grande Encyclopédie*, Paris, 1886-1902, XX, 536.
7. *Ibid.*, XXVII, 403.
8. P. 404.
9. Hippolyte Taine: *Histoire de la littérature anglaise*, Paris, 1911, p. xv.
10. Martino, p. 23. "La moral n'avait plus rien à faire avec la littérature, pas plus qu'avec la science; cela ressortait du système de Taine, et il ne s'était point gêné pour l'affirmer brutalement. 'Le vice et la vertu, disait l'*Introduction* à l'*Histoire de la littérature anglaise* (1864), sont des produits comme le vitriol et le sucre.' Zola fera de cette phrase, qui scandalisa, l'épigraphe de la deuxième édition de *Thérèse Raquin*, son premier roman naturaliste."
11. Taine: *Histoire de la littérature anglaise*, pp. xxii, xxv, xxvii.
12. Martino, p. 21: "Taine a été en effet le vrai philosophe du réalisme, son théoricien; c'est lui qui a donné la formule du positivisme en matière littéraire. Il a définitivement persuadé ses contemporains de ce que les idéologues et Auguste Comte enseignaient depuis longtemps: savior, que la psychologie n'était qu'un chapitre de la physiologie, que l'étude des caractères était celle des temperaments, que le milieu physique presse de tous côtés sur notre destinée, que l'histoire des individus, comme celle des nations, est soumise au plus rigoureux des déterminismes. . . .

"La théorie du roman naturaliste, chez Zola, n'a guère été, à l'origine, qu'un effet des idées de Taine; Zola n'a jamais renié cette influence; Maupassant et Bourget se sont aussi réclamés de Taine, comme d'un maître."
13. *La Grande Encyclopédie*, VI, 363-364: "Le déterminisme, dans la pensée de Claude Bernard, consistait dans ce principe, que chaque phénomène est invariablement déterminé par des conditions matérielles définies qui en sont les causes prochaines. Si l'on reproduit une fois exactement les conditions matérielles de sa première apparition, le phénomène suivra. . . .

"Distinguer les faits des hypothèses . . . —Chercher le déterminisme rigoureux du phénomène, c'est-a-dire les conditions de sa production certaine. —N'adopter une explication qu'après avoir tout fait pour la détuire et avoir constaté sa résistance aux tentatives de destruction. . . ."
14. *Ibid.*, p. 263: ". . . l'*Introduction à l'étude de la Médecine expérimentale*, publiée en 1865, livre qui produisit une grande sensation et ouvrit à son auteur les portes de l'Académie française."
15. *Ibid.*, VI, 364.
16. Martino, p. 42.
17. Martino, pp. 26-27: "En moins de deux ans il était transformé; il s'était fait une nouvelle manière de romancier. Ce fut celle que pouvait déterminer sa brève carrière de critique, ses lectures et ses admirations les plus récentes: une combinaison du réalisme des Goncourt et de celui de Flaubert, avec plus de brutalité; des formules de Taine appliquées dans la rigueur de leurs termes; et enfin d'un certain nombre de notions empruntées aux sciences naturelles.

"*Thérèse Raquin* et *Madeleine Férat* sont les premiers livres de cette nouvelle manière. . . .

"*Thérèse Raquin* eut une seconde édition (1868), à laquelle Zola ajouta une préface fort significative, où il définissait sa conception du roman scientifique."

18. Matthew Josephson: *Zola and His Time*, New York, 1928, p. 139.

19. *Ibid.*, p. 141.

20. Martino, p. 29: "C'est ensuite la théorie de l'*impregnation*, empruntée à un médecin, le Dr. Lucas, mais surtout à Michelet: 'La femme fécondée, disait celui-ci, une fois impregnée, portera partout son mari en elle.' C'est cette affirmation, aussi peu scientifique que possible, que Zola retient pour *Madeleine Férat*. Enfin, dernière suggestion essentielle, il a admis, avec Taine qu'un sentiment violent, comme le remords, n'est en réalité qu'une suite de desordres organiques, de détraquements, des hallucinations . . . Dès ce moment-là Zola pouvait employer . . . le mot naturaliste.' "

21. Martino, pp. 39-40: "Toute sa science, en fait d'hérédité, il l'a demandée à un livre du Dr. Prosper Lucas, qu'il lut en 1868-1869, et sur lequel il prit de trés abondantes notes, qui nous ont été conservées. . . .

"Il s'est reclamé du Dr. Lucas dans la préface d'*Une page d'amour* (1878), en déclarant que c'était ce livre qui lui avait servi 'à etablir l'arbre généologique des Rougon-Macquart,' la charpente de l'oeuvre qui fut dessinée avant qu'un seul des romans de la série ait été écrit."

22. Martino, p. 38: ". . . les *lois* que affirment l'origine purement physiologique des sentiments et des émotions: il les demanda au livre du Dr. Ch. Letourneau, *Physiologie des passions* (1868) . . . ."

23. Quoted by Martino, p. 30.

24. Martino, p. 45: "Zola, apparemment, n'aurait pas donné un tel crédit a de douteuses observations sur l'hérédité . . . s'il n'avait pas vécu dans une atmosphère intellectuelle saturée de darwinisme, ou plûtot de la légende du darwinisme."

25. Zola: *Le docteur Pascal*, François Bernouard, Paris, 1927, p. 107.

26. Zola: *Le roman expérimental*, p. 16.

27. *Ibid.*, p. 19.

28. *Le naturalisme français*, p. 42.

29. *Le roman expérimental*, p. 81.

30. Martino, pp. 6-7: "Le naturalisme est très nettement . . . un des héritiers de la tradition du XVIIIᵉ siecle, un des continuateurs de l'esprit idéologique; et le romantisme a été, avant toute chose, une révolte du sentiment, finalement infructueuse, contre l'esprit idéologique."

31. Josephosn: *Zola and his Time*, p. 142.

32. Zola: *Les romanciers naturalistes*, François Bernouard, Paris, 1927, p. 64.

33. *Le roman expérimental*, p. 80.

34. *Les romanciers naturalistes*, p. 75.

35. *Ibid.*, p. 76.

36. P. 78.

37. P. 77.

38. P. 108.

39. Pp. 108-109: "Balzac, dans ses chefs-d'oeuvres: *Eugénie Grandet, Les Parents Pauvres, Le Père Goriot*, a donné ainsi des pages d'une nudité magistrale, où son imagination s'est contentée de créer du vrai. Mais, avant d'en arriver à cet unique souci des peintures exactes, il s'était longtemps perdu dans des inventions les plus singulières, dans la recherche d'une terreur et d'une grandeur fausses; et l'on peut même dire que jamais il ne se débarrassa tout à fait de son amour des aventures extraordinaires, ce qui donne à une bonne moitié de ses oeuvres l'air d'un rêve énorme fait tout haut par un homme éveillé."

40. P. 109.

41. P. 110: "Balzac est encore pour nous, je le repète, une puissance avec laquelle on ne discute pas. Il s'impose comme Shakespeare, par un souffle créateur qui a enfanté tout un monde. Ses oeuvres, taillées à coup de cognée, à peine dégrossies le plus souvent, offrant le plus étonnant mélange du sublime et du pire, restent quand même l'effort prodigieux du plus vaste cerveau de ce siècle."

42. Pp. 110-111.
43. P. 17.
44. *Les romanciers naturalistes*, p. 202.
45. *Ibid.*, p. 201.
46. Zola: *Mes Haines*, François Bernouard, Paris, 1927, p. 66.
47. *Le roman expérimental*, p. 50.
48. Zola: *L'Oeuvre*, François Bernouard, Paris, 1927, p. 175.
49. *Les romanciers naturalistes*, p. 77.
50. *Le roman expérimental*, pp. 167, 169.
51. *Ibid.*, p. 166.
52. P. 86.
53. P. 105.
54. Zola: *L'Oeuvre*, p. 206.
55. *Le roman expérimental*, p. 103: "Il disparait donc, il garde pour lui son émotion, il expose simplement ce qu'il a vu. Voilà la réalité; frissonez ou riez devant elle, tirez-en une leçon quelconque, l'unique besoin de l'auteur a été de mettre sous vos yeux les documents vrais. Il y a, en outre, à cette impersonalité morale de l'oeuvre une raison d'art. L'intervention passionnée ou attendrie de l'écrivain rapetisse un roman en brisant la netteté des linges, en introduisant un élément étranger aux faits, qui détruit leur valeur scientifique."
56. *Ibid.*, pp. 85-86.
57. Pp. 31-32.
58. P. 102: "Même parfois ce n'est pas une existence entière, avec un commencement et une fin, que l'on relate; c'est uniquement un lambeau d'existence."
59. Pardo Bazán: *La literatura francesa moderna*: III. *El naturalismo*, (*Obras completas*, Vol 41), Madrid, 1914, pp. 125-126.
60. Pardo Bazán: "Emilio Zola," *La Lectura*, II, pt. 3 (November, 1902), 287.
61. Zola: *Mes Haines*, François Bernouard, Paris, 1927, p. 55.
62. Zola: *L'Oeuvre*, Francois Bernouard, Paris, 1927, p. 206.
63. Eugène Asse in *La Revue internationale* for Nov. 1888. Quoted in Zola: *Le Réve*, François Bernouard, Paris, 1927, p. 252: "Ce chef de l'école naturaliste est, avant tout, un poète . . . Qu'est-ce qui caractérise, en effet, le poète? C'est la faculté de grandir les objets, de faire plus grand que nature: voyez Homère, Milton, Victor Hugo; de rendre aussi le beau plus beau, le laid plus laid encore. C'est aussi le don d'animer les choses inanimées. . . ."
64. Pardo Bazán: *El naturalismo*, p. 109.
65. Alberto Gerchunoff: "Notas sobre Emilio Zola," *Nosotros*, IX (February, 1913), 352.
66. *Ibid.*, p. 353.
67. Pardo Bazán: *La Cuestión palpitante*, (*Obras completas*, Vol. 1), Madrid, 1888, p. 213.
68. Pardo Bazán: "El Doctor Pascual," *Nuevo Teatro Crítico*, Nov., 1893, p. 121. Also in *España Moderna*, September, 1893, p. 173.
69. *La Cuestión palpitante*, p. 212.

NOTES TO CHAPTER II

1. Leopoldo García Ramón: "Cartas de Paris," *Revista Contemporánea*, LXIV (November, 1886), 481.
2. Andrés González-Blanco: *Historia de la novela en España desde el romanticismo a nuestros días*, Madrid, 1909, p. 465.
3. García Ramón: "Cartas de Paris," *Revista Contemporánea*, LXIV, 48: ". . . y fácil sería demostrar, . . . que sus grandes virtudes literarias, la claridad del concepto, la profundidad del pensamiento, la energía, la gracia y la novedad de las imágenes, la elegancia y pureza de estilo y muchas también de sus virtudes morales, han nacido o han desenvuelto al

calor de esas lecturas. Tiene mi amiga tan bondadosa y atractiva indulgencia, no sólo en cuestiones literarias . . . sino en las cosas corrientes de la vida, que no me cansaré de alabarla. Y esta indulgencia, secundada, indudablemente por su excelente salud, es otro resultado de las primeras y bien digeridas lecturas."

4. Espasa: *Enciclopedia universal ilustrada*, XLI, 1438.

5. González-Blanco: *Historia de la novela*, p. 465.

6. *Ibid.*, p. 466: "De estos años no nos da la autora más datos para su historia, si no es que entonces comenzó a hilvanar nuevamente tímidos versos, publicados en el *Almanaque* de Soto Freire y en la *Soberanía Nacional*, de Madrid, y que en el *Almanaque* de ésta salió a luz su primera tentativa en prosa novela corta, en la cual creyóse ver 'la relación de una tragedia verdadera ocurrida entonces.' "

7. *Ibid.*, p. 468.

8. i.e., from her marriage in 1868 to 1876, when appeared her *Estudio crítico de las obras del P. Feijóo.* Cf. González-Blanco, p. 469: ". . . aquel lapso de tiempo, calculado en ocho años. . . .

9. González-Blanco, p. 469: "Como hemos de creer que fuese improductiva esta época, cuando ella misma nos confiesa que aquellas *excursiones encantadoras* del verano, a través de Galicia, a caballo, en coche y a pie, 'Empezaron a convertir mis ojos hacia el mundo exterior, me revelaron el reino de la naturaleza y me predispusieron a ser la incansable paisajista actual, prendada del gris de las nubes, del color de los castaños, de los ríos espumantes presos en las hoces, de los prados húmedos y de los caminos hondos de mi tierra'?"

10. Prologue to *La Dama joven*, Barcelona, 1907, p. iii.

11. Espasa: *Enciclopedia*, XLI, 1438. The encyclopedia quotes from Pardo's *Apuntes autobiográficos*, which were published at the beginning of her *Los Pazos de Ulloa* in its first edition only (1886): "Mi congénito amor a las letras sufrió largo eclipse, obscurecido entre las distracciones que ofrecía Madrid a la recién casada de diez y seis años, que salía de una vida austera, limitada. al trato de la familia y de amigos graves, al bullicio cortesano y a la sociedad elegante."

12. When one of Pardo's children died, she dedicated a small book of verse to him under the title *Jaime.*

13. Robert Osborne in his book *Emilia Pardo Bazán: Su vida y sus obras* has reproduced Doña Emilia's official baptismal record to prove her birthday was Sept. 16, 1851. Hence she truly *had* completed her sixteenth year when she was wed on July 10, 1868. We can only conclude that Gómez-Carrillo misquoted her or else the lady was fibbing about her age. This has led to some confusion since even the Espasa *Enciclopedia* gives her birth date as 1852.

14. Gómez-Carillo: "Mme Pardo Bazán à Paris," *Mercure de France*, LX (April, 1906), 458-459.

15. José León Pagano: *Al través de la España literaria*, Barcelona, 1904, pp. 124-127.

16. González-Blanco: *Historia de la novela*, p. 471: "Se empapa de Kant, Hegel, Fichte y Schelling, retrocediendo luego hasta Platón y Aristóteles; y con todo ordena sus lecturas, distribuyendo las horas, gozando así en la reposada lectura 'momentos de sereno bienestar y adquiriendo, sobre todo, el hábito del trabajo constante, la afición a la lectura seguida, metódica y reflexiva, que pasa de solaz y toca en estudio.' "

17. Prologue to *La Dama joven*, p. vi: "Mi inteligencia curiosa, ávida de abarcarlo todo, limitada en su afán por la imposibilidad práctica de conseguir nada de provecho en ciencias que reclaman la vida entera del que aspira a profundizarlas, ha intentado jugar con el martillo del geólogo, el compás del astrónomo y el soplete del químico, y los ha soltado con desaliento, como suelta el niño un arma grave, convenciéndose de que le faltan fuerzas, no ya para manejarla, sino para empuñarla un minuto. La gran poesía de la ciencia positiva la siento allá en serenas regiones intelectuales, a semejanza de los que sin saber latín perciben armonía maravillosa en los versos de Virgilio."

18. *Historia de la novela*, p. 472.

19. Benito Pérez Galdós: *Arte y crítica,* "Conferencias de Emilia Pardo Bazán en el Ateneo" (*Obras inéditas*), Madrid, 1887, pp. 205-206.

20. Boris de Tannenberg: *L'Espagne littéraire,* p. 309: "L'ambition l'avait séduite autrefois de doter son pays d'un livre qui lui manque, une *Histoire de la littérature espagnole.* Ce livre nécessaire, nul n'est mieux préparé qu'elle a l'écrire; nul ne réunit si bien toutes les qualités requises. . . . A-t-elle abandonné ce projet? Espérons qu'elle y reviendra."

21. Gómez Carillo: "Mme Pardo Bazán à Paris," *Mercure de France,* LX (April 1906), 461. He quotes Pardo: "Je suis très communicative et c'est en France que j'ai trouvé la société intellectuelle qui correspond le mieux à mon goût. Après ma conférence de Paris je fus couverte de fleurs; chaque conférence que j'ai donné en Espagne ne m'a valu que des déboires: cela n'a pas peu contribué à me rendre française."

22. Manuel Gálvez: "Emilia Pardo Bazán," *Nosotros,* XXXVIII (May 1921), 31-32.

23. *Ibid.,* p. 32. "Agregaré aquí que poseía también otras dos cualidades indispensables al crítico: la serenidad del espíritu y un perfecto sentimiento de la justicia. Es curioso observar como en plena discusión sobre el naturalismo, en medio de la general malevolencia, de la estupidez, de la ignorancia, no perdió nunca su serenidad y su sentimiento justiciero. Explicó la nueva doctrina con una perspicacia, sobriedad e imparcialdad verdaderamente notables. En ninguna de las páginas de esa obra maestra que es *La Cuestión palpitante* y que todos los espíritus cultos debieran conocer, demostró indignación ni sectarismo, ni aun excesivo entusiasmo. Y combatía sola, puede decirse; y teniendo en su contra a toda España: a la sociedad aristocrática a que pertenecía, al clero, a los grandes escritores, y la prensa, la cual, como ocurre en estos casos, no dejó de exibirse grosera, incomprensiva e ignorante. Juzgó la doctrina como si ella fuese une extraña y no una discípula: señalando sus méritos y sus errores."

24. Pardo Bazán: "Emilio Zola," *La Lectura* II, pt. 3 (November, 1902), 278.

25. Gómez de Baquero: "*La evolución de la novela,*" *Cultura española,* X (1908), 396: "Esto no obstante, la influencia de la Sra. Pardo Bazán ha sido poderosa. Ha dado al naturalismo español una autoridad que difícilmente habría adquerido, de ser otro su campeón. El hecho de que una dama de ideas tradicionalistas, o que al menos tenía un pasado de ideas tradicionalistas, si bien templadas por un espíritu tolerante y moderno; de elevada clase, historiador de santos y poetas cristianos, defendiese el naturalismo, acalló o amansó muchas prevenciones. La suerte de las escuelas importadas depiende mucho de la calidad de sus importadores."

26. Boris de Tannenberg: *L'Espagne littéraire,* p. 305: "Comme il fallait s'y attendre, elle débuta par le pastiche de Zola. *La Femme tribun* . . . est le roman naturaliste selon la formule."

27. Quoted in Pagano: *Al través de la España literaria,* pp. 117-118.

28. Tenreiro: "Emilia Pardo Bazán: *Belcebú,*" *La Lectura,* XII, pt. 1 (March, 1912), 257: "Mas las dotes insignes de la Condesa de Pardo Bazán estaban destinadas a lucir dentro del marco de la novela de modo más completo que en ninguno de los órdenes de actividad literaria en que ejercitó su pluma la polígrafa ilustre, cuya pluralidad de talentos sólo con la de D. Juan Valera podría ser comparada."

29. Manuel Gálvez: "E. P. B.," *Nosotros,* XXXVIII, 27: "Se la juzgaba principalmente como novelista; sin embargo, no es ésta la actividad literaria en que más ha sobresalido. Yo prefiero en ella al cuentista, y, relativamente a la literatura de su pais, al crítico.

"Porque en cuanto novelista, la señora Pardo Bazán es inferior a Pereda, a Galdós y a Palacio Valdés. No es creador de grandes caracteres, y sus concepciones, si bien jamás vulgares carecen de genialidad. Su verdadero talento reside en la evocación del ambiente, sobre todo del cuadro regional. Imposible olvidar *Los Pazos de Ulloa,* vigorosa novela, comparable a *Peñas Arriba,* de Pereda."

NOTES TO CHAPTER II

30. Romera-Navarro: *Historia de la literatura española*, p. 422, speaking of Feijóo, says: "Los ocho tomos de su *Teatro crítico universal* (1726-1739) componen una vasta enciclopedia donde el autor señala, en casi todos los ramos del saber y en las actividades de la vida, los errores comunes en aquel tiempo."

31. An example of this is Pardo's article on Zola's *Docteur Pascal*; it appeared first in *España Moderna* for September 1893 and appeared in the *Nuevo Teatro Crítico* for November 1893. An article comprising the prologue for her translation of Edmond de Goncourt's *Les frères Zemganno* appears in *España Moderna* for March 1891 and also in *Nuevo Teatro Crítico* shortly after. The book appeared in June 1891. Furthermore, when her *Biblioteca de la Mujer* published a translation of John Stuart Mill's essay *On the Subjection of Women,* Pardo's prologue came out in her *Nuevo Teatro* shortly before the book was published in June 1892.

32. In the *Teatro Crítico* for October 1891 appears a study of Alarcón, and in April 1893 there is one on Campoamor; both of these form part of her volume of criticism entitled *Retratos y apuntes literarios* (1908).

33. *Nuevo Teatro Crítico* for September is reviewed in the July number of *Revista contemporánea*.

34. de Tannenberg: *L'Espagne littéraire*, p. 309.

35. Pardo Bazán: "Boris de Tannenberg: *L'Espagne littéraire,*" *La Lectura*, III, pt. 3 (September, 1903), 107.

36. González-Blanco: "Emilia Pardo Bazán," *La Lectura*, VIII, pt. 1 (April, 1908), 421.

37. Cf. note 34 above for reference to the de Goncourt translation. The other work was A. Vitu's *Paris*, translated by Pardo Bazán and issued in instalments all through the year 1891. The edition was profusely illustrated and much commented upon in book reviews in *Revista contemporánea*.

38. Luis Morote: *Teatro y novela*, Madrid, 1906, pp. 213-215.

39. Gómez de Baquero: "Crónica literaria: Emilia Pardo Bazán: *Cuentos sacroprofanos,*" *España Moderna*, July 1899, p. 119: "Como todos los escritores que han escrito mucho y han conseguido gran notoriedad, varias veces y por parte de diversas clases y gentes ha experimentado la ilustre novelista los efectos de la feroz intolerancia a que son dados muchos españoles. . . . Ahora mismo, con motivo de su conferencia, *La España de ayer y la de hoy,* levantó contra ella un conato de tempestad de *chauvinisme,* que no sería excesivo calificar de bárbaro. . . ."

40. There has been some confusion as to just how Doña Emilia got her title of Countess. Ronald Hilton, writing in the November 1951 edition of *Hispania,* explains as follows: "Her father was named Conde de Pardo Bazán by the Pope for having voted against religious freedom in the Cortes of 1869. . . . Doña Emilia's father died in 1888, and she inherited the papal title. However, she refused to use it, and it was not until 1908 when King Alfonso XIII bestowed on her the title of countess in honor of her literary activities that she began to sign herself Condesa de Pardo Bazán." (pp. 327-328)

41. González-Blanco: "Emilia Pardo Bazán," *La Lectura*, VIII, pt. 1 (February, 1908), 156.

42. Tenreiro: "Emilia Pardo Bazán: *Dulce dueño,*" *La Lectura*, XI, pt. 2 (August, 1911), 443.

43. Gutiérrez-Gamero: *Gota a gota el mar se agota*, Barcelona, 1934, p. 237.

44. During her last years occurred the tragic incident of her appointment to the chair of modern literature in the University of Madrid (1916). It was an appointment which she had long desired but it was a hollow triumph, for only one student consented to attend her lectures. Evidently the male resentment of her was still continuing. Never daunted, however, the Countess went ahead and lectured to her one student. Her voluminous lecture notes were later collected into a volume entitled *El lirismo en la*

poesía francesa, which was published posthumously as part of her *Obras completas*.

45. Manuel Gálvez: "Emilia Pardo Bazán," *Nosotros*, XXXVIII (May, 1921), 34.

NOTES TO CHAPTER III

1. Zola: *Le Ventre de Paris*, François Bernouard, Paris, 1927, p. 216.
2. Zola: *La Faute de l'Abbé Mouret*, François Bernouard, Paris, 1927, pp. 18-20.
3. Zola: *Le Docteur Pascal*, François Bernouard, Paris, 1927, p. 56.
4. Zola: *Le Roman expérimental*, François Bernouard, Paris, 1927, p. 77.
5. Translation by Rodrigo Soriano, editor of *La Epoca*, of what Zola said to him in an interview. Quoted in Pardo Bazán: *La Cuestión palpitante (Obras completas)*, I, 24-25.
6. González-Blanco: "Emilia Pardo Bazán," *La Lectura*, VIII, pt. 1 (April, 1908), 421.
7. Pardo Bazán: *La Cuestión palpitante*, p. 60.
8. The Chapter referred to are: IX Los Vencedores, beginning at p. 141, X Flaubert, beginning at p. 155, XI Los hermanos Goncourt, beginning at p. 169; XII Daudet pp. 183 to 195. Zola's name appears ten times in Chapter IX and almost every mention of him involves a reference to something he said in *Les Romanciers naturalistes*. In Chapter X he is mentioned once; in Chapter XI, five times; in XII, eleven times, with frequent reference again to statements made in *Les Romanciers naturalistes*. Chapter IX treats of Stendhal and Balzac, who are the subjects of Zola's first two essays in *Les Romanciers*; the three following chapters also are in corresponding order.
9. Pardo Bazán: *La Cuestión palpitante*, pp. 209-210.
10. *Ibid.*, pp. 211-212.
11. *Ibid.*, p. 62.
12. *Ibid.*, p. 70.
13. *Ibid.*, p. 67.
14. Pardo Bazán: *Polémicos y estudios literarios*, (*Obras completas*), VI, 138.
15. *La Cuestión palpitante*, p. 208.
16. *Ibid.*, p. 209.
17. Zola: *Le Roman expérimental*, pp. 85-86.
18. *La Cuestión palpitante*, p. 64.
19. Pardo Bazán: *Polémicos y estudios literarios*, p. 139.
20. Juan Valera: *Apuntes sobre el nuevo arte de escribir novelas* (*Obras completas*), XXVI, 195 "Tampoco, en realidad, voy yo a lanzar los rayos de la crítica contra los naturalistas franceses en la práctica, esto es, en sus novelas. La pereza me impide leerlas. . . . Mi crítica va contra los preceptos desatinados, contra las enormidades antiestéticas, y nada más." Of this book Pardo Bazán says: "De las polémicas . . . una . . . sobre el *nuevo arte de escribir novelas*, contra mi *Cuestión palpitante*. Y no es exacto que le llame polémica; debiera llamarle impugnación o, para mejor rigor en expresarme, pieza de concierto sobre motivos sugeridos por mi libro. . . ." "Don Juan Valera," *La Lectura*, VI, pt. 3 (November, 1906), 197.
21. Juan Valera: *Apuntes sobre el nuevo arte de escribir novelas*, p. 35.
22. Pardo Bazán: *La literatura francesa moderna*, III, *El naturalismo* (*Obras completas*), XLI, 302.
23. Pardo Bazán: "*El Doctor Pascal*, última novela de Emilio Zola," *España Moderna*, September, 1893, p. 173.
24. Pardo Bazán: (*Prefacio*) *Un viaje de novios* (*Obras completas*), XXX, 7.
25. *La Cuestión palpitante*, p. 214.

26. *Ibid.*, p. 180.
27. Pardo Bazán: "Zola y Tolstoy," *Nuevo teatro crítico*, May, 1891, pp. 52-53.
28. *La Cuestión*, pp. 74-75.
29. Pardo Bazán: *"Fernando Brunetière,"* *La Lectura*, VII, pt. 2 (July, 1907), 238.
30. *La Cuestión*, p. 169.
31. *Ibid.*, p. 177.
32. *Ibid.*, p. 181.
33. *Ibid.*, p. 185.
34. *Ibid.*, pp. 224-225.
35. Pardo Bazán: *El naturalismo*, (*Obras completas*), XLI, 103.
36. Pardo Bazán: "La novela novelesca," *Nuevo teatro crítico*, June, 1891, p. 41.
37. *La Cuestión*, p. 241.
38. Pardo Bazán: "Zola y Tolstoy," *Nuevo teatro crítico*, May, 1891, p. 39.
39. Pardo Bazán: "El Desastre," *Nuevo teatro crítico*, September, 1892, p. 92.
40. *La Cuestión*, p. 193.
41. *Idem: Polémicos y estudios literarios*, pp. 124-125.
42. *Ibid.*, p. 137.
43. *Ibid.*, p. 125.
44. Zola: *Le Roman expérimental*, p. 105.
45. *La Cuestión*, pp. 139-140.
46. Pardo Bazán: (*Prefacio*) *Un viaje de novios*, p. 11.
47. *Idem:* (*Prefacio*) *La Quimera*, p. 10.
48. *Le Roman expérimental*, pp. 173-174.
49. *La Cuestión*, p. 66.
50. *Ibid.*, p. 222.
51. *Ibid.*, pp. 223-224.
52. "Zola y Tolstoy," *Nuevo teatro crítico*, May, 1891, p. 54.
53. (*Prefacio*) *Un viaje de novios*, p. 8.
54. *La Cuestión*, p. 186.
55. *Ibid.*, p. 215.
56. From an article in *La Vie littéraire*, signed Fabrice W., and quoted in the François Bernouard edition of Zola's *Son Excellence Eugène Rougon*, p. 429.
57. *La Cuestión*, p. 227.
58. *Ibid.*, p. 229.
59. "Zola y Tolstoy," *Nuevo teatro crítico*, May, 1891, pp. 53-54.
60. *El Naturalismo*, pp. 104-105.
61. *Ibid.*, p. 108.
62. F. Díaz Carmona: "La novela naturalista," *Ciencia cristiana*, IV (1884), p. 80.
63. *El Naturalismo*, p. 113.
64. *Ibid.*, pp. 124-125.
65. (*Prefacio*) *Un viaje de novios*, p. 6.
66. *Ibid.*, p. 7.
67. *Ibid.*, p. 8.
68. *El Naturalismo*, p. 104.
69. (*Prefacio*) *Un viaje de novios*, p. 8.
70. *La Cuestión*, p. 6.
71. "La novela novelesca," *Nuevo teatro crítico*, June, 1891, p. 40.
72. Pardo Bazán: "Emilio Zola," *La Lectura*, II, pt. 3 (November, 1902), 279, 287.
73. Pardo Bazán: "Fernando Brunetière," *La Lectura*, VII, pt. 2 (July, 1907), 234.
74. *El Naturalismo*, p. 99.
75. *Ibid.*, p. 105.

76. Pardo Bazán: "Tolstoi," *La Lectura*, X, pt. 3 (December, 1910), 282-283.
77. *El Naturalismo*, p. 308. "Zola no fué un crítico excelente, porque, en otras cosas, le faltó la convicción. La confesión de este escepticismo del maestro, recogida por Goncourt, es en extremo curiosa. Hallándose reunidos, se dió Flaubert a atacar los prefacios, las doctrinas, las profesiones de fe de Zola, a lo cual respondió éste:
" 'Me río lo mismo que usted de esa palabra naturalismo, pero la repito porque hay que bantigar las cosas a fin de que parezcan nuevas . . . Una cosa son mis libros, otra mis artículos. De mis artículos no hago cuenta. No sirven sino para levantar polvareda en torno de mis libros. He apoyado un clavo en la cabeza del público, y voy dando martillazos. . . . A cada uno, entra el clavo un centímetro. Y mi martillo es la Prensa.' "
78. *Ibid.*, p. 309.
79. *Ibid.*, p. 99.
80. *Polémicos y estudios literarios*, p. 137.
81. Pardo Bazán: *"El Doctor Pascual*, última novela de Emilio Zola," *España Moderna*, September, 1893, p. 179.

NOTES TO CHAPTER IV

1. Blanco García, Francisco: *La Literature española en el siglo XIX*, Madrid, 1910, p. 539.
2. de Tannenberg, Boris: *L'Espagne littéraire*, Paris, 1903, p. 305.
3. González-Blanco, Andrés: *Historia de la novela en España desde el romanticismo a nuestros días*, Madrid, 1909, p. 489.
4. Pardo Bazán: *La Tribuna, (Obras completas*, Vol. 8), p. 56.
5. *Ibid.*, p. 195.
6. *Ibid.*, pp. 164-165.
7. Pardo Bazán: *(Prólogo a) La Dama joven*, Barcelona, 1907, p. iii.
8. Pardo Bazán: *(Prólogo a) La Tribuna*, p. 7.
9. *La Tribuna*, pp. 12-13.
10. *Ibid.*, p. 54.
11. Zola: *Le Ventre de Paris*, François Bernouard, Paris, 1927, pp. 93-94.
12. Pardo Bazán: *La Cuestión palpitante, (Obras completas*, Vol. 1), p. 225.
13. Pardo Bazán: *La Tribuna*, p. 162.
14. *Ibid.*, p. 57.
15. *Ibid.*, p. 195.
16. *Ibid.*, p. 87.
17. *Ibid.*, p. 195.
18. *Ibid.*, p. 253.
19. Leopoldo Alas (Clarín) : *Sermón perdido*, Madrid, 1885, p. 115.
20. *Ibid.*, p. 114.
21. *(Prólogo a) La Tribuna*, p. 6.
22. Zola: *Le Roman expérimental*, François Bernouard, Paris, 1927, pp. 16, 19.
23. Pardo Bazán: *La Dama joven* (Collection including *Bucólica*), p. 89.
24. *(Prólogo a) La Dama joven*, pp. iii-iv.
25. Pardo Bazán: *Los Pazos de Ulloa, (Obras completas*, Vol. 3), pp. 118-119.
26. Lorenzo Benito: "Los Pazos de Ulloa," *Revista Contemporánea*, LXV (February, 1887), 398.
27. *Los Pazos de Ulloa*, p. 30.
28. Zola: *La Faute de l'Abbé Mouret*, François Bernouard, Paris, 1927, p. 26.

29. *Ibid.*, pp. 36-38.
Frère Archangias haussa les épaules . . .
—Ecoutez, monsieur le curé, reprit-il enfin, je suis trop bas pour vous adresser des observations; seulement, j'ai presque le double de votre âge, je connais le pays, ce qui m'autorise à vous dire que vous n'arriverez à rien par la douceur. . . .
Et il partit en courant, son rabat sale volant sur l'épaule, sa grande soutane graisseuse arrachant les chardons. . . .
Le prêtre continua sa marche. Frère Archangias lui causait parfois d'étranges scrupules; il lui apparaissait dans sa . . . crudité, comme le véritable homme de Dieu. . . . Et il se désespérait de ne pouvoir se dépouiller davantage de son corps, de ne pas être laid, immonde, puant la vermine des saints. . . .
Compare this from *Los Pazos*, pp. 57-58.
. . . y al abad de Ulloa . . . le exasperaba Julián, a quien solía apodar *mariquitas*, porque para el abad de Ulloa, la última de las degradaciones en que podía caer un hombre era beber agua, lavarse con jabón de olor y cortarse las uñas: tratándose de un sacerdote, el abad ponía estos delitos en parangón con la simonía. . . .
30. *Los Pazos*, p. 26.
31. *Ibid.*, pp. 97-98.
32. *Ibid.*, p. 185.
33. Lorenzo Benito: "Los Pazos de Ulloa," *Revista Contemporánea*, LXV (February, 1887), 399-401.
34. *Los Pazos*, pp. 133-134.
35. *Ibid.*, pp. 222-224.
36. *Ibid.*, pp. 225-226.
37. *Ibid.*, pp. 230-231.
38. *Ibid.*, p. 234.
39. *Ibid.*, p. 239.
40. *Ibid.*, p. 318.
41. Lorenzo Benito: "Los Pazos de Ulloa," *Revista Contemporánea*, LXV, (February, 1887), 402.
42. *Los Pazos*, pp. 37-38.
43. F. Vézinet: *Les Maîtres du roman espagnol contemporain*, Paris, 1907, pp. 213-214.
44. *Ibid.*, pp. 212-213.
45. Manuel Gálvez: "Emilia Pardo Bazán," *Nosotros*, XXXVIII (1921), 33-34: "Y no sólo fué doña Emilia de su tiempo, sino que fué un escritor europeo. . . . Ello es que en España los únicos escritores universales, traducidos con éxito al francés, al inglés, al alemán y a otras lenguas, son aquellas que han recibido la poderosa influencia inglesa o francesa: Palacio Valdés, Valle-Inclán, Blasco Ibáñez, Emilia Pardo Bazán, Jacinto Benavente. . . ."
46. Zola: *La Faute de l'Abbé Mouret*, pp. 260-261.
47. *Ibid.*, p. 266.
48. Zola: (*Ebauche de*) *La Faute de l'Abbé Mouret*, p. 418.
49. Pardo Bazán: *La Madre Naturaleza*, (*Obras completas*, Vol. 4), p. 283.
50. *La Faute*, p. 254.
51. *Ibid.*, pp. 250-251.
52. *La Madre*, p. 244.
53. Zola: *Le Roman expérimental*, pp. 188-189.
54. *La Faute*, p. 249.
55. *La Madre*, pp. 265-266.
56. *Ibid.*, p. 231.
57. *Ibid.*, p. 134.
58. *Ibid.*, p. 162.
59. *Ibid.*, p. 276.
60. *Ibid.*, p. 370.

61. *Ibid.*, p. 375.
62. Pardo Bazán: *Insolación* (*Obras completas*, Vol. 7), p. 22.
63. *Ibid.*, p. 28.
64. *Ibid.*, p. 40.
65. *Ibid.*, p. 43.
66. *Ibid.*, p. 47.
67. *Ibid.*, p. 53.
68. *Ibid.*, p. 63.
69. *Ibid.*, p. 68.
70. *Ibid.*, p. 71.
71. *Ibid.*, p. 76.
72. *Ibid.*, p. 101.
73. *Ibid.*, p. 131.
74. *Ibid.*, p. 136.
75. *Ibid.*, p. 185.
76. F. Vézinet: *Les maîtres du roman espagnol contemporain*, Paris, 1907. p. 230.
77. Pardo Bazán: *Morriña* (*Obras completas*, Vol. 7), p. 223.
78. Juan Valera: "*Morriña* por Emilia Pardo Bazán" (*Obras completas*, Vol. 28), p. 10.
79. *Ibid.*, pp. 17-18.
80. Blanco García: *La Literatura española en el siglo XIX*, Madrid, 1910, p. 543: "Mil veces protestó la gran escritora coruñesa contra las extremosidades y groserías y contra los principios filosóficos de Zola, aun al admitir parte de sus procedimientos, y he aquí que, por la resbaladiza pendiente de la lógica, viene a parar en la sima del determinismo al escribir, no sólo *La madre Naturaleza*, cuya conclusión trae a la memoria los mitos y leyendas helénicos de Edipo y Mirra, sino también *Insolación* y *Morriña*, a pesar de que las travesuras amorosas de la primera naración vienen a finalizar en la Vicaria, y de que la segunda flotan vagos celajes de idealismo."
81. *Morriña*, pp. 292-293.
82. *Ibid.*, pp. 291, 255.
83. *Ibid.*, p. 250.
84. *Ibid.*, pp. 256-257.
85. *Ibid.*, p. 217.
86. *Ibid.*, p. 225.
87. *Ibid.*, p. 253.
88. *Ibid.*, pp. 265-267.
89. *Ibid.*, pp. 268-269.
90. *Ibid.*, p. 288.
91. *Ibid.*, pp. 290, 294.
92. *Ibid.*, pp. 358-359.
93. Pardo Bazán: *La Piedra Angular* (*Obras completas*, Vol. 2), p. 219.
94. Pardo Bazán: "Notas literarias," *Nuevo teatro crítico*, September, 1891, p. 95.
95. Leopoldo Pedreira: "*La Piedra angular*," *Revista contemporánea*, LXXXV (January, 1892), 118.
96. *La Piedra Angular*, p. 72.
97. *Ibid.*, p. 70.
98. Zola: *L'Assommoir*, François Bernouard, Paris, 1927, pp. 242, 247.
99. *La Piedra Angular*, p. 69.
100. *Ibid.*, p. 299.

NOTES TO CHAPTER V

1. Zola: *La Faute de l'Abbé Mouret*, François Bernouard, Paris, 1927, pp. 173-174.
2. Pardo Bazán: *Un Viaje de novios* (*Obras completas*, Vol. 30), pp. 169-170.

3. *Ibid.*, p. 94.

4. *Ibid.*, pp. 209-210.

5. Pardo Bazán: *El Cisne de Vilamorta*, Madrid, 1928, pp. 5-6.

6. Lorenzo Benito: *"El Cisne de Vilamorta," Revista contemporánea*, LVIII (July, 1885), 12: "El prólogo . . . no la perdonaré a V. nunca el haberlo escrito, porque . . . yo no puedo menos de decir que me ha engañado V. como a un chino . . . Salir al paso de los críticos que puedan acusar a V. de que *El Cisne de Vilamorta* es un tributo pagado a la escuela romántica como en desagravio de las ofensas que V. pudo inferirla con *La Tribuna* representa o un apocamiento de espíritu (imposible en V.) ante las severidades de cierta crítica académica que reniega de su siglo . . . o un ligero remordimiento que a V. asalta por no ajustarse a los estrechos preceptos de la religión naturalista . . . Ya sé yo que V. me contestará que no hay tal, sino que los personajes son románticos por temperamento, y que . . . no es ésta razón para excluirlos del mundo del arte . . .; pero si he de decir la verdad, confesaré que tampoco este argumento encuentro que justifique el prólogo, porque yo dudo, y conmigo otros muchos, que sean románticos los personajes de *El Cisne de Vilamorta*."

7. Pardo Bazán: *(Prólogo a) La Dama joven*, Barcelona, 1907, p. viii.

8. Blanca de los Ríos: "Elogio de la Condesa de Pardo Bazán," *Raza Española* No. XXX (1921), p. 27.

9. *Ibid.*, p. 28.

10. *Ibid.*, p. 32.

11. Zola: *L'Oeuvre*, François Bernouard, Paris, 1927, p. 380.

12. Pardo Bazán: *La Quimera (Obras completas*, Vol. 29), p. 536.

13. *Ibid.*, p. 440.

14. Gómez de Baquero: "La Evolución de la novela: La última manera espiritual de la Sra. Pardo Bazán: *La Quimera y La Sirena negra*," *Cultura Española*, No. X (1908), p. 397.

15. *Ibid.*, p. 399.

16. Pardo Bazán: (Prólogo a) *La Quimera*, p. 8: "Y discurriendo acerca de este efecto, doy en creer que la intención de la sátira estorba el paso a la verdad, como la caricatura al parecido, y que para pintar lo que fuere . . . es rigor atenerse a la verdad sencilla (no a la verdad *nimia*) y entrar en la tarea con ánimo desapasionado."

17. *La Quimera*, p. 287.

18. *Ibid.*, pp. 296-297.

19. *Ibid.*, pp. 308-309.

20. *Ibid.*, p. 394.

21. Gómez de Baquero: "Crónica literaria: Emilia Pardo Bazán: *La Quimera*," *España Moderna*, October, 1905, p. 170.

22. *L'Oeuvre*, p. 265.

23. *La Quimera*, p. 240.

24. *Ibid.*, pp. 243-244.

25. *L'Oeuvre*, pp. 90, 198.

26. *La Quimera*, p. 413.

27. *Ibid.*, pp. 206-207.

28. Zola: *Le Docteur Pascal*, François Bernouard, Paris, 1927, p. 46.

NOTES TO CHAPTER VI

1. Julio Cejador y Frauca: *Historia de la lengua y literature castellana*, Madrid, 1918, IX, 271.

2. *Ibid.*, IX, 274.

3. Luis Araujo-Costa: "Emilia Pardo Bazán y la literature francesa del siglo XIX," *Raza española*, No. XXX (1921), p. 52.

4. Pardo Bazán: *La literatura francesa moderna: El naturalismo, (Obras completas*, Vol. 41), p. 125.

5. *Ibid.*, p. 104.

6. José A. Balseiro: *Novelistas españoles modernos*, New York, 1933, p. 274.

7. *Ibid.*, p. 268.

8. *Ibid.*, p. 265.

9. *Ibid.*, p. 269.

10. *Ibid.*, p. 268.

11. Gómez de Baquero: "La Evolución de la novela: La última manera espiritual de la Sra. Pardo Bazán: *La Quimera* y *La Serena negra*," *Cultura Española*, No. X (1908), pp. 396-397.

12. Gómez de Baquero (Andrenio): *De Gallardo a Unamuno*, Madrid, 1926, p. 154.

13. Pardo Bazán: *La España de ayer y la de hoy* (*L'Espagne d'hier et celle d'aujourd'hui*), polyglot edition, Madrid, 1899, p. 51.

14. Balseiro: *Novelistas españoles modernos*, pp. 268-269.

15. Pardo Bazán: *Retratos y apuntes literarios*, (*Obras completas*, Vol. 32), p. 190.

16. Although the date of *Retratos y apuntes literarios* is 1908, this essay on Alarcón first appeared in *Nuevo teatro crítico* for October, 1891.

17. Manuel Gálvez: "Emilia Pardo Bazán," *Nosotros*, XXXVIII (1921), 33.

18. *Ibid.*, p. 34.

19. Emilio González López: *Emilia Pardo Bazán, novelista de Galicia*, New York, 1944, p. 55.

20. *Ibid.*, p. 58.

21. *Ibid.*, p. 177.

BIBLIOGRAPHY

Included in this partial bibliography are not only the articles and books referred to in the Notes but also numerous works and studies which have appeared in the last fifteen years and which could have a bearing on our subject. Since the editions of the works of Zola, Pardo Bazán and their critics to which the Notes refer have long been out of print, I have indicated the best of the currently available editions as well.

Alas, Leopoldo (Clarín): *Sermón perdido,* Madrid, 1885.

Araujo-Costa, Luis: "Emilia Pardo Bazán y la literatura francesa del siglo XIX," *Raza española,* No. XXX (1921).

Balseiro, José A.: *Novelistas españoles modernos,* New York, 1933. Also reissued by Las Americas Publishing Co. N.Y.C. 1963.

Benito, Lorenzo: *"El cisne de Vilamorta,"* *Revista contemporánea,* LVIII (July 1885).

Benito, Lorenzo: *"Los pazos de Ulloa,"* *Revista contemporánea,* LXV (Feb. 1887).

Blanco García, Francisco: *La literatura española en el siglo XIX,* Madrid, 1910.

Bravo-Villasante, Carmen: *Vida y Obra de Emilia Pardo Bazán,* Madrid, Revista de Occidente, 1962.

Brown, Donald F.: "Pardo Bazán and Zola: Refutation of Some Critics," *Romanic Review,* XXVII, p. 273 (1936).

Brown, Donald F.: "Two Naturalistic Versions of Genesis: Zola and Pardo Bazán," *Modern Language Notes,* LII, p. 243 (1937).

Brown, M. Gordon: "La condesa de Pardo Bazán y el naturalismo," *Hispania* XXXI, p. 152 (1948).

Cejador y Frauca, Julio: *Historia de la lengua y literatura castellana,* Madrid, 1918, Vol. IX.

Chandler, Arthur A.: "The Role of Literary Tradition in the Trajectory of Emilia Pardo Bazán" Dissertation Abstract XVI 1450 (Ohio State 1956).

Contreras, Matilda: "Two Interpreters of Galicia: Rosalía de Castro and Emilia Pardo Bazán," Dissertation Abstract XXI 2703, (Pittsburgh 1960).

Davis, Gifford: "The 'coletilla' to Pardo Bazán's *Cuestión palpitante,"* *Hispanic Review,* XXIV (1956).

Díaz Carmona, F.: "La novela naturalista," *Ciencia cristiana,* IV (1884).

Eddy, Nelson W.: "Pardo Bazán, Menéndez y Pelayo and Pereda Criticism," *Romanic Review,* XXXVII p. 336 (1946).

Espasa: *Enciclopedia universal ilustrada,* XLI, 1438.

Gálvez, Manuel: "Emilia Pardo Bazán," *Nosotros,* XXXVIII, (May 1921).

García Ramón, Leopoldo: "Cartas de Paris," *Revista contemporánea,* LXIV (Nov. 1886).

Gerchunoff, Alberto: "Notas sobre Emilio Zola," *Nosotros,* IX (Feb. 1913).

Giles, Mary E.: "Color Adjectives in Pardo Bazán's Novels," *Romance Notes* (U. of N.C.) 10 (1968) p. 54.

Giles, Mary E.: "Impressionist Techniques in Descriptions by Emilia Pardo Bazán," *Hispanic Review,* XXX (1962) p. 304.

Giles, Mary E.: "Pardo Bazán's Two Styles," *Hispania,* XLVIII, (1965) p. 456.

Gómez de Baquero: "Crónica literaria: Emilia Pardo Bazán: *Cuentos sacroprofanos,"* *España Moderna,* July 1899.

Gómez de Baquero: "Crónica literaria: Emilia Pardo Bazán: *La Quimera,"* *España Moderna,* Oct. 1905.

Gomez de Baquero: "La evolución de la novela: La última manera espiritual de la Sra. Pardo Bazán: *La Quimera* y *La Sirena negra,"* *Cultura española,* No. X (1908).

Gómez-Carillo: "Mme Pardo Bazán à Paris," *Mercure de France,* LX (April 1906).

González-Blanco, Andrés: "Emilia Pardo Bazán" *La Lectura,* VIII, pt. 1 (Feb. 1908).

González-Blanco, Andrés: "Emilia Pardo Bazán," *La Lectura,* VIII, pt. 1 (April 1908).

González-Blanco, Andrés: *Historia de la novela en España desde el romanticismo a nuestros días,* Madrid, 1909.

González López, Emilio: *Emilia Pardo Bazán, novelista de Galicia,* New York, 1944.

La Grande Encyclopédie, Paris, 1886–1902, Vols. VI, 263, 363 & XX, 536.

Gutiérrez-Gamero: *Gota a gota el mar se agota,* Barcelona, 1934.

Hilton, Ronald: "Doña Emilia Pardo Bazán and the Carlist Movement" *Modern Language Forum,* XXXVII, p. 101, (1952).

Hilton, Ronald: Doña Emilia Pardo Bazán the the 'Europication' of Spain," *Sumposium* VI, No. 2, Nov. 1952.

Hilton, Ronald: "Doña Emilia Pardo Bazán, Neo-Catholicism and Christian Socialism," *The Americas* XI, No. 1, July 1954.

Hilton, Ronald: "Emilia Pardo Bazán and the Americas," *The Americas* IX, No. 2, Oct. 1952.

Hilton, Ronald: "Emilia Pardo Bazán's Concept of Spain," *Hispania* XXXIV, Nov. 1951.

Hilton, Ronald: "Emilia Pardo Bazán et le mouvement féministe en Espagne," *Bulletin Hispanique* LIV, No. 2, (1952).

Hilton, Ronald: "Pardo Bazán's Analysis of the Social Structure of Spain," *Bulletin of Hispanic Studies* XXIX, p. 1, (1952).

Hilton, Ronald: "Pardo Bazán and Literary Polemics about Feminism," *Romanic Review* XLIV, No. 1, (1953).

Hilton, Ronald: "Pardo Bazán and the Spanish Problem," *Modern Language Quarterly* XIII, p. 292 (1952).

Hilton, Ronald: "Spanish Preconceptions about France, as Revealed in the Works of Emilia Pardo Bazán," *Bulletin of Hispanic Studies* XXX, p. 193 (1953).

Josephson, Matthew: *Zola and His Time,* New York, 1928.

Kirby, Harry Lee, Jr.: "Evolution of Thought in the Critical Writings and Novels of Emilia Pardo Bazán," *Dissertation Abstract* XXIV, 299 (Illinois 1963).

Kirby, Harry Lee, Jr.: "Pardo Bazán, Darwinism, and *La Madre Naturaleza,*" *Hispania* XLVII, 733, 1964.

Knox, Robert B.: "Artistry and Balance in *La madre naturaleza,*" *Hispania* XLI, 1958.

Kronik, John W.: "Emilia Pardo Bazán and the Phenomenon of French Decadentism," *PMLA* LXXXI, 418 (1966).

Lima, Fernando de Castro Pires de: "A condessa Emilia Pardo Bazán e o folclore galaico-português," *Panorama,* No. 14, p. 39 (Lisbon 1964).

Lott, Robert E.: "Observations on the Narrative Method, the Psychology, and the Style of *Los Pazos de Ulloa,*" *Hispania* LII, p. 3, (1969).

Martino, Pierre: *Le naturalisme français,* Paris, 1923.

Mazzeo, Guido E.: "La voluntad ajena en *Los Pazos de Ulloa* y *La Regenta,*" *Duquesne Hispanic Review* IV, p. 153, (1965).

McLean, Edward Fletcher: "Objectivity and Change in Pardo Bazán's Treatment of Priests, Agnostics, Protestants, and Jews" *Dissertation abstract* XXII, 873 (Duke 1961).

Morote, Luis: *Teatro y novela,* Madrid, 1906.

Osborne, Robert: "The Aesthetic Ideas of Emilia Pardo Bazán," *Modern Language Quarterly* XI, p. 98, (1950).

Osborne, Robert: "Emilia Pardo Bazán y la novela rusa," *Revista Hispánica Moderna* XX, p. 273, (1954).

Osborne, Robert E.: *Emilia Pardo Bazán: Su vida y sus obras,* Mexico, Andrea, 1964.

Pagano, José León: *Al través de la España literaria,* Barcelona, 1904.

Pardo Bazán: *Bucólica, Obras completas* Madrid, Aguilar, 4th Ed. 1964, Vol 1, p. 926.

Pardo Bazán: *El cisne de Vilamorta,* Madrid, 1928. Also in *Obras completas,* Madrid, Aguilar, 1956, Vol. 2.

Pardo Bazán: *La cuestión palpitante, Obras completas,* Madrid, 1888, Vol 1. Also Salamanca. Biblioteca Anaya, 1966.

Pardo Bazán: "*El Doctor Pascual,* última novela de Emilio Zola," *España Moderna,* Sept. 1893. Also in her *Nuevo Teatro Crítico,* Nov. 1893.

Pardo Bazán: "Emilio Zola," *La Lectura* II, pt. 3, (Nov. 1902).

Pardo Bazán: *La España de ayer y la de hoy (L'Espagne d'hier et celle d'aujourd'hui),* polyglot edition, Madrid, 1899.

Pardo Bazán: "Fernando Bruntière," *La Lectura* VII, pt. 2, (July 1907).

Pardo Bazán: *Insolación,* old *Obras completas* Vol. VII. Also Buenos Aires, Espasa Calpe, 1955. Also *Obras completas,* Madrid, Aguilar, 4th Ed. 1964, Vol. 1, p. 412.

Pardo Bazán: *La literatura francesa moderna:* III. *El naturalismo, Obras completas,* Madrid, 1914, Vol. 41.

Pardo Bazán: *La madre naturaleza,* old *Obras* Vol. 4. Also *Obras,* Madrid, Aguilar, 4th Ed. 1964, Vol 1, p. 285.
Pardo Bazán: *Morriña,* old *Obras, Vol.* 7. Also *Obras,* Madrid, Aguilar, 4th Ed. 1964, Vol. 1, p. 473.
Pardo Bazán: "La novela novelesca," *Nuevo teatro crítico,* June 1891.
Pardo Bazán: "Notas literarias," *Nuevo teatro crítico,* Sept. 1891.
Pardo Bazán: *Los pazos de Ulloa,* old *Obras,* vol. 3. Also Madrid, Aguilar, 1959. Also *Obras,* Madrid, Aguilar, 4th Ed. 1964, Vol. 1, p. 165.
Pardo Bazán: *La piedra angular,* old *Obras,* Vol. 2. Also *Obras,* Madrid, Aguilar, 1956, Vol. 2.
Pardo Bazán: *Polémicos y estudios literarios,* old *Obras,* Vol. 6.
Pardo Bazán: (Prólogo a) *La dama joven,* Barcelona, 1907.
Pardo Bazán: *La quimera,* old *Obras,* Vol. 29. Also *Obras,* Madrid, Aguilar, 4th Ed. 1964, Vol. 1, p. 705.
Pardo Bazán: *Retratos y apuntes literarios,* old *Obras,* Vol. 32.
Pardo Bazán: "Tolstoi," *La Lectura* X, pt. 3, (Dec. 1909).
Pardo Bazán: *La Tribuna,* old *Obras,* Vol. 8. Also Madrid, Taurus, 1968. And *Obras,* Madrid, Aguilar, 2nd Ed. 1956, Vol. 2, p. 101.
Pardo Bazán: *Un viaje de novios,* old *Obras,* Vol. 30. Also *Obras,* Madrid, Aguilar, 4th Ed. 1964, Vol. 1, p. 67.
Pardo Bazán: "Zola y Tolstoy," *Nuevo teatro crítico,* May 1891.
Pattison, Walter T.: *El naturalismo español,* Madrid, Gredos, 1965.
Pedreira, Leopoldo: *"La piedra angular," Revista contemporánea,* LXXXV, (Jan. 1892).
Richards, Henry Joseph: "True and Perverted Idealism in the Works of Emilia Pardo Bazán," Dissertation abstract XXVI, 4672, (Minnesota 1964).
Ríos, Blanca de los: "Elogio de la Condesa de Pardo Bazán," *Raza española* No. XXX (1921).
Rubia Barcia, J.: "La Pardo Bazán y Unamuno," *Cuadernos americanos,* Año XLX, CXIII, p. 240, (1960).
Sánchez, Porfirio: "Emilia Pardo Bazán: A Contrast Study Between the Novelist and the Short Story Writer," Dissertation abstract XXV, 1924, (U.C.L.A. 1964).
Scone, Elizabeth L.: "Cosmopolitan Attitudes in the Works of Emilia Pardo Bazán," Dissertation abstract XX, 2809, (New Mexico 1959).
Taine, Hippolyte: *Histoire de la littérature anglaise,* Paris, 1911. Also, Paris, Hachette, 1921.
Tannenberg, Boris de: *L'Espagne littéraire,* Paris, 1903.
Tenreiro: "Emilia Pardo Bazán: *Dulce dueño,"* *La Lectura,* XI, pt. 2, (Aug. 1911).
Tenreiro: "Emilia Pardo Bazán: *Belcebú,"* *La Lectura,* XII, pt. 1, (Mar. 1912).
Valera, Juan: *Apuntes sobre el nuevo arte de escribir novelas,* old *Obras* XXVI. Also, *Obras completas,* Madrid, Aguilar, 3rd. ed., 1961, Vol. 2, p. 616.
Valera, Juan: *"Morriña por Emilia Pardo Bazán,"* old *Obras,* XXVIII. Also, *Obras,* Madrid, Aguilar, 3rd. ed., 1961, Vol. 2, p. 794.
Vezinet, F.: *Les maîtres du roman espagnol contemporain,* Paris, 1907.
Zola, Emile: *L'Assommoir,* Paris, François Bernouard, 1927. Also, *Oeuvres complètes,* Edition sous la direction de Henri Mitterand, Paris, Cercle du livre précieux, 1962, Vol. 3.
Zola, Emile: *Le docteur Pascal,* Paris, F. Bernouard. 1927. Also, *Oeuvres,* Paris, Ed. Mitterand, 1962, Vol. 10.
Zola, Emile: *La faute de l'abbé Mouret,* Paris, F. Bernouard. 1927. Also *Oeuvres,* Paris, Ed. Mitterand, 1962, Vol. 3.
Zola, Emile: *Mes haines,* Paris, F. Bernouard. 1927. Also, *Oeuvres,* Paris, Ed. Mitterand, 1962, Vol. 10.
Zola, Emile: *L'Oeuvre,* Paris, F. Bernouard, 1927. Also, *Oeuvres,* Paris, Ed. Mitterand, 1962, Vol. 5.
Zola, Emile: *Le roman expérimental,* Paris, F. Bernouard, 1927. Also, *Oeuvres,* Paris, Ed. Mitterand, 1962, Vol. 10.
Zola, Emile: *Les romanciers naturalistes,* Paris, F. Bernouard, 1927. Also, *Oeuvres,* Paris, Ed. Mitterand, 1962, Vol. 11.
Zola, Emile: *Le ventre de Paris,* Paris, F. Bernouard, 1927. Also, *Oeuvres,* Paris, Ed. Mitterand, 1962, Vol. 2.